# Imperatives

# Imperatives

C.L. HAMBLIN

*Foreword by*
*Nuel Belnap*

Basil Blackwell

Copyright © The Estate of the late C.L. Hamblin 1987

First published 1987

Basil Blackwell Ltd

108 Cowley Road, Oxford, OX4 1JF, UK

Basil Blackwell Inc.
432 Park Avenue South, Suite 1503
New York, NY 10016, USA

*British Library Cataloguing in Publication Data*
Hamblin, C.L.
  Imperatives.
  1. English language — Mood
  I. Title
  425        PE1290
  ISBN 0-631-15193-1

*Library of Congress Cataloging in Publication Data*
Hamblin, C.L. (Charles Leonard), 1922-1985.
  Imperatives.
  1. Grammar, Comparative and general – Imperative.
2. Commands (Logic) 3. Semantics (Philosophy)
I. Title.
P281.H36 1987     415      86-13980
ISBN 0-631-15193-1

Typeset in 10 on 12pt Sabon
by Columns Reading
Printed in Great Britain by
T.J. Press Ltd,
Padstow, Cornwall.

# Contents

Foreword by Nuel Belnap     vii

1   The Varieties of Imperative     1

2   Grammar-Logic     46

3   Three Reductionist Theories     97

4   Action-State Semantics     137

5   The Consistency of a Set of Imperatives     167

6   Imperfect Ability     200

7   Imperatives in Dialogue     218

Bibliography     242

Index     255

# Foreword

Grant importance to the imperative; of all speech forms the imperative is the last one that we would let them take away. Not that *information* is trifling, either in the gathering via questions or in the broadcasting via assertions, but in spite of the supremacy of the assertion in the imagination of academic students of language, *action* is that of which we would primarily say, lose not its name.[1] Be therefore a little astonished that the book in your hands is the first sustained treatment of this topic.

And delight yourself with its excellence. C.L. Hamblin, who died too young and too soon after completing this work, came to his topic having previously contributed wonderfully to philosophy (at his academic home in the University of New South Wales), linguistics, and computer science. And in this book Hamblin draws from within the province of philosophy itself not only upon 'dialectical systems,' or 'the logic of dialogs,' which is a sub-field of philosophical logic that he created, but also – non-trivially – upon many parts of formal and informal logic, upon the history of philosophy (both ancient and modern), upon the philosophy of language, ethics, and law, upon philosophy of mind, philosophy of science, and philosophy of action, and upon metaphysics. He was master not only of twenty-five languages, but of much else that he shows us to be relevant to our understanding of imperatives, and vice versa.

Throughout this book Hamblin encourages by his examples two striving tendencies: hunt for the data (examples) and search for appropriate theories (generalizations). Since in the philosophy of language it is easiest either to ignore or tyrannize the data while pushing ungainly theories, or to overwhelm with careless or subtle observation while mocking all possibility of structure, one is continually refreshed

---

1. 'Verily,' said a Persian, ''tis the sorest of all human ills, to abound in knowledge and yet have no power over action' (Herodotus).

by Hamblin's patient use of the method he thinks of as 'case law'. 'Not so fast, Jack' could summarize one of his principal lessons for us. His closely reasoned rejection of the frequent attempts summarily to 'reduce' imperatives to something else (say, to a creature of standard truth-conditional semantics) is but part of this lesson, which is taught constructively by the way in which he makes us see the need to invoke special materials and techniques in coming to understand the variety and structure and logic of imperatives. Another part is his rejection of those who would tell us that although there are plenty of cases, there is no law, no prospect of theory, no hope. Hamblin suits Alfred North Whitehead's repeatable motto, 'Seek simplicity, and distrust it.'

Hamblin's own beginning of a non-reductionist semantic theory of imperatives claims that if we are properly to understand them, we must supplement the equipment normally employed by philosophical logicians in coming to grips with indicatives.

1. A theory strong enough to illuminate imperatives must contain some apparatus for dealing with the passing of time and with the consequent concept of change of state. Such apparatus is thought to be useful for indicatives, but Hamblin argues that there is no theory of imperatives without some such.

2. A semantic theory of imperatives must distinguish what happens from what is done; it must mark the difference between state or process and action.

3. Hamblin argues that two forms of causation must enter into our considerations, one giving us a handle on future physical states, the other on what persons will or would do.

4. The concept of agency is said to be essential.

5. Some element of intention, not hidden in the mind, however, but expressed in action through a strategy.

Of course all of these items have been proposed at one time or another as useful to our understanding of natural language; Hamblin's thesis here is that when it comes to imperatives, they are not only useful but essential. The thesis does not go without saying; let it be tested.

Hamblin himself provides many of the materials for such testing. There is a sustained account of all the ways that negation can enter into our imperative habits, and a consequent story about the numerous forms that consistency of imperatives can take, and what they might mean. There is a beginning of a discussion of the difficult concept of ability as it relates to imperatives and their logic, and an all too brief introduction to a dialectical understanding of imperatives and of the consequent (says Hamblin) interior mental states of intention, willing, and the like in terms of publicly available interchanges. (Hobbes says that 'the language of desire is *Imperative*'; a dubious thesis.) And there is a tremendous amount of grammatical, logical, and linguistic reflection on what does and does not make sense about imperatives. Who, for instance, would have thought that a study of imperatives would show that the familiar distinction between 'knowing that' and 'knowing how' is fundamentally flawed?

The work is all unfinished, as case law invariably is. It will be a long time, however, before the following lapses: do not take yourself to be competent concerning imperatives (neither their logic, nor their grammar, nor their significance for any area of philosophy) without relying on this volume. There is much to learn, and to do.

*Nuel Belnap*
*University of Pittsburgh*

# 1
## The Varieties of the Imperative

---

Imperatives pervade our lives. An imperative is uttered every time someone invites a caller to:

Come in

or

Sit down

in shopping,

Give me three of the large ones

in the giving of route-directions,

Turn left at the lights

or recipes,

Have the dough dry and springy.

We use them in the mutual organization of our lives in the workplace:

Go off to lunch and finish it later
Cut as close as you can to the ten-centimetre mark

and at home,

Bring in a pint of milk when you come
Do be careful with that leaky vase
Don't wait up.

They confront us in traffic signs:

Stop
Keep left

in advertisements,

Don't delay, buy yours today

and election slogans,

Cast your vote for freedom and progress.

The card in the board game says:

Go to jail. Do not pass 'Go'. Do not collect $200.

In practical terms, imperatives are not only among the most frequent of utterances; they are also, surely, the most important. If the human race had to choose between being barred from uttering imperatives and being barred from uttering anything else, there is no doubt which it should prefer.

Just *how* frequent are they? No general answer is possible, but I offer the following scraps. Fries, (*The Structure*,* p.51) who managed to get access to a body of recorded telephone conversations in the days when the making of such recordings was still legal, estimated the imperatives, defined as 'single free utterances that are regularly followed by "action" responses', to be of the order of 7 per cent of the 'meaningful utterances'. Joos, (*The English Verb: Form and Meaning*, p.16), dealing with material chosen from published, mainly American, literature, and the transcript of an English court case, counted occurrences of *verbs*, and found imperatives, which he classifies as a subclass of 'presentatives', or plain finite verbs lacking the infinitive *to* marker, to be much rarer than Fries would suggest – about 1 per cent, so far as can be judged from a rather unclear statement of totals. But it is, of course, impossible to be satisfied with either of these figures; the writers both use atypical definitions on material in which you would not expect to find imperatives in large numbers. In an admittedly amateur attempt to do better, I did a rough count in Shakespeare, and found a rich 20 per cent or so. Remember the famous ones?

Out, damned spot!
If music be the food of love, play on. . .
. . . lend me your ears!
O, swear not by the moon, the inconstant moon, . . .

There is a book-length study of Shakespearean imperatives by Ukaji, *Imperative Sentences in Early Modern English*. Even most dramatists, corrupted by a literary education, probably write relatively fewer imperatives than Shakespeare; but it is a fair guess that he better represents our everyday speech.

---

*References in text are identified by author(s) and, where necessary, abbreviated titles.

My intuitions define *imperative* broadly, as will appear, and as this figure possibly suggests; anyway, this is good preliminary methodology. But I am unwilling, so early in this book, to offer a short, or any, definition. Some kind of definition will appear gradually as we proceed; but the similarities, grammatical and functional, between examples will be a better guide than any that could be set down. I do not want to make a case for any particular use of the word *imperative* other than what I take to be the usual and natural one. Grammar is the first test of this, but, starting from locutions that are imperative in grammatical form, we shall be led to others that resemble them in function, and to others that are not imperative at all but are related to them in logic. *Para-imperative* will do, when we are in doubt, as a catch-all for these; and it will be with the substance of this enlarged class, rather than with verbal niceties in its description, that we shall deal.

It will not be necessary, at first, to discuss (as some logicians would immediately wish) whether the examples are examples of *sentences*, bare forms of words; or the *utterances*, with a context of speaker or occasion; or of other logically more abstract entities, counterparts, say, of the *propositions* of traditional logical theory. It is possible that none of the obvious characterizations will fit. In the end, though our interest is in entities having logical properties, much more of the context of utterance needs to be read into imperatives than is usually read into their supposed brothers, indicatives or declaratives. But it would even be wrong to prejudge whether imperatives and indicatives are distinct. I think, in an important sense, they are; but there would be no contradiction in supposing that an area of logical interest and concern, requiring analysis in a particular way, could overlap other such areas and encompass entities that could be helpfully analysed also in alternative ways.

One special reason for studying imperatives concerns attitudes that run very deep in our culture. In particular, it concerns the important distinction between *theoretical* and *practical* knowledge, reflected in our tendency to distinguish between *pure* and *applied* studies and, often enough, to have separate institutions for their prosecution. The propositions of pure science are conceived as uncompromisingly indicative in form; but the applied scientist, in the end, gives people instructions to do things in this or that appropriate way, and the most direct way to express instructions is in the imperative. We shall come to scientific imperatives, and to the para-imperative language in which they are commonly wrapped, in a moment; and also, in due course, to theories that challenge this perhaps over-facile characterization of the pure-applied distinction. But the main point, here, is a different and more preliminary one. Lacking a developed logic of imperatives, that would enable us to give *any* account of what it is for an imperative to be rational, or well-based, or scientifically sound, we approach any discussion of their place or merits with tied hands. Do scientists exceed their authority when they issue instructions? Or is it possible for imperatives to be part of a scientific theory, dovetailed with indicatives or other entities? The standard (Kantian) answer, that scientists are concerned only with 'hypothetical' imperatives, will seem unconvincing when we look at details.

Philosophers, too, have expressed themselves in imperatives often enough. Among the sayings of the Seven Sages were:

> Know thyself

and

> Nothing in excess.

William of Ockham gave us:

> Entities are not to be multiplied beyond necessity.

Hume told us how to deal with any book not containing either statements of empirical fact or logico-mathemtical reasoning, namely,

> Commit it, then, to the flames

and Kant gave us his famous Categorical Imperatives,

> Act only on such maxim as you can wish should become
> a universal law.

Wittgenstein reportedly summed up his attitude to questions of meaning with:

> Don't ask for the meaning, ask for the use

(see Wisdom 'Ludwig Wittgenstein, 1934-1937'), and in any case gave us many other imperatives scattered through his later writings. Anyone who thinks imperatives do not have any foundation in rationality will have to reject all claims any of these imperatives have to be part of the corpus of philosophy.

But, in an older and venerable philosophical tradition that includes the sayings of the Seven Sages and is still in force in societies outside the (broadly) western, there has never been any doubt that philosophers may be called on to give *advice* in areas of their expertise; and this advise has generally been regarded not only as (in principle) rational, but as the best approach to rationality that is to be hoped for in what are, usually, difficult and debatable areas. This does not mean that we regard a philosopher, however expert, as having a right to issue imperatives at random or as he wishes; rather the reverse. Philosophical imperatives need to be seen as requiring rational justification just as much as philosophical indicatives would. Of the various conclusions that might be drawn from this fact, let us be content, for the moment, with one: we need to be much more aware of the logic of imperatives – at least, of the fact that imperatives *have* a logic – than we apparently are.

It will be useful to start by classifying imperatives in a quasi-sociological way, according to the kind of 'authority' they carry – whether social or academic – and according to the aims and expectations putatively entertained by their issuers and recipients.

Most obviously, COMMANDS presuppose some kind of legal or coercive authority. They are treated by many writers as the leading or typical, if not sole, members of the imperative family, in spite of the fact that the description does not sit easily on most of the everyday examples. (Hardly any of the examples with which we began this chapter could reasonably be called *commands*.) To start with, this is a verbal point. As a term applied to imperatives COMMAND is now old-fashioned, and there is nothing in my experience that I naturally describe as somebody's commanding someone to do something. (You may *command* a clear view or a knowledge of Chinese. An officer may command a regiment, but not *do* anything.) We say:

Control *ordered* the mission to abort,
The Judge *instructed* the Jury to return a verdict of 'Not Guilty',
The ranger *told* us to keep to the marked paths.

At a more general level, authoritative imperatives are sometimes described as DIRECTIVES or COMMISSIONS.

But there may be more to it than this. It is a reasonable conjecture that *command* was a more popular word a century or two ago when social hierarchies were more rigid. These days there is little real authority as it used to be known, and instead we have a large-scale interplay of relatively small-scale sanctions. The powers of parliament, police, parents, even of animal-owners, are all in principle limited, and their charges have legal rights against them. Only the gunman in a back street, or others who are prepared to exercise a sanction nakedly, can issue the kinds of command that were available to old-fashioned authorities.

But we can still, if we look, find plenty of modern examples of imperatives issued by people in institutionally recognized authority:

Fall out tonight's sentry detail.
Stick no bills.
Stop that dreadful noise, children, at once!

Move further down the car!
Jones, go down to the store and draw two spare tool-kits,
DZ3, drop back on my tail and give cover,
Pull over, driver.

I shall continue to call these COMMANDS. And while we are about it we should not pussyfoot the purely grammatical distinction between imperative constructions and substitute ones that do the same job:

Passengers must not speak to the driver.
Jones, I want you to take charge of 4 Division.
You will approach a short dark man holding a cigar-case and say
to him, 'Are you waiting for the Belfield bus?'

Care is, of course, indicated: but the test of what is or is not a command, or any sort of imperative, is ultimately functional, not grammatical. (How else would we even be able to make the *grammatical* distinction?) Commonly the imperative sense is conveyed, as in two of these examples, by the use of a modal such as *must* or *will*, sometimes, as in the other, by the expression of a wish. This does not mean, of course, that just *any* use of a modal or expression of a wish conveys an imperative; context tells, however fuzzy the concept may be at the edges. Naturally, when an imperative is very indirect – as in, for example,

Johnny, the door's open!

– it may be better to say something else; for example (here), that what we have is an indicative with an imperative implication.

But let us move on. The license to extend our considerations to cover substitute forms is particularly important if we turn next to REQUESTS; because it is a normal feature of them that they be made rather politely. Beside simple imperative forms, we find a wide variety of culture-bound and language-variant expressions:

Pass the salt, please.
Lend me five dollars till Monday.
Wait here a moment, would you?
I wonder if I could trouble you for a light?
Would you be so good as to mind my suitcase?
The Management requests patrons to limit calls to three minutes
when others are waiting.
I would appreciate it if you would let me know in advance.
Could I have one from the front of the pile?
If you could perhaps all just stand a little closer together . . .

Some of these have the form of questions; and it is interesting that the etymology of the word *request* indicates a felt connection with question-asking. *Ask* is also the commonest verb in reporting requests (matching *tell* for orders); we say

> I *asked* her to mind my suitcase,
> He *asked* for the salt.

The *ask/tell* test, though it is not utterly reliable, must be the simplest one for dividing requests from orders. (Presence of *please* is not a good indication; see Geukens, 'The Distinction Between Direct and Indirect Speech Acts . . .'.)

But requests are (is it necessary to argue?) certainly not *typical* questions; and if it is doubted whether they ought to be classified as imperatives – and if the point is more than a mere verbal one, about which I shall not argue more (it is ably argued in Schachter, 'Imperatives') – the answer must be that they have more in common with imperatives than with anything else, and that the alternative contenders differ, in any case, not just from this one but also extensively from one another. It is also not the case, generally, that these forms are unavailable for COMMANDS and for imperatives of other kinds to come. COMMANDS are often given 'politely', in one of the variant forms, and requests abruptly. (Some languages – Hindi, Japanese – have systematically different verb-forms or verbal constructions for 'polite' and 'abrupt' imperatives. But even these do not reliably discriminate requests from COMMANDS, because the 'polite' ones would often be used for polite COMMANDS and the 'abrupt' ones for REQUESTS in informal situations.) Our examples, or most of them, to be typed accurately as REQUEST or COMMAND, need to have read into them typical contexts, without which they could be either, or neither.

On the general question of what have become known as 'indirect speech acts' (not to be confused with sentences in 'indirect speech'!), namely, utterances in which, for politeness or similar reasons, a substitute grammatical form is adopted, there have been some attempts both at classification and at explanation. Mohan, ('Principles, Postulates, Politeness') for example, gives a list of 24 alternative forms for REQUESTS, ranged on an empirically determined 'politeness' scale. Gordon and Lakoff, ('Conversational Postulates'), starting from the postulates proposed by Grice, ('Logic and Conversation') define some 'sincerity conditions' of utterances and suggest (p. 65):

One can convey a request by (i) asserting a speaker-based sincerity-condition or (ii) questioning a hearer-based sincerity-condition.

It is a speaker-based sincerity-condition of a REQUEST, for example, that the speaker wants the hearer to conform with it; whence (i) licenses

> I want you to . . .

and similar formulations. Hearer-based sincerity-conditions are that the hearer can, would be willing, and will in fact, conform, whence by (ii) a REQUEST can be expressed by a question of any of the forms:

> Can you . . . ?
> Would you be willing to . . . ?
> Will you . . . ?

and, again, parallel formulations. Lakoff, ('The Logic of Politeness') Heringer, ('Some Grammatical Correlates of Felicity Conditions and Presuppositions') and Davison, ('Indirect Speech Acts and What To Do With Them') add some other points; see also Searle ('Indirect Speech Acts') Green, ('How to Get People To Do Things With Words . . .') and Clark, ('Responding to Indirect Speech Acts'). The original treatment of this problem is that of Sadock, ('Whimperatives'). What is said clearly also applies to polite COMMANDS, though it needs reformulation to deal with some of the other kinds of imperative we shall come to. It is also, however, very incomplete and limited in explanatory power, and says little to license even some of the formulations in our examples just given, or to reject a wide variety that need to be rejected. In particular, it says nothing of a general character about formulations using modals; these must apparently be 'root modals' in the sense of Hoffman, ('Past Tense Replacement and the Modal System') not 'epistemic' ones. Besides *can* and *will* as already mentioned, *must, may, might, should* and *would* are all usable. We shall return to the question of modals in a later chapter.

To distinguish COMMANDS from REQUESTS, one good rule is: Formulate a description in indirect speech. It is not the only one. In a very few cases, content will do it; for example,

> Lend me five dollars

must be a REQUEST, not a COMMAND, for reasons associated with the nature of the institution of lending. But the distinction is, above all, sociological. REQUESTS are made by those who have no authority to give COMMANDS, at least on the matter at issue. The junior officer who says:

> Stand at ease, please

is an army joke. Very exceptionally, when a request is made by someone in a position to give a command, it requires special, careful formulation:

> Gentlemen, I do not *order* you not to talk to the Press, but I *ask* you for the good of the Regiment, . . .

But even this case is misleading if it is taken at face-value. The description in indirect speech demands hedging; 'Well, he didn't *order* us, but . . .' And perhaps talking to the Press is a democratic right over which the speaker's authority only doubtfully extends, or a problematic democratic right to which he feels called to give lip-service.

REQUESTS, in short, can and perhaps must be made from a position of inferiority, or at best equality; COMMANDS not. But we ought to notice, in passing, a feature COMMANDS and REQUESTS have in common, that does not extend to all the varieties of imperative we shall meet later: they are made or issued in the putative interest of the utterer, independently of the interest of the addressee. This does not mean that the utterer really wants what he says, since the command or request can conceivably be one that he feels obliged to issue for some other reason. It also does not mean that the interest of the addressee is not served by it, which it no doubt very often is. But essentially, and typically, the object of a command or request is to get the addressee to do or bring about something the issuer wants done, which the addressee would not be disposed to do otherwise. Departures from this norm are aberrations.

A related variety of imperative, that shares this feature, is the one that occurs in hard-bargaining situations:

> Take your hands off me!
> More porridge!
> You must pay me for the damage.

I think we would call these DEMANDS. They lack the authoritative backing of commands, but are altogether too peremptory for requests. DEMAND is an altogether better description than COMMAND or ORDER for many imperatives in modern life. Trade unions make demands on employers, and employers make counter-demands. (Neither is boss.) If my neighbour makes a noise in the middle of the night I shall first request, then demand that he desist, and if necessary demand that the authorities do something about it. These are cases in which (as we said) there is a large-scale interplay of small-scale sanctions. The 'commands' of the gunman are ambiguously in this category despite their coercive nature. Boyd and Thorne, ('The Semantics of Modal Verbs') note some detailed grammatical points separating *demand* from *command* and *order*. Morris ('Imperatives and Orders') contrasts 'personal orders' with 'authoritative orders' and discusses the nature of the sanction that must accompany an order of the former variety. Hare, (*The Language of Morals)* noted by Broadie, ('Imperatives') tries to make the difference between the words *command* and *order* reflect this distinction, or something like it; a COMMAND, he says, needs authority, but an ORDER only needs power. But in this he is surely not reflecting average English usage.

INVITATIONS are, of course, not the same as requests, though terminology commonly conflates or even exchanges the two. For example,

> We invite you to leave a donation in one of the boxes provided in the foyer

is more request than invitation, whereas,

> Mr and Mrs J. Smith request the pleasure of the company of . . . at . . .

is invitation, not request. Are invitations imperatives? Yes, unless the simplicity of the commonest examples is misleading; we say:

> Come at eight.
> Have one of these.

On the other hand, unlike COMMANDS, DEMANDS and REQUESTS, they are not designed to serve exclusively the interest of the issuer. The interest, rather, is mutual, and we shall have to put them in a different or borderline category.

COMMANDS, DEMANDS and REQUESTS, for the sake of a label, could be called *wilful* imperatives. By contrast, a second category, consisting mainly of ADVICE, INSTRUCTIONS (in one sense) and RECIPES, is *non-wilful* and is concerned not with the interests or wishes of the utterer but with those of the addressee. (Imperatives as a whole have sometimes been regarded as products of 'the will' – for example, by Jespersen, (*The Philosophy of Grammar*, p.320) echoing the long German idealist tradition that started with Kant – but this is misleading if it suggests that issuers of imperatives are always trying to impose their wills.)

The distinction between COMMANDS and ADVICE (he called it COUNSEL) was made long ago by Hobbes, (*Leviathan*, 25). The force of advice derives not from its support by some legal or coercive authority, but on its being *good* advice, or *reasonable*; and a counsellor, as Hobbes says, is in principle quite a different sort of person from a commander. It carries, we might say, rational authority rather than the social authority of the issuer; or, in the words of K. Baier ('Ability, Power and Authority') its authority is *principle-related* rather than *principal-related* (see Holdcroft, *Words and Deeds . . .* , p. 70.)

The simplest advice goes naturally into imperative form:

Turn left at the lights and go straight on past the Town Hall.
Take three of these immediately and try to get a good night's rest.
Bring out the melody a little more clearly in the left hand.
Always cut your fingernails round and your toenails square.

(The last of these, I was told, was once part of a code issued to Boy
Scouts.) In other cases the imperative is more disguised:

If I were you I wouldn't tell Julia.
I think your most promising plan is to invest in nickel exploration.

ADVICE can be practical, scientific (or unscientific), prudential, moral. It
can also be factual, and indicative in form, though in this case it is
usually so-called only because the addressee is expected to want to act
on it, or to take it into account in planning eventual action.

A SUGGESTION is a light or loose piece of advice,

Get all the *x*-terms on the left-hand side.
You could ask him to phone the recommendation through.
Why not try the caramel custard?

(But SUGGESTIONS, too, can often be factual. The Gordon-Lakoff rules,
again, are no help with the indirect forms; but on *Why not . . . ?* see
Lee, 'The Performative Analysis of "Why not V"?') If we say that the
difference between *non-wilful* imperatives and *wilful* ones consists in
the former's relying on rational authority rather than social, we can say
that SUGGESTIONS differ from ADVICE in the same way as REQUESTS differ
from COMMANDS and DEMANDS. The issuer of a SUGGESTION, that is to
say, doesn't put his own rational authority behind it, but addresses it as to
a rational superior or equal. COMMANDS, on this reckoning, correspond
with ADVICE that is oracular and carries a presumption of overriding
expertise; DEMANDS with ADVICE which, however hard pressed, is
regarded or regards itself as being in potential competition with other
ADVICE and leaves room for contention. (But the parallel between rational
authority and social authority has limits.)

The word INSTRUCTION has two different kinds of ambiguity. First, it
is sometimes used in reference to commands, rather than to non-wilful
imperatives resembling advice; and second, even when instructions are
non-wilful – as in the case of the 'instruction book' issued with a piece
of apparatus – there may be much factual material besides actual
specification of which switches to operate and levers to push. However,
the grammatical imperative is clearly at home with this latter material:

Assemble plug with striped lead attached to long pin.
Turn on, allow warm-up period of 1 min. before pressing knob D.

Consequently the best thing to say is that, although the word

INSTRUCTION has a range of uses, over at least part of that range instructions are imperatives of the same general type as ADVICE.

That ADVICE, SUGGESTIONS and INSTRUCTIONS are imperative at all is something many philosophers – in spite of the grammatical evidence – seem to find it difficult to accept. But before we go on to consider their objections, let us consider RECIPES, in which the grammatical imperative is again clearly at home:

Take 200gm, of butter, melt, rub lightly into the flour, . . .

And the word *recipe* itself is by origin imperative, being Latin for *take*. We are sometimes inclined to think of recipes more as stating established facts about methods of manufacture, ingredients, oven temperatures and the like; and, in fact, in English sometimes, and in other languages regularly, alternative formulations make this judgement more plausible. Scandinavians, for example, may use their convenient passive, to say in effect,

The butter is rubbed into the flour, . . .

In some other languages an impersonal subject is favoured, *One rubs* . . . or *You rub* . . . , or even (for example, in Polynesian) first-person plural, *We rub* . . . These formulations make a recipe resemble a description of an existing practice rather than a prescription for a contingent future one; and it is, after all, a normal feature of a recipe that it should express an ongoing practice, real or envisaged. A recipe is, as has sometimes been said of moral advice, universalizable; it tells you not just what to do on *this* occasion, but rather what to do (and what anyone should do) on *all* occasions of a certain sort, namely, occasions that call for a batch of waffles or whatever.

But this only says that a RECIPE is a certain sort of universal imperative, not that it is not an imperative at all. (And some INSTRUCTIONS, and certain kinds of ADVICE, are universal in the same way.) A description of an existing practice, moreover, is *not* necessarily itself a recipe, since the practice could be unsystematic or obviously faulty, and consequently not fit to be considered as recipe-material. A RECIPE, in short, is more than a mere description; it is an endorsement, for future repetition, of what is described. (We shall pick up 'academic', and to that extent unendorsed, recipes later as being, at least, para-imperatives. On RECIPES, and particularly on the question of their inductive reliability, see Stopes-Roe, 'Recipes and Induction . . .', who refers to Ryle, 'Comment on Mr Achinstein's Paper', and Achinstein, 'From Success to Truth'. It is asserted by Field, 'Note on Imperatives' that Kant's 'rules of skill' are, properly, RECIPES rather than imperatives of another kind.)

The answer to those who want to say that what I have called *non-wilful* imperatives — ADVICE, INSTRUCTIONS, RECIPES — are really indicative is to show that the differences in kind between these and the *wilful* ones — COMMANDS, DEMANDS and REQUESTS — are not the same as the differences between indicatives and imperatives. To say that non-wilful imperatives are different from COMMANDS and REQUESTS is not to admit that they are not imperatives; least of all, to admit that they are indicatives, in any sense that would imply that they do not raise separate logical questions and need special treatment.

There is one feature of non-wilful imperatives that certainly puts them closer to indicatives than COMMANDS and REQUESTS are. Non-wilful imperatives are *accountable* in the sense that they are supposed, like indicatives, to be capable of being provided with a rational backing or justification. Advice can be *good* or *bad* in the sense of having a sound rational backing, or not. COMMANDS and REQUESTS, it is true, may be good or bad, and their issuers may choose to give reasons to back them up; but these issuers are not required to do so, and, if they do, they in some sense change the character of their utterances. A commander also might have to account to his superiors for the commands he gives; but the interests of those to whom such a command is issued, if it is a command in the full old-fashioned sense, are not what the command is essentially intended to serve, and if they ask,

Why?

they may as well be told,

Do it, that's all!

Cases in which we consider subordinates to have a right to question COMMANDS are, precisely, cases in which we regard the authority of the commander as less than absolute. Another way of putting this is to say that a commander has *discretion* where a commandee has not. It is the same with REQUESTS; I may request what I like, of whom I like, and persist with my request without explanation for as long as I like. Although giving a good explanation may be wise, in the sense of helping to get my request granted, refusing to do so would not in any way alter the nature of the request as request.

By contrast, an adviser who refused to give reasons for his advice and said:

I'm telling you to do it; that's all

would very soon find his advice redescribed as arbitrary, or *wilful*, and ultimately as, say, a demand.

Non-wilful imperatives, then, need to be reasoned for. This means that they need the ramified kind of *logic* within which can be demonstrated which reasons support which imperatives; and it is, perhaps, pardonable that logicians have tried to find this logic by conflating non-wilful imperatives with the only sort of entities for which a comparable logic already exists. But to show that such a conflation is a blind alley we need only look a little more carefully at the distinction between *theoretical* and *practical* knowledge and inference, or between *pure* and *applied* studies. The dichotomy can be traced back to Aristotle, though his distinction is nowhere drawn on very clear lines or made a matter of fundamental doctrine. The scholastics took it up – Aquinas repeatedly distinguishes *speculative* from *practical* intellect and knowledge – and Kant made the respective studies of *pure* and *practical* reason the major division of his works. Clearly these people draw the line in quite different places, and we need to see it as a family of distinctions sharing, perhaps, a simple-minded intuition. We need to look here both at the distinction relevant to science and epistemology (and philosophy), and to those that have been made in connection with ethics and the philosophy of law.

Pure science (the simple account runs) is concerned with the pursuit of truth, in the shape of laws of nature and relevant empirical facts coming under them. The pure scientist establishes these laws and facts disinterestedly, without special regard to whether they are practically useful. The philosopher also once used to be thought of as such a pure scientist, and most people would still think of him as disinterestedly concerned, above all, with truth. It is not generally thought, any longer, that the philosopher's job is to set up 'laws' resembling the laws of nature, or that he has a right to be remote from practical concerns. But that is just part of a certain tension in our modern view of the academic culture. Let us turn to the other camp.

Academic applied scientists, despite their name, do not themselves *apply* science, or not very much. They leave that to a range of engineers, practitioners, technicians, tradesmen and ordinary people. Their job is rather to tell these other people how to do it. (In practice, of course, there is much overlap; it is only for the sake of a simple account that I speak as if there were none.) But the most natural way of telling someone how to do something is in the imperative mood:

Do it such-and such a way;

and it seems to follow that the professional business of the applied scientist is the formulation of a stock of scientifically sound imperatives, for the guidance of the engineers, technicians and others. It should go without saying that his imperatives are of the *non-wilful* variety; for

only those who think that all imperatives are COMMANDS would draw
the conclusion that applied scientists, to be able to issue them, need to
stand in any position of social authority apart from what might be
given them by their knowledge or expertise. The imperatives issued by
philosophers should also, surely, be thought of in the same way. The
distinction between *wilful* and *non-wilful* varieties of imperative in fact
serves to bring scientific and philosophical imperatives into our
conceptual scheme without strain; we can see them as resembling
indicatives in being potentially rational, without being pressed to see
them as indicative in grammatical or logical form.

The difficulty, as many people have seen it, is that our ideas of what
is necessary to validate an imperative as *scientifically sound* are, to say
the least, sketchy and ill formed. In particular, since the object of the
distinction between pure and applied science is to enable us to say that
the contribution of the applied scientist is the working out of the
application of the knowledge the pure scientist disinterestedly compiles,
what is the logic by which the applied scientist derives a set of
imperatives from a set of indicatives?

The traditional but, I think, inadequate solution to the problem starts
by noticing that many practical imperatives of the sort the applied
scientist might issue are prefixed with what, despite their varying
linguistic form, we may as well call *hypothetical* clauses:

> If increased speed is desired, program frequently used loops in
>     basic machine language . . .
> For a firmer mix, use additional cement up to the proportion of
>     one in three . . .
> If desired, dissolve tablet in a warm drink such as cocoa. . .
> To make fine pancakes, take flour, eggs, . . .

(I choose lowly examples. They sufficiently illustrate the general point.)
The proposed solution to our difficulty takes this pattern as general; *all*
technological imperatives, it would be said, have the hypothetical form,

> If you want to achieve such-and-such, do so-and-so;

and, moreover, hypotheticals of this kind are really indicatives in
disguise and can be rewritten,

> If you do so-and-so *you will* achieve such-and-such.

It follows that a hypothetical of this kind is really just a statement of
cause-and-effect of the kind produced by the pure scientist. This is, in
effect, the solution of Kant, (*Fundamental Principles of the Metaphysics
of Ethics*, p. 40) who separated out a certain class of imperatives he
called *rules of skill* and said that, being hypothetical, they raise no

problem compared with the true and irreducible imperatives, the categorical ones.

It is possible to pull this theory apart piece by piece, in the way all reductionist philosophical theories can be pulled apart. Rules for doing something are *not* always literally in hypothetical form, and to make the solution work we need to search around for suitable unique hypothetical clauses which are 'understood' when the rules are stated. But let us grant, for the sake of argument, that it is always clear what a given rule is a rule for doing, and that we can therefore always find such a clause.

From the fact that a given hypothetical imperative rule is a 'good' rule it does not follow that its translation into indicative form gives a respectable pure–scientific law of cause and effect. It will do so, in general, only if the hypothetical, in a very strict sense, completely specifies both what the rule is a rule for doing and what is to be done in order to do it. And as soon as any degree of complexity is encountered, these requirements are quite unrealistic. The bridge-builder who wants a prescription for a 'good' bridge wants one that is strong enough not to fall down, within certain budget limits, long-lasting, easy to maintain and aesthetically pleasing; but he can achieve a design that satisfies these requirements – if at all – only by an involved process of planning and balancing that could never be justified in terms of reduction to a pure–scientific cause–and–effect analysis. And if he can not do so he may even need to face the very different questions of which requirements to sacrifice, and to what degree. To the extent that his finished design can be regarded as a non-wilful imperative it will no doubt be true that, if he is asked to justify it, he will produce various pieces of reasoning that invoke pure–scientific laws. But he could never derive all the features of his design at once in this way, and to say that the design is 'in theory' so derivable is consequently to indulge in metaphysics.

So the solution cannot be sustained in detail; practical application of science is just not like that. In fact the most startling consequence of the proposal, taken literally, is the lowly role it assigns the applied scientist; he becomes a mere indicative–to–imperative translation machine. No theoretical apparatus is provided by which he may validate, check out, balance or otherwise operate with the hypothetical imperatives that are his stock–in–trade. We are invited to picture him spending his days in his office receiving laws of cause–and–effect from the pure scientist, performing on each the trivial operation of rewriting it in hypothetical imperative form, and passing the result on down the line.

Many people, though obviously rejecting this picture, might be disposed to entertain a compromise one; concede, perhaps, that the applied scientist brings more to his discipline than the laws and facts produced by the pure scientist, but deny that his activities taken him outside the province of traditional, indicative logic. The applied scientist, it might be said, merely adapts, selects or develops certain areas of pure science in detail, these areas being chosen for their human usefulness or value. Within his specialty – that is, subject to the constraints imposed by his initial appraisal of a set of problems or pursuits as humanly valuable or useful and hence worth his specialized attention – he may be as disinterested, truth-oriented and indicatively logical as his pure brother. His choice of a specialty merely enables him to go deeper, with more practical effect, into matters that may form the basis of action.

But even this account undervalues the directed, inventive and problem-solving aspects of the applied scientist's activity. No doubt it is true that he brings values as well as pure–scientific knowledge to the problems with which he deals; but it is *not* true that the values are simple, well-formed and previously-chosen ones and that it is only in the realm of pure knowledge that his battles are waged. Some of the values he brings – the 'utility' appraisals – are, perhaps, uncontroversial, of the kind that all reasonable men would accept; and others may be so much a matter of individual choice and difference of opinion that his conclusions had better mention them and be conditionalized with clauses of the form *If you want so-and-so*. But there remains a large middle ground, where the applied investigator *forms* practical policy, in accordance with (we hope) an expertise that he develops and accumulates in much the same way as he is supposed to develop and accumulate a ready grasp of the relevant facts and laws. In finding 'good' ways of proceeding to certain ends he is required even to reappraise, continually, the ends themselves; and, particularly, in the process of satisfying incidental or consequential value-requirements, he is expected to make sound, sometimes inventive, value-judgements of his own, that those without his background are in no position to make or even, perhaps, appreciate. All this is part of his trade, and to say so is to say no more than that he is, like the rest of us, a member of the human race.

The conception of the applied scientist as a pure scientist who happens to work within a certain utilitarian specialty is reasonable, perhaps, in certain areas. The applied mathematician who works on electromagnetic field problems is not a very different person from the pure mathematician who works on the theory of groups. But elsewhere it is totally misleading. And there is a certain danger in failing to realize that the applied scientist deals in values, since we may fail to make allowance for the fact that he makes decisions for us. (He often fails to notice it himself.) The upshot is that we need a developed theory of just what it is he does.

This conclusion does not in itself imply that we need any radical supplementation of the logic with which we are familiar, since it could turn out that a comparatively trivial translation of his imperatives and value-judgements could bring them within his scope. In fact we shall find the reverse, that the unfilled need is a major one. But it would be wrong, in another way, to suppose that a 'theory of imperatives' (as I shall continue to call it) must be something radically distinct and separate from any theory developed up to now. There are not two logics, as if there were two languages, but one language with (at least) two logically different but related kinds of entity in it. If we wished, we might avoid mention of imperatives altogether and speak about, say plans of action, their execution, their aims and worth or value. But since there is no developed 'logic of action', or of 'plans', or even of 'value', we would not avoid any problems by avoiding the imperative mood, or point up any different issues from the ones raised here.

So let us broaden the discussion beyond science and look at the dichotomy of the theoretical and the practical as it affects ethics and law. The imperative theory of ethics, in its baldest and most uncompromising form, says that anyone who utters a moral judgement, such as,

> Stealing is wrong,

has really done no more than utter an imperative, such as,

> Don't steal.

For a forthright statement of this view see Carnap, (*Philosophy and Logical Syntax*, pp. 23ff); an older version is in Brentano, (*Vom Ursprung sittlicher Erkenntnis*). According to Hare, (*The Language of Morals*, e.g. p. 163) ethical statements *imply* imperatives. For a detailed review of the conflation see Segerstedt ('Imperative Propositions and Judgements of Value'). We shall return to this subject in chapter 3.

The corresponding theory of law needs to be just a little more complicated, since someone who says:

> Stealing is illegal

usually merely reports indicatively that existing laws of the land prohibit stealing. But (the theory would say) the force of a law against stealing, if any, is no more than that of the same imperative:

> Don't steal,

backed by the authority of some sort of (usually) corporate law-giver or state legal apparatus. The classical statements of the imperative theory of law are those of Bentham, (*An Introduction to the Principles of Morals and Legislation*) and John Austin, (*The Province of Jurisprudence Determined*, p. 32). For some discussion of these statements see D'Arcy, *Human Acts*.

It has sometimes (for example, Olivecrona, *Law as Fact*, ch. 1) been urged against the imperative theory of law that there is in general no one who can be singled out as the 'issuer' of the supposed commands; and the same objection could surely be made against the imperative theory of ethics. But the objection misses the point if the theories are seen as primarily concerned just with what sort of logical or grammatical entities moral and legal judgements are. There could be, it is true, a 'strong' form of either theory, to the effect that moral or legal utterances are no more than commands issued by someone (or some assemblage of persons) that stands in or arrogates a position of authority over us; but I shall assume that this cynical view is one we need not discuss. The question is rather whether – particularly, since we now recognize the existence of non-wilful, accountable imperatives – it is plausible to regard imperatives, rather than indicatives, as these theories' raw material.

The answer, so far as it concerns us at the moment, is rather simple. Ethics paints on a large canvas and is partly concerned with the 'evaluation' of past, and perhaps even present and contingent future, actions and states of affairs that are not urged, recommended or otherwise enjoined as are those that form the content of imperatives. The statements of ethics are often 'academic' in raising issues without practical implications or relevance. But, at the point of application, where,

> Stealing is wrong

or, more directly,

> It would be wrong for you to take that

is put to a prospective thief, there is hardly anything to choose between the indicative and an imperative formulation. And in the same way there are circumstances (though rarer) in which the promulgation of an injunction or prohibition that has the force of law can be put nearly interchangeably in imperative form – the obvious examples are signs such as,

> Stick no bills.
> Don't walk.

– or as indicatives that spell the legality or illegality out; say,

The posting of bills on this wall is prohibited.
You are not permitted to cross at this point.

Moreover, the studies of ethics and the law would not be what they are if they had no 'points of application' of this kind at which the imperative force of their material is transparent; and it follows that, properly conceived, they can benefit from – need – association with an analysis that throws light on what imperatives are and do.

But it does not follow that the imperative theories of ethics and of law must be accepted in all their detail; least of all, with all the implications that they are sometimes asked to carry. One of these, in particular, is very relevant here; the imperativity of ethical and legal utterances *could* be (and has often vaguely been) held to imply that they need never be taken quite seriously from the logical point of view. Moralists who, traditionally, regarded locutions such as

Stealing is wrong

as indicative were forced to discuss the merits of doctrines in which there were logically structured and interlocking moral judgements, and worry about their consistency and ultimate rationale; but imperatives (the claim would run) are summary in their logical relations, have no rationale beyond the fact of their utterance by whoever utters them, and do not fit together into any objective doctrine of the kind the moral philosopher traditionally sought. Legal pronouncements similarly; for what worries the philosopher of law is, again, the question of rational system and, particularly, the relation of law to ethics; and a mere imperative (says the theory) need have none.

None of this need be said even about those moral or legal utterances that undeniably *are* imperative. (Let us accept that there may be more to be said about the others.) The imperative theories, in so far as this is their claim and aim, rest on the mistaken assumption that imperatives are non-accountable, that is, *wilful.* Imperatives, it would be thought, all resemble COMMANDS and raise no question of justification beyond the fact of their utterance by one or another actual or would-be commander; *rational* justification, or accountability, is not in question. But if this is a mistake – if many imperatives are not like COMMANDS or their wilful brothers at all, but are as rationally accountable as indicatives – the theories stand in a very different light. To those who hoped to explain away problems of truth and rationality they have no point. To others, they may be acceptable where they were not before, namely, because they give a newer and richer grasp of what the rationality of ethical and legal theories is all about. In particular, it is connected with action and practical judgement.

A further philosophical contention, that is common enough to sustain the claim that it should be regarded as rather characteristic of twentieth century philosophy, is a species of the same mistake. It comes in various forms, but they arise as a result of disillusionment with the claims of philosophers of earlier centuries to be able to set up high-level and abstract philosophical doctrines. Philosophy, it would now often be said, has no doctrines of its own, and makes no claim to be able to state any proprietary truths. Instead, it is a doctrine-free 'critical' activity and should perhaps be called methodology. In the same vein, even indicative-mood statements by philosophers, under attack as unscientific, have sometimes been defended as being 'methodological', or as being procedural rules, or the like. (Carnap, 'Testability and Meaning', Ayer, *Language Truth and Logic* and others so defended their verifiability principle of meaning.) All philosophy, it would sometimes be said, is really scientific method.

Those who put forward this view regard it as improper or unacceptable that philosophers should attempt to set up any – even, presumably, logical or critical truth – that are part of their own discipline and not part of anyone else's. But they do, apparently, regard it as proper that philosophers should give ADVICE – that is presumably characteristically philosophical – to scientists and others. And they think that ADVICE should meet certain standards of worth or rigour. The claim is consequently the strange one that philosophers *do* have access to a source of sound and rational imperatives in spite of the fact that they have no access to any comparable source of indicatives.

I shall assume that we ought to set this contention aside. But there is one implication that might remain. If philosophers are in the ADVICE-giving business at all – as the examples of philosophical imperatives given earlier suggest – they should know what they are doing when they compare and contrast, sift, justify and interrelate the material that goes into the task. If the advice is to be systematic, philosophers, above all, ought to be capable of appreciating what it is for advice to fit together into a system. The actual systems philosophers build may not be complete and all-embracing ones, but they cannot consist, either, of isolated critical comments. Once again the need for a logic is clear.

The demand for a logic is not necessarily a demand for any analogue of an 'epistemological' foundation. As, arguably, we do in the case of our knowledge of fact, we might start our imperative philosophizing in the middle. So long as we are capable of appreciating some of the principles on which the sifting, discussion and refinement of plans, advice, moral principles, proposals for action, and evaluation are based, we have begun to understand how proposed sets of imperatives can be subjected to rational tests, and consequently how our middle-range beliefs or tenets – neither high-level 'first principles' nor grass-root 'elementary' or 'protocol' entities – can be put in order. The larger and more synoptic questions can wait.

Our division of imperatives – *wilful* and *non-wilful*, COMMANDS, REQUESTS, ADVICE, . . . – is close in character to one in terms of what has become known as *illocutionary force*; I shall speak just of *force*, and use this more or less as a technical term. The verbs *request, advise,* . . . automatically differentiate reported imperatives, as when we say,

> He ordered them to shut down inessential facilities.
> They advised us to take the alternative road round the shorefront.

(Sometimes, of course, an inappropriate main verb is used, and we are in our rights in reclassifying.) These verbs can also all be used as *performatives*, as in,

> I order you to return to base.
> I advise you to take care on bends.

(A performative verb is one, roughly, whose use in the formulation I (*hereby*) *do so-and-so* actually constitutes the doing of whatever-it-is. *Promise* is a performative verb because saying *I promise*, in normal circumstances, constitutes the giving of a promise; *advise*, similarly, because saying I *advise (whatever-it-is)* is a normal way of giving advice; whereas, say, *sit* is not, because saying *I sit* is nothing whatever to do with actually sitting.) In fact, most of the modern writers who have made any distinction between different kinds of imperative at all have done so in connection with a discussion of performatives and illocutionary force, by listing different performative verbs; though few of them have attempted any taxonomy of imperatives themselves, of the sort in which we have been engaged. Naturally, many have made some distictions; see, for example, Searle, (*Speech Acts*, p. 66-7). Holdcroft, (*Words and Deeds. . .* , p. 74), has a slightly different classification in which the dichotomy 'hearer interested/not hearer interested' intersects the dichotomy 'sanctioned or authoritive/not-sanctioned or authoritive'. COMMANDS and REQUESTS are both 'not hearer interested', the former authoritative, the latter not; virtually all *non-wilful* imperatives are 'hearer interested, non-authoritative', one or two of them authoritative as an alternative. There is no recognition of variations in accountability, that is, rational justifiability. The same applies to suggestions by Vendler, (*Res Cogitans: An Essay in Rational Psychology*, p. 21). Some points about classification are made by Green ('How to get People To Do Things with Words . . .'), p. 120-5).

J.L. Austin, (*How to do Things with Words*, p. 150-61) the inventor of the terms *performative* and *illocutionary*, noting the resemblance of imperatives to performatives of the kind just mentioned, merely labelled all such performatives, together with certain others that will concern us in a moment, as *exercitives*, defined as the 'exercising of powers'.

Others, notably Searle, 'A Classification of Illocutionary Acts' and Vendler, (*Res Cogitans*) have revised Austin's scheme to the extent of separating imperative exercitives from others; and Searle finds that Austin's categories are built on a conflation of several different sorts of distinction, of which one, which he calls *illocutionary point*, reintroduces something very close to what earlier writers (such as Reichenbach, *Elements of Symbolic Logic*) had called *logical mood*. For general discussion and criticisms of Austin see T. Cohen, ('Illocutions and Perlocutions') and L.J. Cohen, ('Do Illocutionary Forces Exist?'), Burch, 'Cohen, Austin and Meaning', and Graham, (*J.L. Austin: A Critique of Ordinary Language*).

We have already had occasions to use the word *force* to make what might be described as distinctions of *mood*, namely, in speaking of the *indicative force* or *imperative force* of certain utterances such as moral ones. This seems a legitimate use, and suggests that distinctions of logical mood are, broadly, of the same character as our 'sociological' ones within imperative mood proper. (See McGinn, 'Semantics for Nonindicative Sentences', p. 303-4. A radical distinction between imperative and indicative mood is implicit in much other work, particularly on meaning; for example in the attempt by Schiffer, *Meaning*, to broaden Grice's theory of meaning, Grice, 'Meaning', to cope with imperatives as well as indicatives. On the Grice-Schiffer analysis of imperatives see later, ch. 7).

But it is also clear that divisions by *mood* and by *force* mingle and overlap. SUGGESTIONS and ADVICE, for example, can be either indicative or imperative, and in some cases they seem to straddle the line, in the same way as moral or legal utterances. The same applies to WARNINGS, which can be imperative,

> Don't go down to the woods today,

or indicative,

> It could be stormy later.

Indicative warnings are only properly so-called because they have implications for action, which is to say, some force as imperatives; and imperative warnings, being *non-wilful* – a subspecies, we might say, of ADVICE – can and often do, rest for their justification, heavily on implied indicatives. Moral and legal utterances are not the only ones that can hover between moods.

Since we must now go on to enlarge our field of view to take in various kinds of locution not so clearly imperative as the front-runners, it becomes necessary to say more in justification of our principles of selection. One of Searle's criteria, though it is a little vague in application, is worth mentioning here; some words are uttered with the intention of matching some circumstance in the world, some in order that a circumstance in the world shall come to match them. Broadly, indicatives have the object of matching words to world, imperative the reverse. Further, again broadly, logicians understand the former project well, the latter badly; and this book aims to improve their performance at it. But, to the extent that it succeeds, what it says will be relevant to the consideration of any locutions with the same 'direction of match' as imperatives; and we may as well rope them in and let their presence influence the project. On the other hand, there may be other principles of selection than this, and I proceed, as before, largely by letting likenesses and differences of examples speak for themselves.

There are a few stragglers which, though genuine imperatives in any but the narrowest sense of that word, do not fit our grand dichotomy or any of the categories laid out so far. We have already mentioned INVITATIONS. Another is what I think we should call WISHES; they include

Get well!
Have a good day!

and, I suppose,

Go to the Devil!

(See Schachter, 'Imperatives', p. 637). Atypically, I dignify these by exclamation-marks. (In some languages exclamation-marks are regularly used to mark imperatives, but in English their more typical function is to mark, literally, exclamations, and it is a confusion to class imperatives as that. Imperatives do not need to be uttered loudly, or sharply, or fervently.) WISHES, at least of the type of the first two examples, are putatively, like INVITATIONS, in the interest of both utterer and addressee, but none of the previous categorizations fits them.

Another kind not so far classified is exemplified by

Help!
Mind your head!
Run!
Ssh!

Are these REQUEST, ADVICE, EXHORTATION and DEMAND respectively?

The suggestion is much too specious. In some cases the interest of the addressee provides a rationale, in others that of the issuer. But, because of the immediacy or urgency, the question of rationale is academic; compliance is expected as not much more than a reflex action, and categorization, along with the debate over merits, can wait. Another example might be that of the string of instructions given by the control tower to a pilot who is being 'talked down' blind in a fog. When Field, 'Note on Imperatives' says authoritative commands are 'just like button-pushing' he must have imperatives of this kind in mind rather than those issued in less specialized situations. Let us call them IMMEDIATE imperatives and bear them in mind for possible special logical treatment.

Note in passing that some languages (Latin, Bengali) distinguish 'present tense' from 'future tense' imperatives. The distinction made is a complex one and the names are not always apt, but the general idea is that the former are supposed to be acted on immediately or soon, the latter after a period of time. The two forms do not make precisely the same distinction as that between IMMEDIATE and other imperatives, but their existence provides evidence of a felt distinction and inclines us to look for a logical analysis.

In a separate category again are FORMAL imperatives,

> Let $x$ be the length of the fish.
> Consider what would happen if a tanker sank in the Straits.
> Suppose the letter has gone astray.

There is no 'act', in these cases, that an addressee is being asked to perform; they are not even quite like,

> Think, man, think!

which clearly enjoins a mental act and can be COMMAND or ADVICE. Perhaps RHETORICAL would be a better name for them. Note that *Suppose* often introduces locutions which are better classified as SUGGESTIONS; thus

> Suppose you paint the side-rails before screwing the legs on.
> Suppose we call in on the way to the theatre.

The 'supposing' is formal, but its content – with *you* or *we* subject – gives the locution as a whole an alternative imperative character. Occasionally there is ambiguity and the utterer has to explain,

> No, I don't mean let's do it; I just mean suppose we did,

or

Well it would be a good idea, wouldn't it?

But finally, in considering miscellaneous true imperatives, we should notice that many ordinary imperatives are unclassifiable not so much because they are not covered by our main headings as because they are unspecific between them. If one's spouse says

Bring in some fresh bread when you come home,

this is not clearly not a REQUEST, but the word suggests too one sided an interest on the part of the speaker to be a good description of it. But COMMAND and DEMAND imply, to say the least, abnormally rocky marital relations. ADVICE suggests a one-sided interest in the other direction; there's a difference (says Mayo, 'Varieties of Imperatives') between *advising* and merely *saying what to do*. SUGGESTION is too weak, and INVITATION too strong. On the other hand it is clear that the example shares features of most of these categories and differs from them, as it were, only negatively. Social authority is not involved because co-operation between speaker and hearer, in a common interest, is regarded as pre-established. Rational justifiability is similarly presupposed or waived. As in the case of IMMEDIATE imperatives – though for a slightly different reason – argument about detail, even to the extent that would establish a place in the taxonomy, is out of place.

This leads to the comment that a major difficulty in generalizing about imperatives is terminological. Even the word *imperative*, that must do duty to cover all these instances, is not quite ideal since it has a suggestion of COMMAND – Latin *imperare* – or of urgency or strong pressure, as in

It is imperative that we go at once.

Nearly all the associated terms need to be varied depending on which variety of imperative we are talking about; COMMANDS are *given* or *issued*, REQUESTS are *made* or *submitted*, ADVICE is *given* or *offered*. (PLANS, which we shall come to in a moment, are *drawn up*.) COMMANDS, moreover, are *obeyed*, whereas requests are *granted* (or *refused*), DEMANDS are *met*, ADVICE is *accepted* or *taken* or, like RECIPES and INSTRUCTIONS, *followed*. There is virtually no neutral terminology that is good English, and my researches suggest that in other languages the situation is much the same. An ordinary-language philosopher of the old school might conclude that the varieties of imperative really do have nothing, or very little, in common. Unfortunately, I find that they do, and that I must sometimes make do with strained English. The happy state, by contrast, of indicative logic is, in any case, partly due to the fact that it has had upwards of two thousand years to find its feet.

Are QUESTIONS imperatives? Various people have thought so. (For references see Llewelyn, 'What is a question?', who cites Bosanquet, *Logic, or the Morphology of Knowledge* and Hare, 'Imperative Sentences'; Bosanquet got it from Sigwart, *Logik*.) The 'questions' in an examination paper are often in the grammatical imperative, as in

Write an essay on the causes of the Second Punic War,

though it has been doubted whether this kind of example is fair. (See Field, 'Note on Imperatives'.) Two more recent accounts of questions have given detailed imperative analyses. That of Åqvist, 'A New Approach to the Logical Theory of Actions and Causality', says, roughly, that to ask the question,

Do fish have ears?

is to say,

Bring it about that I know that fish have ears, or that I know that they haven't,

where *Bring it about that* is an imperative operator; and Belnap, (*An Analysis of Questions*) – for discussion of the relative merits see D. and S. Lewis, review of Olson & Paul, (*Contemporary Philosophy in Scandinavia*), and Åqvist ('On the "Tell Me Truly" Approach to the Analysis of Interrogatives'), and for a general appraisal Hintikka, ('Questions about questions') – says that it is to say

Tell me that fish have ears or tell me that they haven't.

Both analyses can be extended to deal with questions of arbitrarily greater complexity. See also J.R. Ross, ('On Declarative Sentences').

In a later chapter we shall explore reductions of imperatives to indicatives, and some of the tests developed there can be applied to Åqvist's and Belnap's reductions also. Perhaps all that needs to be said here is that the verdict, whatever it is, is not of much concern in connection with the logic of imperatives; if it were the logic of questions we were dealing with it might be a different matter. Note, however, that approval of the reduction would not necessarily reduce questions to REQUESTS; answers to questions may just as easily be effectively commanded, demanded, invited, suggested and so on. In fact, with the complexities of imperatives laid before him, the logician of questions might find the so-called reduction two-edged.

Among locutions that, though they can hardly be called imperative as they stand, have consequences in action for addressees, are:

The next meeting will be on Wednesday 25th at 10.

The following examiners are appointed: Philosophy 103, Dr S Smith; Philosophy 104, Prof J Jones.

The Lion and Sun Society will have at its disposal a further 15 million ri'als.

In virtue of the power conferred on me, I hereby award you the degree of Bachelor of Arts with Honours.

I vote against.

(According to J.L. Austin, *How to do Things with Words*, these are 'exercitives' of the same category as orders and advice; according to Searle and Vendler they demand a separate characterization. Searle, 'A Classification of Illocutionary Acts', p. 13, calls them 'declarations'; Vendler, *Res Cogitans*, p. 21-3, includes them with a fairly wide class of others as 'operatives'.) Voting, of course, is often not verbal, but is done by raising a hand or marking a ballot-paper. These locutions decree, or, in the last case, contribute to a decree, that certain notional states of affairs shall obtain, without referring in any explicit way to what anyone is supposed to do about it. But the standing rules or conventions about meetings are such that, once a time is fixed, members are under the same kind of obligation to attend as if they had been explicitly summoned; the appointment of examiners brings them under the standing instructions affecting examiners; and voting, besides having consequences for whoever has the job of counting votes, contributes force to whatever action is supposed to flow when the issue is decided. Often people other than an appointee, votee, or other person directly affected, incur parallel obligations.

In some respects these locutions are like definitions of terms, significant only in so far as other things are said using the terms defined. The statements,

A gockle is a person with at least one stillborn uncle.

All gockles who survive to middle-age contract dyspepsia.

are empirically empty singly, the first because purely verbal, the second because it contains an undefined term; together they make a single, testable statement. In the same way, the pair of locutions,

X is appointed common-room rouseabout.

It is the duty of the common-room rouseabout to defrost the refrigerator.

can together be regarded as implying a direction to X to defrost the refrigerator, an injunction that is contained in neither singly. The difference is that the first member of the pair is itself not a mere *statement* of a meaning, since it relies for its force on the social authority of the utterer – he must be someone empowered to make or declare this kind of appointment – in the same way as the force of a COMMAND or DEMAND. It has sometimes been urged against the imperative theory of law that statutes and legal documents often contain little but decrees that have the function of defining subjects' legal statuses, powers and authorities. In fact such enactments carry the same kind of imperative force indirectly, when teamed with general enactments or conventions regarding standing duties; and a satisfactory theory of them might go some way towards making us happier about a relevantly emended version of the imperative theory of law.

Some part of what needs to be said about APPOINTMENTS, VOTINGS and DECREES will be plainer when we come to consider imperative inference in a later chapter.

In the case of imperatives proper, what seems to be implied by saying that their 'direction of match' is from words to world is that they look forward to, and seek, the performance of specified actions of the addressee or other subject, or the effecting of maintenance of specified states of affairs; or, if negative, non-performance or non-effecting or non-maintenance. There are a few respects in which this rubric is not general enough for a definition, and it is open to various broad, narrow or eccentric interpretations. But all the examples given so far can be brought under it somehow.

We turn now to some parallel or fringe entities that lack or vary some typical ingredient. Let us first consider,

> All right; *go* to the football match. (But don't expect me to be here when you get home.)

Far from seeking that the addressee go to the football match, the speaker clearly wants him or her *not* to; the locution does not urge, request, order or advise, but merely (in this case with ill-grace) withdraws or denies some bar or objection (see Schachter, 'Imperatives', p. 637). The grudging tone is not essential; we can equivalently have,

> Bill; borrow *my* lawnmower,
> Take the money ( – but leave me my charge cards).

These are close to being INVITATIONS, perhaps SUGGESTIONS; but, as I read them, they neither urge, ask nor entice, but rather *allow* or *permit*.

This reading would be obligatory if phrases such as *if you like* or *if you want to* were added, or if the formulation were a modal one with *may, can, could*, . . . We say,

> You can borrow my lawnmower if you like.
> Take the money if you must, . . .

(But an *if*-clause of this kind, attached to an imperative, does more than just conditionalize it. The issuer of,

> Smoke if you wish

does not tell his addressees that if they have a desire to smoke they *must* or *should* do so. See Hare, 'Wanting: Some Pitfalls', 1971.) The unadorned imperative form is used mainly when the addressee clearly *does* want to do or bring about whatever-it-is.

I shall call these PERMISSIVES or, in suitable cases, CONCESSIVES or AUTHORIZATIONS. But it would be misleading, in one way, to see them as ranged alongside COMMANDS, ADVICE and the others as yet another variety of imperative. This is because they themselves fall into sub-categories that run parallel with the 'sociological' ones.

The issuer of,

> Smoke if you wish

putatively claims authority to permit smoking; and that is, equivalently, authority to forbid it. If he did not claim this authority he would have to say merely something like

> You can smoke as far as I'm concerned.

In effect, this kind of permissive can be issued only by someone who has the authority to command. On the other hand, the permissive

> You can take the money (but please don't tear up my bus pass)

implies a speaker who is in a position not to command, but only to request. The first is a COMMAND-PERMISSIVE, the second a REQUEST-PERMISSIVE. Our initial example

> *Go* to the football match

apparently neutralizes a possible DEMAND, and is a DEMAND-PERMISSIVE. In the same way we can have ADVICE-PERMISSIVES,

> Put it into Commonwealth bonds if you like (but I wouldn't touch gold stocks).
> It will be all right to leave the finishing coat till next week.

INVITATION-PERMISSIVES,

> (It starts at eight, but) come earlier if you like;

RECIPE-PERMISSIVES,

> . . . . or more, or less, to taste . . .

and so on. Only one or two of the minor varieties refuse analogues; I cannot think up a plausible example of a wish permissive, or of a formal permissive. Negative permissives are straightforward wherever affirmative ones are:

> You don't have to contribute if you don't want to.
> It isn't necessary to stir for more than a minute or two.
> All right, *don't* then!

It has, of course, been recognized by logicians for a very long time that the concept of permission is related to that of obligation. (Modal 'squares of opposition' were drawn at least as long ago as the thirteenth century, and there is a deontic 'square' of the same kind in Höfler, 1885; see Chisholm, 'Supererogation and Offence: A Conceptual Scheme for Ethics'.) What you are *obliged* to do is, precisely, what you are *not* permitted *not* to do. 'Deontic' logics are built using complementary operators *It is obligatory that* . . . and *It is permitted that* . . . The parallel, within any of the 'sociological' categories, with imperatives and permissives is clear; but just one comment must be made. To say that something *is* obligatory, or permitted, is not the same as to enjoin or permit it, and a deontic logic, so read, no more provides a logic of permissives than a logic of indicative moral, evaluative, deontic or necessity terms provides a logic or imperatives. PERMISSIVES are locutions that permit, not locutions that talk about permission. Perhaps some or most deontic logicians think this is what they are talking about but, if so, they do not usually make the fact clear.

An occasional ambiguity in permissives, which will occupy us later, should be noted, since it casts light on their nature. What a speaker intends to permit is often that a *specific person* be given discretion to choose what is done. Compare,

> Henry go to the party, if you wish

with

> Henry go to the party, if *HE* wishes.

The first gives the discretion to the addressee, the second to Henry. The simpler

> Henry may go to the party

does not separate the alternatives, and is usable only when it is not necessary to do so.

When an imperative is reported with the use of one of the verbs COMMAND, REQUEST, ADVISE (etc), the direct object of the verb – that specifies the 'content' – is of the generic form to do *so-and-so* or *to achieve such-and-such*. (Or a corresponding negative, or one of a small range of closely allied forms.) But imperatives are not the only entities whose concern with action is so reflected. I can *formulate a plan* or *work out a program* to do something, or I can *resolve, intend, promise, hope* or *know how*; and I can think about or refer to other people who similarly have these *plans, hopes* and so on. Part of what we say about imperatives applies to these other entities too. But let us notice three ways in which they may (and generally do) fall short of being imperatives in the full sense.

1. In the first place they may be hypothetical, or refer wholly to the past, or they may be remote from the active concern of any speaker or hearer that is currently speaking or hearing them. These are even in one sense 'real' imperatives; it is just that they have no application here and now. Napoleon's orders to his troops were certainly imperatives, but though I speak of them as such they are not *my* imperatives nor directed at anyone who hears me.

I mention this sort of 'academic' imperative only to set it aside as distinct from the next two. All the examples in this book are, of course, 'academic' in this way, just in virtue of being only examples in a book.

2. The envisaged action may be action not of the addressee or of any third person, but of the speaker. This is the case with PROMISES, VOWS and UNDERTAKINGS, which Austin called 'commissives'.

3. The concern of a locution with action can be 'academic', but in quite a different way from that mentioned. Thus the statements of ethics or law can be concerned with the evaluation of actions independently of any commitment to performing them or attempt to urge them or others. This is especially clear when the action referred to is a past one, or a purely hypothetical one, whose morality or legality is in question. It is not always clear where we draw the line between an 'academic' evaluation and an imperative, since evaluations can slide gradually into being commitments, or can be half-hearted ones. But it is in this vein that we need to consider as para-imperatives PLANS, PROJECTS, PROPOSALS, SCHEMES, PROGRAMS and DESIGNS.

4. Finally, there are the mental accompaniments of proposed action, of imperatives and of para-imperatives like the above – DECISIONS, INTENTIONS, RESOLUTIONS, DESIRES, INCLINATIONS and many others. (In the case of some of these terms it is necessary to select among varying senses.) Their relevance to the logic of imperatives is approximately the same as is the relevance of beliefs, doubts, opinions and knowledge to that of indicatives.

Vendler, (*Res Cogitans*, ch. 3) develops this parallelism in detail. Against each of his groups of performative verbs – with one important exception – he sets, (a) a group of mental act verbs, representing mental acts typically accompanying or preceding the uttering of the performatives, and (b) a group of mental state verbs, representing utterers' typical states of mind. For example, against the group of 'expositives', which refer to the making of statements and include *state, affirm, contend* and so on, he sets (a) mental act verbs such as *find out, notice* and *realize*, and (b) mental state verbs such as *know* and *believe*. Against 'commissives', that is, *promise, undertake, vow,* . . . he sets (a) mental act verbs *decide, resolve,* . . . and (b) mental state verbs *want, intend, plan* and some others. The curious exception is the category of 'exercitives', namely, imperatives *order, request* and so on. About these Vendler says that because they are 'other-directed' they have no mental act or mental state counterparts.

But it can surely not be held that the issuing of imperatives has no typical accompaniment of mental acts and states; and to give as a reason for the alleged absence of mental verbs the fact that imperatives are 'other-directed' is hardly adequate, since all locutions are that. Imperatives, in fact, are typically the expression of a wish, intention or plan that the *addressee* (or someone connected with him) should do what is enjoined. In short, the mental act verbs *resolve* and *decide*, and the mental state verbs *wish, intend,* . . . , do a double duty; they belong against 'commissives' when the envisaged action is the speaker's, and against 'exercitives' when it is action of someone else. Perhaps they are not all equally amenable to both tasks. As we shall see, subtleties can be found in their grammar, which make the distinction for us.

PROMISES, UNDERTAKINGS, VOWS, PLEDGES and COVENANTS obviously form a family, and UNDERTAKINGS, provided we understand them as undertakings *to do* something-or-other, are perhaps the most neutral and typical members of it. (A PROMISE is sometimes understood as more solemn and binding than a mere UNDERTAKING, and what does or does not constitute a PROMISE has sometimes been held to depend on special forms of words, speaker competency, or whether you have your fingers crossed behind your back.) I cannot find any good evidence that PROMISES, UNDERTAKINGS or any of the others are ever made in grammatically imperative form; the usual expression is a simple *I will* or near variant, which context must distinguish from a prediction, a statement of INTENTION (which would not belong to this family), or an expression of epistemic certainty:

> I'll be there about six.
> I won't oppose you if you move to have it deferred.
> Under no circumstances will I retreat from that position.

or

> The airline will honour all existing bookings.

You can have it tomorrow.

or, of course, in explicit performative form,

I promise to pay the bearer five pounds.

Should THREATS be in this list? They are certainly often made in the same future-tense form,

If you continue to park across my driveway I'll pour glue in your carburettor.

But note the (typical) conditional form, and that the object is to get the *addressee* to act in a certain way. Although it has been argued (by Grant, 'Promises' and Árdal, 'And That's a Promise') that THREATS are no more than unwelcome PROMISES, there are some significant differences. (See Peetz, 'Promises and Threats', who says threats are at most statements of unwelcome intention; recontested by Ardal, 'Threats and Promises: A Reply to Vera Peetz'. On some complications see Lyons, 'Welcome Threats and Coercive Offers'.) Note that *threaten* is in any case hardly a performative verb; it would be eccentric to issue a threat by saying *I threaten to . . .* Vendler, (*Res Cogitans*, p. 207) calls a number of similar verbs 'shadow performatives'.

A description of these locutions as *para-imperative* needs to be supported by an indication of their similarities to, or connections with, imperatives proper. But these are many. Let us first of all note that a common way of making an UNDERTAKING is by agreeing to an imperative. *A*, say, says to *B*,

Lend me five dollars, would you?

and *B* says,

Yes, okay.

meaning,

Yes, I will lend you five dollars.

In effect, *B* has agreed to the same imperative as *A* uttered; but *B's* reply, though the *I will* that is prefixed to its paraphrase seems no more than a necessary grammatical adjustment to introduce the right subject-pronoun, is not literally the imperative he agrees to, but an UNDERTAKING with the same content.

Second, this being so, UNDERTAKINGS can occur with any *force* available to imperatives. The example given was of an undertaking to carry out a REQUEST, but we could as easily have chosen the obeying of a COMMAND, the taking of ADVICE, or the acceptance of an INVITATION,

UNDERTAKINGS are in consequence strong or weak, accountable or non-accountable (in the sense that someone who changes his mind about taking ADVICE ought to have a reason concerning its merits), subject to this or that special commitment-feature. In practice, perhaps, these varieties merge, and an UNDERTAKING tends to be treated on its merits independently of the circumstances of its origin. But any of the distinctions can be made if necessary.

There is also even a PERMISSIVE analogue of UNDERTAKINGS, as when someone says

> I may call in on Peter later.

Again, the formulation has multiple ambiguities; it is not clear that it does not represent a permissive intention, or a weak prediction. But, again, careful formulation would make discrimination possible, and the result could have any force of the same range.

UNDERTAKINGS (and PROMISES, VOWS, . . .), then, are of importance in complementing imperatives at a certain point of their logic. One of the ways this occurs is in the analysis of so-called first-plural imperatives in *Let's* such as,

> Let's have dinner out tonight.
> Let's give him a little surprise.

These involve the difficult concept of joint action, which we shall take up later. But the joint actors are not the multiple addressees of an ordinary imperative; they include the speaker, who lays out a course of action for himself and his addressee or addressees jointly. Consequently, if the joint action the *Let's* locution adumbrates can be analysed at all into actions of individuals, the locution needs to be seen as a (possibly complex) blend of an imperative with an UNDERTAKING. Various forces of the interlocking elements – which need not match – can, in theory, combine to give a bewildering range of possible forces to the result; but I shall leave the elucidation of this subtle matter to others.

Are UNDERTAKINGS, of one or another variety, the first-person equivalents of second-person imperatives? Is their relation as simple as that?

Before answering, let us look at some other contenders. One writer who has tried to develop a first-person-second-person parallelism is Castañeda, ('The Logic of Obligation'), 'Imperatives, Decisions, and "Oughts"' and 'Outline of a Theory on the General Logical Structure of the Language of Action'), who calls the first–person equivalents of imperatives 'resolutives'. Unfortunately this term is rather strongly suggestive of a false doctrine, to the effect that someone who *resolves* or *decides* something is engaged in an activity corresponding with the issuing of imperatives; whereas, as we have already seen, *resolve* and *decide* are mental act verbs, not (like *order, request* and so forth) performatives. The reasoning, perhaps, is that a resolution or a decision is an act of will that accompanies one's own actions, analogous to the act of will that accompanies the issuing of a command or request. (There is, in fact, a tradition to this effect; Aquinas says a voluntary action is 'an act commanded by the will', and Kenny, (*Action, Emotion and Will*, p. 207) accordingly describes *desire* as the 'saying in one's heart' of a command, and later, p. 216, says that,

> I will do *A*

is a form or possible form of command.) But imperatives are to be conceived, basically, as linguistic utterances; and it becomes relevant to ask whether the *expression* of a resolution plays the required role for us to regard it not merely as a para-imperative but as, in effect, some kind of imperative proper. What, in any case, is the test?

It is true that we do sometimes issue imperatives to ourselves. Towards the end of a particularly arduous walk or climb I might mutter,

> Come on, Charles Hamblin. Keep at it. Left foot, then right. Keep your spirits up.

But there is no good reason to describe this either as a first-person imperative – its grammar is that of a second-person one, and I address myself as if I were someone else – or, of course, as a resolution or statement of intention or anything of that kind. (At most it may be aimed at *producing* a certain resolution, in the psychological sense of that word. Imperatives of this kind are discussed by Grant, 'Imperatives and Meaning', who refers to Wittgenstein, *Investigations*, para. 243.) Talking to oneself can serve an important purpose, but its merits should not be sought by examining the actual words uttered; it is not clear that the chanting of a formula, say *Ohm mani padme hum*, would not do as well. As Wittgenstein said about private languages, there are no objective tests; what is right is whatever *seems* right. To exaggerate a little, talking to oneself is just like chanting a magic formula anyway.

A better, because less pointless, example would be that in which someone writes himself a memo. The shipwrecked sailor writes in his notebook, which perhaps he never expects anyone else to read,

1. Find chickens, or goats, for company.
2. Make needles, to sew sails, for boat.
3. Construct boat.

Since these look forward to actions to be performed they are certainly para-imperatives of some kind; but are they genuine imperatives? There seem to be three possibilities:

1. they are second-person imperatives as in the previous example, and the sailor is addressing himself as if he were someone else:
2. they are first-person imperatives of the kind we are looking for; or
3. the verbs are non-descript or, to give them a grammatical name, 'infinitive' (or something). In this case the notes might be abbreviations of sentences beginning *I must* or *I should*. (He could, after all, have headed his list 'Things I must do.') It is not clear how we are to choose between these alternatives.

(Actually there are some fairly simple grammatical tests, at which we shall look in the next chapter, but they do not totally resolve the issue.) One consideration, however, points towards alternative (3). Imperatives are generally understood to create some sort of pressure, personal or rational, for the enjoinee to do what they say; but these create none at all. The sailor will not be disobeying himself, or refusing his own request, or even rejecting his own advice, if, having written the notes, he in the end does nothing at all but bask on the shingle. By contrast even PROMISES and other UNDERTAKINGS *commit* those who utter them. (There has been much discussion of Prichard's thesis. (*Moral Obligation*, ch. 7) concerning this obligation. Grant, 'Promises', for example, insists that a promise creates not an obligation but only a situation in which we are obliged. It has even been said that the obligation arises only from the promisee's aroused expectations; see Kading, 'How Promising Obligates', criticized by Robins 'The Primacy of Promising'. But basically no one denies the obligation's existence.) Consequently any PROMISE is closer to being an imperative (and a first-person one) than are the sailor's notes.

If alternative (3) is accepted (as, granting some ambiguity, I recommend), the sailor's notes are not first-person imperatives, because they fail the pragmatic tests of imperativity. They may still be regarded as 'first-person', in whatever sense that designation has – the speaker, at least, considers himself as the person supposed to do what the list sets out – and they are certainly para-imperative, and within our ambit. But we would do better to consider them along with PLANS, to which we shall come in a moment.

Among explicitly first-person formulations that have sometimes been put in for the title of first-person imperative are those in *Let*, as in

Let me tell you a little story.
Let me think about that for a moment.

Unlike the sailor's notes, these do announce an intended act to someone else, for comment and co-operation. But their existence does not do much to alter anything else we have said. In the first place, the idiom has a faintly obsolescent air, except in its 'full' sense in which *Let* is a second-person imperatives and *Let me* means *Don't prevent me*. If *Let me* is to do duty as a first-person imperative it must be taken in a weaker sense than that; but the difficulty is to be sure just how much *can* be read into it. If the man who says,

Let me tell you a story

is to be understood as *undertaking* to go on to tell a story, in the sense in which he would be remiss if he did not do so, then what we have is merely another way of expressing UNDERTAKINGS. If not, it should, perhaps, be taken as a statement of INTENTION, and is a para-imperative of a kind we shall also in a moment consider; or else it is of the same para-imperative family as PLANS, like the sailor's notes. ('Let me do the following' would be as good a heading as any other for the sailor to put on his list.) If it is none of these, perhaps it has no very definite character at all, but just hovers over or between them.

Do we finally conclude that UNDERTAKINGS must be the true first-person imperatives? Searle, ('A Classification of Illocutionary Acts', p. 11) says:

Since the direction of fit is the same for commissives as directives, it would give us a simpler taxonomy if we could show that they are really members of the same category. I am unable to do this because, whereas the point of a promise is to commit the speaker to doing something (and not necessarily to try to get himself to do it), the point of a request is to try to get the hearer to do something (and not necessarily to commit or obligate him to do it).

UNDERTAKINGS create, in the speaker, a kind of obligation that is at best an imperfect parallel of any that imperatives create in an addressee. The addressee of an imperative is, it is true, obligated if he *accepts* the imperative, but acceptance, as we saw, amounts to his making an UNDERTAKING of his own. Imperatives, on the other hand, have the function of trying to get addressees to conform, or (if non-wilful) of indicating to them a course of action that would benefit them; but UNDERTAKINGS have neither of these functions. A PROMISE, it has been said (by Grant, 'Promises'; see also Peetz, 'Promises and Threats' and Atiyah, 'Promises and the Law of Contract'), pragmatically implies the existence of a promisee who desires what is promised, and a prediction of conformity by the promiser, or at least an intention to conform; but none of these properties has a good parallel among imperatives. (On whether the addressee *must* want fulfilment there has been discussion by Searle, (*Speech Acts*, p. 58) Schneewind, ('A Note on Promising') and Armstrong, ('Meaning and Communication', p. 431); but Grant's point about *pragmatic* implication remains largely unaffected.) If there is a kind of locution whose utterance has the function of trying to get the speaker himself to conform, it is the self-addressed second-person imperative, or the morale-building magic formula; but neither of these is a candidate.

And anyway, what law of grammar or logic dictates that imperatives *must* have first-person analogues? Why should the existence of a form of linguistic transaction involving two or more people, in which the speaker specifies actions for performance by the others, imply the existence of a parallel linguistic phenomenon that is not a transaction of that kind at all, but involves, as speaker and agent, one person only? Aren't my relations to my own actions different from my relations to actions of other people? Granted that if other people have ideas about what I should do they need means to tell me about them, and I, as linguistic recipient, must typically be in the position of having to take note of them; but if they merely have ideas about what they should do themselves, their need to tell me about them – if any – is surely of quite a different nature. In short, though it might be possible to devise a limited characterization of imperatives that would permit the drawing of a parallel, only a doctrinaire view of grammar that ignores pragmatic realities could lead anyone to regard the existence of such a parallel as mandatory; and we had better confine ourselves to the consideration of those realities and stop chasing phantoms.

PLANS, provided they are plans to *do* something (unlike, for example, maps), sufficiently represent a category that includes not only SCHEMES, DESIGNS and PLOTS but also certain kinds of SKETCH, MENU, ITINERARY, TIMETABLE, SCRIPT, SCORE, SCENARIO and so forth. RECIPES, too, which we considered earlier, could alternatively be pigeon-holed here. PLANS (and some of the others) may be wholly non-verbal, as in the designer's drawing of a house or bridge or a circuit-diagram. Or they may be verbal, even grammatically imperative, as in,

> Here is my plan: Dusty go in quiet-like to the main switchboard; Ches and I use the front door, and Skipper double-parks the escape van at the side . . .

(Actually, I've mixed the verbs. Some of them are third-person imperatives, or subjunctives or something; some are indicative. It is characteristic that, in sense, they are non-descript and neutral as between these alternatives. Note also that one of the subject is first-person. Joos's 'presentative' verbs, (*The English Verb*, p. 31-8) capture this category – he allows that subjects may be included, as in *Dusty go in* . . . – if it were not that usage slips easily from plain verb-forms to narrative present, or even to infinitive with *to*,

Jenkins to pick up car from pool.

PLANS essentially involve a degree of worked-out detail, and discussion of their merits can proceed very much along the same lines as discussion of non-wilful imperatives. When a PLAN is 'put into effect' it will often, in fact, become the content of an imperative, as when the architect's drawing is given to the builder as an instruction, though it is not then necessarily a non-wilful one. But it may also be used for various non-imperative purposes; the drawing may be given to the finance company as an undertaking concerning intentions for the purpose of negotiating a mortgage, and after the house is built it may be sent to friends to show what the house *is* like, or, perhaps, *would have been* like if the builder had done his job. Their 'direction of match', that is to say, is characteristic of their use, and may vary from one occasion to another; compare Anscombe's shopping-list (*Intention*, p. 56), drawn up to guide selection, but *the same list* as one compiled by a detective interested in reporting on what was bought. Architects draw plans, too, for other purposes than to have them put into effect; to demonstrate a possible technique, or for aesthetic appreciation, or even to show how a job should *not* be done.

In one sense PLANS, like ethics and law, have 'points of application' at which such parts of them as are relevant are imperative; that is, someone who 'follows' a plan treats it as being or implying a set of imperatives. (Ethical and legal codes are themselves, we might say, in part PLANS; though to say this seems to divest them of their proper force, to regard their framers as guided by considerations of political engineering rather than by considerations that apply autonomously to individual cases.) But which variety of imperatives? As soon as we ask this question we see that there are no grounds on which it could be answered; PLANS, themselves, are neutral, and only acquire a force when someone orders, requests, advises or invites putting them into effect. The reason they must be called *para-imperative* only (and another reason for not classifying ethical and logical codes with them) is that they are forceless.

Can it make sense, then, to classify them with imperatives rather than with indicatives? Are they dry-run imperatives with other, parasitic uses? Or are they indicative descriptions of possible courses of action or ends, lacking intrinsic imperative force? It doesn't matter very much which we say. It is tempting to argue that the relative mood-neutrality of the word *plan* fits it, better than any of the words describing imperatives proper, for the description of the kind of entity we deal with when we discuss imperative logic. The important thing about an imperative – it could be said – is that it is a PLAN for action; everything else about it – the fact that it is issued by a given person to another, at a given time and place, with a given force (and even in a given mood!) – is external to it. (Vermazen, 'The Logic of Practical "Ought"-Sentences', apparently so regards PLANS in his formulation of the logic of *ought*-sentences.) Tempting, but premature; for we shall see later how important it is not to undervalue the logical peculiarities of imperatives, as this contention could easily do. The word *plan*, too, is inept for describing imperatives that involve little deliberation or conscious detail – that is, imperatives that enjoin simple acts and, above all, IMMEDIATE imperatives such that there is little chance of deliberation by the addressee.

Besides planning *to do* something, one may plan *that something* shall be the case, or even *that someone else* shall do something. PLANS, that is to say, may themselves indifferently involve first, second or third-person actions, or results to be achieved by action incompletely specified. Adopted, they may acquire more precise force in these respects too. But before we investigate this range of differences further, let us move on to some other para-imperative varieties.

An INTENTION is also generally an intention *to do* something; for even an intention that something shall be so, or that someone else shall do something, is an intention to take steps, under at least some circumstances, to make it so or to engineer that other person's acts. Consequently the logical content of an INTENTION is like that of an imperative. But INTENTIONS also enter into the analysis of imperatives in several ways. First, the issuer of an imperative performs a deliberate act, and must be regarded as having an INTENTION regarding its consequences; the standard one would be that his addressee take steps to carry it out, and presumably this is always part of the act, though his 'real' INTENTION may be ulterior and different. Second, since the carrying out of the imperative by the addressee(s) is supposed to be, in normal cases, deliberate, rather than just a matter of reflex action, the imperative is typically calculated to engender certain INTENTIONS in them. The Rylean point perhaps needs to be made about both these sorts of INTENTION that they are not necessarily something separate from and causative of the acts themselves; to say that something is done intentionally, or deliberately, implies the existence of an INTENTION to perform it, but only, as it were, analytically.

But INTENTIONS (or should we pedantically spell it 'INTENSIONS'?) are also bound up in the acts themselves. Some actions, that is to say, are what they are *only* because appropriate intentions accompany them.

Consider fishing, which notoriously does not imply catching fish. To sit attached by a thread to a piece of bent wire that hangs in water is not to fish, since a person could get into this configuration by accident or for irrelevant reasons. Fishing implies at least a forlorn hope of outcome, a readiness to react to *possible* contingencies involving available quarry, and an understanding of why. So fishing is, again notoriously, as much a state of mind as anything else.

This point is sometimes put by saying that different descriptions of what may be extensionally the same actions may have different intensions. (See J.L. Austin, 'Three Ways of Spilling Ink', discussed by Mannison, 'Doing Something on Purpose But Not intentionally'; and Kraemer, 'Intentional Action, Chance and Control': Lowe, 'Neither Intentional nor Unintentional'; Gustafson, 'Expressions of Intentions' and 'The Range of Intentions', notes that even subtle stresses within a sentence can be important to the description of an act.)

It follows that an imperative that literally enjoins fishing, though it may be carried out by performing no overt act beyond sitting on a bank with a thread etc., is more than an imperative to carry out that overt act. But it would also be inadequate to describe it as enjoining only that overt act plus an accompanying state of mind. (In any case, *can* we reasonably enjoin this kind of state of mind?) The INTENTION of the injunction to fish can be specified only by spelling out a structured set of conditional imperatives such as,

If something tugs, tug back

(and so on), covering all relevant eventualities, including even those that may be known not to be going to arise. Someone *fishes*, not merely if what he actually does conforms with these, but if what he does *would* go on conforming with them even in different circumstances.

INTENTIONS, then – and WISHES, DESIRES, RESOLVES, DECISIONS, AIMS and PURPOSES, whose similarities are mostly greater than their differences – join our catalogue. Note, with Vendler, that they fall into two subcategories, roughly, mental states and mental acts. But the proviso that we are dealing not with psychological states or acts, but with the clearly formulated or formulable possible logical contents or objects of those states or acts, needs to be insisted upon. There are many uses of the various words that do not meet the requirement; to say of someone that he has good INTENTIONS may be merely to say that he has an amiable or well-meaning disposition, and be quite different from saying, for example, that he has good PLANS. In speaking of *formulated* or *formulable* intentions we are speaking of intentions spellable out like a fishing program, that is, of intentions that have become like plans.

So let us return to the distinction between INTENTIONS of the first two kinds mentioned, (1) the INTENTIONS with which a deliberately-issued imperative is issued, and (2) the INTENTION the addressee – or, for that matter, other agents – are supposed to be going to have when they carry out deliberate conforming action. The second of these is part of the content of the first; the issuer *intentionally* enjoins that the addressee *intentionally* conform. (And in a chain of command there are as many intentions as there are commanders, plus one.) Although it doesn't make sense to tell or ask someone to do something intentionally or deliberately, this is not because he cannot do so but because he cannot do anything else. And now let us look again at the gap in Vendler's table; he put all the intention and decision verbs in columns against 'commissives', but left the columns against 'exercitives' empty. So long as the intentions (etc) are confined to being those whose content can be expressed in simple infinitives, as in

They intend *to arrive* early,
He decided *not to have* another cup of coffee,

namely, to those in which subject and agent are the same, this is unexceptionable. But INTENTIONS and the others, not to mention also UNDERTAKINGS and PLANS and the other members of their respective families, can also – like imperatives, Vendler's 'exercitives' – concern acts of other agents. Let us call contents of this second sort *that-someone*-contents, to mark the fact that their usual expression is of this form, as in:

Jerry hoped desperately *that she* would be in when he phoned,
The grizzler intended *that Jones* should call back in the office afterwards.
It was planned *that everyone* would travel in the same bus.
I promise you *that the bank* won't hold your papers longer than necessary.

The commonest alternative form, that applies to a few verbs, is as an infinitive with subject, as in:

They wanted *me to* let them play through.

Both these forms stand in contrast to the plain *to*-content that goes with a simple commissive such as:

I promise to tell you soon,

in which the promising and the telling are done (or to be done) by the same person.

Now since *promise* and other verbs in the commissive category can take *that-someone*-contents as well as the more ordinary plain *to*-contents, whereas imperative verbs such as *order* and *request* can only take the former, Vendler's classification seems vindicated. But it is possible to question whether this is the best way of looking at things; isn't there a sharp difference between PROMISES (or PLANS or INTENTIONS) concerning other people's actions and the same things concerning actions of one's own? Aren't INTENTIONS, and the like, concerning other people's actions as 'other-directed' (in Vendler's words) as imperatives? Don't they, in fact, constitute the mental states that typically *accompany* the issuing of corresponding imperatives? But if this is so, INTENTIONS-*to* and INTENTIONS-*that-someone* differ in exactly the way commissives and 'exercitives' do, and INTENTIONS-*that-someone*, together with DECISIONS-*that someone* and so on, can fill the gap in Vendler's table.

This leaves PROMISES-*that-someone*, or in general UNDERTAKINGS-*that-someone*, hanging; they are neither imperatives nor true commissives. In fact they are of only marginal interest to us here. It is worth while noting, however, that there are independent grounds for regarding them as locutions of a rather special and peculiar kind. (There are two subvarieties; I can promise *on behalf of* someone, or I can promise on *my own* behalf to compel or unfailingly influence that person.) Granted that influence, even power, over other people's actions is possible, and a commonplace; there remain questions of where the responsibility for action lies, and consequently of how UNDERTAKINGS concerning such action are to be analysed. The issue has been discussed by Harrison, ('Knowing and Promising'). On *promising-that* in general, see also Fillmore, ('Subjects, Speakers and Roles').

As a final contribution to our list of para-imperatives, let us notice INFLUENCINGS themselves, or what we might more neutrally call GETTING-TO; thus PERSUASIONS, ENTICINGS, SEDUCTIONS, PROMPTINGS and INCITINGS. None of the verbs *persuade*, etc., are performative; they refer rather to the results of performances than to the performances themselves. But since an obvious (though not the only) way to influence, persuade or seduce people is by the use of imperatives to the desired effect, connections with everything else we have said can be easily drawn.

The reader may appreciate a summary table. I've made it brief, suppressed many possible variant entries, and made connections mainly using notes.

1. Imperatives proper:
   (a) Wilful, non-accountable: COMMANDS, REQUESTS, DEMANDS;
   (b) Non-wilful, accountable: ADVICE, INSTRUCTIONS, SUGGESTIONS, RECIPES (or under 3b?), WARNING(?);

(c) Straddling (a) and (b): INVITATIONS;
(d) Stragglers: FORMAL or RHETORICAL, WISHES, MALEDICTIONS, EXHORTATIONS, IMMEDIATE imperatives, *Let's* (connections with 3(a));
(e) Imperative in effect(?): APPOINTMENTS, VOTINGS and DECREES.

2. Permissives: COMMAND-PERMISSIVES, REQUEST-PERMISSIVES etc., AUTHORIZATIONS (sometimes like le).

3. Para-imperatives (3(a)–(c) all with *to*-contents or *that-someone*-contents).
(a) First-person: UNDERTAKINGS, PROMISES, VOWS (Subdivisible as COMMAND-UNDERTAKINGS, etc.?);
(b) Forceless: PLANS, SCHEMES, PLOTS;
(c) Mental act and state: INTENTIONS, DECISIONS, WANTS;
(d) Gettings-to: PERSUASIONS, INCITINGS.

Not anywhere specific in this list: ETHICAL and LEGAL.

Regarding the division of imperatives and para-imperatives we have been discussing, the remainder of this book falls into two parts. For several chapters I shall be concerned not with the separate varieties at all, but with what they have in common; and the discussion on which we have been engaged is relevant only as a survey of material. We can analyse, as it were, the kernel or content of the imperative – the action (though the word is not sufficiently general) that the imperative enjoins – without worrying about the way in which it enjoins it (or whether that word, either, is an adequate description of its relation to it). This part of the book is, for the most part, relevant to the various para-imperatives in the same way as to the imperatives proper; except that I have sometimes had to treat PERMISSIVES in relation to imperatives of assumed corresponding force. It is also, though I think it breaks new ground, relatively orthodox in its logical approach and assumptions.

For the remainder, we turn to differentiation, which must be in terms of use, or of what I have elsewhere called *dialectic*; though meaning that term not at all in Hegel's or Marx's sense, but rather in a modern development of Plato's as the logic of dialogue. Within a framework of this kind, the imperatives differentiate themselves, and are differentiated from locutions of other kinds; though they are also, of course, seen together with them as separate parts of a common practical process.

# 2

# Grammar-Logic

Alexander Broadie ('Imperatives') unseriously suggested that an imperative should be defined as any sentence whose verb would be in the imperative mood if it were translated into Latin. The joke is near the bone. Our grammatical and logical categories have been determined for so long by Latin grammar that it is still only with an effort of will that we rid ourselves of what ought to be obvious falsehoods.

The mistakes so generated are compounded by the fact that there has been very little detailed study of imperatives at all, whether of Latin ones or of any other. There are just a few signs of a change; the last few years have seen a readiness, among a few grammarians and logicians, to start studying them from the beginning again. Among recent, reasonably diversified, treatments may be mentioned that in Quirk (*A Grammar of Contemporary English*, sections 7.72-7.77 and elsewhere); that of Schachter; ('Imperatives') and of Stockwell, Schachter and Partee (*The Major Syntactic Structures of English*, ch. 10).

The assumption that what determines a sentence as imperative is the mood of the main verb is especially inept in the case of English and similar languages with few or no inflexions. A *mood* (same word as *mode*) is by origin an inflexional category; and the verbs in English imperatives have no special distinguishing mark at all, being everywhere the same as the infinitive or, with the sole exception of the verb *be*, the ordinary non-third-person-singular present. At least in a language such as English it ought to be obvious that whether a verb is or is not imperative depends on the sentence in which it occurs; or, more accurately, in normal cases on the locution-act towards whose performance it contributes. It is whole sentences, not isolated verbs, that are imperative or indicative, and even then they need to be seen in a context of use.

I proceed, still, without a definition of *imperative* or *indicative*, preferring to continue to refine intuitive concepts by comparing examples. At this level it is artificial to separate grammar from elementary logic – that is, from the logic of form and of connectives – and I divide the material of this chapter into short sections under a miscellany of mingled grammatical and logical headings.

PLAIN-PREDICATE IMPERATIVES

The simplest and commonest kind of imperative in English consists of a plain predicate without a subject, as in:

Close the door.
Move further down the car.
Take the first turning on the left.

The verb is, as we noted, in the plain or infinitive form without special ending. Imperatives *can* have subjects, as:

John move upstage.
Henry and Mary bring the lunch.
Somebody get a doctor.

But the ordinary imperative does not do so; it is complete without.

It has sometimes been debated (Thorne, 'English Imperative Sentences', Levenston, 'Imperative Structures in English', Joos, *The English Verb; Form and Meanings*), whether plain-predicate imperatives really lack a subject or whether the subject is an understood *You*. In the case of the typical imperative there is not much to choose between the contentions. Since the person (or persons) supposed to carry out what the imperative enjoins is (are) the addressee(s), and since an imperative has to be conceived of as being addressed, at least in principle, to some person or group, the meaning is clear without an expressed subject. So the dispute is doctrinaire, turning on the question of whether a verb *must* have a subject. Note, however, that English is fortunate or unfortunate in having only one second-person pronoun that can be 'understood'. In the case of languages that have more than one, those who argue for an 'understood' subject may be faced with the problem of saying which.

For what they are worth, there are some linguistic arguments that are often put forward in favour of an understood *You* in the case of English. For one thing, except in the case of certain rather atypical imperatives such as FORMAL ones, *You* may actually be inserted, if wished, for emphasis or contrast, as in:

*You* tell him. (Apparently nobody else is going to.)
You take the high road (and I'll take the low road).

For another (it is said), the only reflexive pronouns that occur in direct or indirect object positions in an imperative predicate are *yourself* and *yourselves*, as in:

> Make *yourself* at home.
> Try it out for *yourselves*.

In this they correspond with indicatives whose subject is *You*. There are some possible uses of other reflexive pronouns in other positions, for example for special emphasis in:

> See if you can speak to the manager himself

but they are possible also in the indicative case and do not upset the correspondence.

J.R. Ross ('On Delcarative', p. 245) notes that although you can crane your neck, hold your breath or go on your way, you cannot crane anyone else's neck (and so on), nor can anyone else crane yours. But instructions:

> Crane your neck.
> Hold your breath.
> Go on your way.

are perfectly meaningful, whence it again seems that *you* is implicit.

Another reason given for saying that, at least, nothing other than *You* can be the subject concerns the availability of tags such as *will you*, *won't you* and *could you*, whether as question-type tags with rising pitch,

> Come a<sub>bout</sub> e<sub>ight,</sub> will you?

or, in the case of *won't you*, as imperative-type with falling pitch,

> Watch out for<sub>pick-</sub>pock<sup>ets,</sup> won't<sub>you!</sub>

It seems from the case of tags attached to indicatives that the pronoun in a tag must pick up the person and number of the subject, as in

> I'll bring it back tomorrow, may I?
> Souths won resoundingly on Saturday, didn't they!

There are various subtleties in the application of tags (see Quirk, *A Grammar of Contemporary English*, and Arbini, 'Tag-questions and Tag-imperatives in English') but, again, typical plain-predicate imperatives behave like indicatives with *You* subject.

I say 'typical'; what are the atypical ones? Let us reconsider the question of first-person imperatives and, in particular, what the shipwrecked sailor wrote in his notebook. This could have contained first-person reflexive pronouns,

Find myself a goat or two,

or even, if he were to spread himself a little, first-person tags,

. . . and look for esparto grass for sandals, shall I?

If we accept the earlier arguments in reference to second-person, we must now say either that some imperatives have understood I (or in some cases *We*) instead of *You*, or that these are not imperatives. And some people, it is true, seem to feel that these forms are 'different', elliptical or even ungrammatical. (A Frenchman who, if shipwrecked, might write himself in *infinitive* note,

Trouver chèvres,

but would reject as ill-formed, say,

Trouve-moi chèvres,

would certainly feel this; and similarly the speakers of many other languages.) But the formal similarities, and even the semantic ones, between these forms and 'typical' imperatives are so great that the interests of simplicity would surely be served by rolling the two together and accepting that the understood-*You* doctrine needs widening.

The verb in the predicate of an imperative – any imperative – is nearly always a single word, *go, jump, play,* . . . , lacking not only an inflexion but also an auxiliary, indicator of number, voice, tense or aspect, or any special particle. Issuers of English imperatives seem to want to get the verbal meaning across shortly and with the least possible fuss. (English is not unique in this respect, but it is not typical. Although virtually every language has a short imperative form for use on urgent occasions or for deliberate abruptness, most of them have, at least, separate form for singular and plural, or for different degrees of formality or familiarity. In many languages the pronoun-subject *You* is normally included, and may itself assume various forms.) Wachtel shows, interestingly, that, for a wide range of languages, the grammatical forms of imperatives, and the ellipses in them, could be explained by supposing them always to be answers to imperative questions of forms such as *What shall I do now?* or *What do you suggest I do?* But it is difficult to see what an assertion that they always *are* answers to such questions could amount to.)

An English passive construction with *be* and passive participle is possible but not very common, except in combination,

Come in and *be fitted* by our expert staff,

or in the negative,

Don't *be offended* by his bluntness.

In virtue of this rareness, it is sugested by Thalberg, ('Mental Activity and Passivity') that availability of an imperative is a test of what is 'active'. Similarly infrequent is a continuous verb in *be* and *-ing*, as in:

Be *standing* by the gate at seven,
Be *working* when the boss comes round.

There are no other possible auxiliary constructions at all, except that a continuous passive, with both constructions at once, is just possible, as in;

If the police spot you, *be being impressed* by something in the distance.

(I cannot think up a less strained example; making it negative doesn't seem to help. The strangeness of many passives and continuous forms links up with the fact that *be* is a stative, not agentive, verb; more on this later.)

A perfect form with *have* and participle – say,

Have finished it by knock-off time(?)

– would be the nearest thing possible to a past tense, as required by some writers (see Dummett, 'Bringing About the Past', Bolinger, 'The Imperative in English' and discussion below) who seem to find such a thing vaguely possible. In this example it would refer to a past relative to a given future time. It happens that English does not need this form, since it has an alternative way of saying the same thing, in the closely similar but grammatically more satisfactory:

Have it finished by knock-off time,

with transposed object and participle. I leave it to the reader, or to some linguist interested in minutiae, to decide whether the first of these is independently acceptable, or whether it is a stylistic variant of the second, or to be regretted. But the *Have* is not the same in the two cases since, in the second only, it can be replaced by *Get*, and cannot be the *have* of the perfect.

It is claimed (by Bosque) that Spanish has an incontestably perfect-tense grammatical imperative form. This carries, however, deontic ('You should have . . .') rather than imperative force.

Auxiliaries such as *will, shall* and *may* have no imperative form, and in any case *will* is not needed for a future tense since an imperative (always – see below) has a future reference without it. But *be going to* and *be about to* (though, for various reasons – see Joos, *The English Verb: Form and Meanings,* pp. 22–5 they must be counted as separate verbs rather than as auxiliaries) are vaguely possible to give a future reference relative to another given future time, as in:

> Now don't be about to jump down my throat before I've even spoken.

Again, a strangeness; and, again, more later. We noted earlier that some languages have separate imperative forms for what are called 'present' and 'future' tenses; but the distinctions between these are also unrelated to the uses of *be going to* and *be about to* in English. The English phrases suggest immediacy or active tendency and may be relativized to an indicated time.

There are not many other restrictions on the predicates that can be used as imperatives, but there are a few. It is of interest to comment on, and explain away, one in particular, namely, that an imperative cannot have a modal adverb such as *probably* or *necessarily* any more than it can have a modal auxiliary. Although we can say:

> He was probably in the library

it does not make sense to order someone

> Be probably in the library.

But is *probably* really part of the predicate in the first sentence? It would be better logic to say that it is not a predicate-modifier but a sentence-modifier, and that a logically more perspicuous form of the imperative sentence would be,

> Probably, he was in the library.

And if this is so no predicate containing *probably* is in question. The non-availability of the imperative is perhaps itself evidence for the verdict. Some other adverbs such as *certainly* and *possibly* are in place only in the more tentative varieties of imperatives such as REQUESTS and SUGGESTIONS. (Katz and Postal, *An Integrated Theory of Linguistic Descriptions,* p. 77, say these can't occur at all, but they're wrong.)

## IMPERATIVES WITH SUBJECTS

There is a fine line to be drawn between an imperative subject and an attrached vocative. The imperative that says to someone other than

John, or to some group of which John is one member, that John is to move upstage would have subject *John* and a characteristic steadily-falling pitch,

$$\text{John}_{\text{move}}{}_{\text{up}}{}_{\text{stage.}}$$

On the other hand, if John is addressed by name and told to move upstage, the name would normally be pronounced with a rise and followed by a pause, after which the imperative would have falling pitch as usual,

$$\text{Jo}^{\text{hn,}}\ \text{move}\ _{\text{up}}{}_{\text{stage.}}$$

The latter is, of course, a plain-predicate imperative of the kind we have already dealt with. Tags also indicate the distinction; thus

John move upstage, would he, please?

but

John, move upstage, would you?

No doubt subject and vocative sometimes merge. But any remaining doubt that there is a distinction to be made between them ought to be dispelled when it is pointed out that there can be *both* a subject *and* a vocative, side by side, as in,

Nobody leave the hall, sergeant.

*Nobody* is subject, *sergeant* vocative. In any case, *Nobody* MUST be a subject rather than a vocative, since the addressee is not, literally, nobody. There is no meaningful locution of the form (with comma)

Nobody, leave the hall.

Among the various persons associated with an imperative we can distinguish:

(a) the issuer
(b) the group for which he is spokesman
(c) addressee(s)
(d) referent(s) of a vocative, if any
(e) logical subject(s).

(c), (d) and (e) are commonly all identical, and distinct from (a) and (b), which are also identical; but what other possible cases are there? Downing, 'Vocatives and Third-person Imperatives in English', says that logical subjects, (e), must be included among addressees, (c); but it is easy to find counter-examples, such as

B Company deploy on the escarpment, Lieutenant.

If there is a vocative, (d), must addressees, (c), be the same as its referents? I shall normally speak as if this were the case, but we shall later need to remember that there is a sense of 'addressee' which includes all intended recipients of an utterance, including those who are bystanders to the immediate transaction. (But excluding *over*hearers.) Since it is possible to apostrophize absentees, (d) and (c) can even be distinct. When it is allowed that there are first-person imperatives, it becomes difficult to see that there are any exceptionless relations between the five categories at all, though we shall later notice a minor one that applies to imperatives in *Let's*.

The logically important point that is made by the distinction between subjects and vocatives is that third-person imperatives (as we may as well call them) are separate in kind from second, and that the person or persons who are supposed to carry out the action the imperative specifies are not necessarily those to whom it is addressed. This does not mean (usually) that those to whom it is addressed are to do nothing about it at all. The addressee is expected to pass the imperative on, by some appropriate means, and perhaps persuade, threaten or cajole the intended agent. In fact there would be something to be said for the view that the imperative:

X do so-and-so,

addressed to Y, is really an elliptical plain-predicate imperative,

Bring it about that X does so-and-so.

But that would be literally untrue of even some quite simple imperatives, such as those in which the subject is among the addressees and needs to be mentioned only in order to be picked out. When John is told to move upstage, the other members of the cast do not need to tell him and are not expected to have to persuade or force him. We shall achieve the intended effect of the reduction in a different way later.

Some logically interesting cases are those in which the subject is specified indeterminately:

Somebody get a doctor,
Two of you carry the table upstairs,
Not everyone go.

What, if I am among a group to which one of these imperatives is issued, am I being asked to do or not do? Or what is the group as a whole, or any determinate subgroup of it, being asked to do or not do? I think we can answer these questions, but only after an excursus. (On a related ambiguity see Sobel, ' "Everyone", Consequences, and General Arguments'.)


### ACTIONS AND THE ACHIEVEMENT OF STATES

But not all predicates are equally at home as imperatives, whether second or third-person. Consider, as imperatives,

> Know the answer to Mary's question,
> Appreciate the music,
> Want to go to town,
> Be tall.

Any of these *might* be used under some circumstances, but they are all unnatural. And this is not because they ask us to do things that are difficult or impossible, so much as because there is something odd about their formulation or grammar. We would not be nearly so worried by them if they were put in the forms,

> Find out the answer to Mary's question,
> Be receptive to the music,
> Get yourself into a mood to go to town,
> Become tall.

(Or *Pretend you are tall*, or something.) Some of these sound as if they might, in some circumstances, be difficult or impossible to carry out, but at least it is clearer what they demand of their addressees.

The source of the difficulty is connected with the fact that the original imperatives enjoined states to get into, rather than actions to perform. In general,

> Be in state S

is an uncomfortable imperative, better expressed as

> Take steps to be in, or get into, or remain in, state S,

where *Take steps* specifies, however vaguely, an action rather than a state. The distinction between *stative* and *agentive* predicates is due in modern times, I think, to Vendler, ('Verbs and Times') though it has been pointed out that it was noticed as long ago as Anselm (*Lambeth Manuscript 59*). The application to imperatives was pointed out by Kenny (*Action, Emotion and Will*, p. 183). See G. Lakoff (*On the Nature of Syntactic Irregularities* and 'Static Adjectives and Verbs in English), who incidentally notes that adverbs of manner affect the distinction; although:

Drive carefully

is agentive,

Drive well

is effectively stative (and unhappy), because it is equivalent to

Be good at driving.

Generally, it is better to speak of a distinction between *predicates* rather than, as most writers, do, *verbs*. Vendler, incidentally, incorporating some terminology from Ryle, (*Concept of Mind* and *Dilemmas*) made a finer four-way distinction between 'activity term', 'accomplishment terms', 'achievement terms' and 'state terms' – both of the last two are uncomfortable in imperative formulations – but we shall in due course deal with his extra divisions in another way.

There are quite a lot of ways in which stative and agentive predicates differ, or tests which may be used to identify a particular predicate as one or the other.

1. Agentive, but not stative, predictes can take a 'continuous' tense; you can say,

I am cutting the tomato

but not normally,

I am knowing the answer

or,

I am being tall.

2. Agentive, but not stative, predicates fall under the genus *do something*: the question,

What did he do?

can be answered,

He wrote a novel

but not,

He wanted his dinner.

This is the point Anselm noted.

3. Agentive, but not stative, predicates can be augmented with the adverb *deliberately*, or with adverbs of manner such as *carefully, enthusiastically*; thus,

He drove to town deliberately

is acceptable, but not,

He had red hair carefully.

4. Someone may be *persuaded* or *reminded* in respect of an agentive predicate such as *to go to bed*, but not in respect of a stative one such as *to understand the instructions* or *to be asleep*.

4. The present tense of an agentive, but not stative, verb can be used with future reference; we naturally say,

The bus leaves in one hour

but not,

The bus has newly-painted mudguards in one hour.

(Rather, *The bus will have . . .*) It should be noted that the tests are all in the direction of providing agentive predicates with a richer logic than stative ones.

But the unhappiness of stative imperatives varies all the way from mild strain to unacceptability, and this needs explaining. A good thing to say seems to be that stative imperatives always have to be interpreted, in one way or another, as agentive ones in disguise, and create difficulties for hearers when this reinterpretation is unobvious. There may be various ways of achieving a given state; and there may be various indirect or metaphorical meanings that the words specifying the state may bear. A further complication is that states vary in their achievability, and that an imperative may be regarded as improper if it enjoins the impossible or the unbearably difficult. An imperative such as,

Be tall

perhaps suffers more from this fault than from the simple fact of being stative, since we could readily gloss it as,

Grow

if it were not that voluntary growing or self-stretching is unusual or painful. The hearer's reaction given this challenge, may be to look around for an alternative interpretation; was he being enjoined to be proud and dignified, perhaps, or to wear built-up shoes? Al alternative common agentive meaning replaces *be* by *seem*, as when an actor is told,

Be being charmed by her beauty

– note that many passives and virually all continuous-tense formations are stative, which partly explains their imperative rarity – and correctly deduces that this means.

Act so as to *give the impression that* you are charmed . . .

Some languages provide the mechanism for a regular grammatical distinction between stative and agentive predicates. Japanese so-called 'adjectives', for example, have all the tenses and other inflexions 'verbs' have – except, significantly, the imperative – and generally express states, freeing the 'verbs' to express actions. I do not suggest, of course, that Japanese or any other language makes the distinction on semantically perfect lines.

Semantic perfection, if we chase it, is in fact extremely elusive. In a semantic sense, not even the simplest and most typical imperatives, such as,

Come in.
Sit down.

are purely agentive or purely stative; they enjoin *effective* actions, namely, actions which achieve appropriate end-states. The addressee of *Sit down* is adjoined to jackknife at hips and knees, but also by so doing to achieve a location on and in contact with an anatomical support. He cannot be regarded as carrying out the injunction to the letter if he fulfils one of these expectations without the other. If the effect of jackknifing, in some zero-gravity situation, is merely that his feet leave the floor, he has not, in the full sense, sat. And the same applies if, uncompliant or paralysed, he does not personally jackknife at all, but is nevertheless bent and placed by others or by a gust of wind. The action and the achievement of the end-state are both essential to the carrying out of the imperative, a fact we fail to notice mainly because they are normally inseparable. But matters are also a little more complicated than this; for when we characterize *jackknifing* as an action separate from the end-state of sitting we beg the question whether this, too, does not have some stative force, the achievement of a certain body-profile; whence the elusive pure actions must have been the tensing of certain muscles. And this, in turn, is partly stative, so that we must chase yet further. The whole issue has been debated at length as the issue of 'basic actions'. (Danto, 'What We Can Do' and 'Basic Actions', Brand, 'Danto on Basic Actions', and Margolis, 'Danto on Basic Action'.)

It is not to our purpose to enter this debate. Provided a predicate has at least a certain minimum agentive force it is fully eligible as an imperative, and may meet all the other linguistic tests of agentivity as well. But the debate has some relevant to a principle I propose to adopt concerning imperatives. It is perhaps the most fundamental principle behind the treatment of imperatives in this book, and I shall call it the *addressee-action-reduction principle.*

The addressee-action-reduction principle is to the effect that the meaning of any imperative can be spelt out in plain-predicate agentives. Some of these may need to be qualified by hypothetical clauses in a way we shall look into later, and, in the case of multiple addressees, it may be necessary to distinguish different imperatives applicable for different ones of them. The principle is, in part, a definition. It says that when, and only when, an imperative has a *clear* meaning the various addressees are each, under every conceivable circumstance, in effective receipt of injunctions in respect of their individual actions. Otherwise the imperative is unclear or incompletely specified.

I do not want to recommend this principle without argument and, from what has just been said, it should be clear that I have reservations about it myself, attaching to imprecision of the term *agentive*. In some respects it is a methodological principle, itself imperative in form; it says: To explicate a difficult or logically puzzling imperative form, try spelling it out in terms of what actions it enjoins of its addressee or addressees. I have already adumbrated this method in two cases above; in saying that third-person imperatives are to be looked at for what they require of their addressees rather than for what they require of their subjects; and in raising the special question of the force of third-person imperatives with indefinite subjects. If the principle has merit, this merit will be displayed by its ability to make useful contributions to the discussion of these examples and others.

If there are no 'basic actions', action-reduction can never be complete. But we can live with this possibility and still use the principle to throw light on many logical obscurities. For that matter, even the theoretical assumption that there *are* basic actions, as a sort of limiting case, can do no logical harm. Compare 'elementary propositions'.

It is important to emphasize the component *addressee* in the name *addressee-action-reduction*. A third-person imperative (say) may be ever-so precise in its specification of the actions required of its proposed agent, but its ADDRESSEE-action-reduction will not contain any such specification in the form of primary imperatives; it will consist of plain-predicate imperatives (possibly conditional, and of various other degrees of complexity) directed to the addressee(s), and, moreover, if there is more than one, to each individually. In the same way, when an imperative refers to a non-immediate action, or to a state to be achieved, the reduction must also contain reference to preparatory actions to the extent that they are necessary to the task. For short, an imperative that specifies an *end* is reduced to imperatives that specify *means*. By insisting on this rigorous interpretation I make the principle more questionable, no doubt, but also methodologically more fruitful. It is a practical man's principle. For any task, it gives the program, or set of alternative programs, appropriate to the performance.

LET'S

You can't say, as imperatives,

He close the door.
They help themselves.
I think a moment.

you must use the forms with *Let him, Let them* or *Let me*. And perhaps even these forms are archaic, though it is not clear that there are any others to replace them. I cannot explain this disinclination to use pronouns other than *You* as imperative subjects, but it is an apparent fact. There is just one exception: *let's* is, in modern times, a first-person plural pronoun.

The freeing of the word *let* to assume exclusively its other meaning *permit* applies, at least in speech in all but very formal situations, to the combination *Let us* as well as the others, but only because the imperative function of *Let us* is being taken over by the abbreviation *Let's*. We do commonly say,

Let's drop in on Frank.
Let's all go to the ball-game.

In effect, *Let's* is evolving into a single, separate first-plural imperative marker word. (Other languages show similar tendencies: Latin-American *Vamos (a)*, Malay-Indonesian *Mari kita*.)

But are first-plural imperatives really imperatives? I do not want to argue the verbal point, but we are beginning to develope a case-law. And the first thing to point out is, perhaps, that we are concerned only with a subsense of 'first-plural', distinguished in many languages more clearly than it is in English. In Pidgin, *yumi*, 'you and me', is addressee-inclusive; but *mipela*, a sort of plural of *mi*, means 'we are distinct from you' and is used when the speaker refers to some group to which he belongs but to which the addressee does not. (I ignore certain other complications.) English *we* does not differentiate these two meanings; but English *Let's* has only or mainly the 'you and me' (or 'you and we') sense. Imperatives in *Let's* refer always, or typically, to proposed joint action of speaker and addressee, possibly with other people. If they referred solely to the speaker or his own group, there could be some argument over admissibility of the word 'imperative' as, in fact, there is in the case of *Let me*. But *Let's* imperatives do have a force – that is, an action reduction – for the addressee or addressees, as part of his or their joint action with the speaker.

The concept of joint action is very complex. The group of participating agents may constitute an organized team, a corporate body that is legally an agent in its own right, or may be a collocation unified by nothing more fundamental than the contingency of being within earshot. (See Gruner, 'On the Action of Social Groups', Londey, 'On the Action of Teams' and earlier Sosa, 'Actions and Their Results' p. Von Wright, *Norm and Action*, raised the problem of simultaneous joint and individual actions.) Many joint actions involve mutual signals of intention or of tasks part-performed, or mutual influences of other kinds such as moral support or persuasion. And actions of any agent may be conditional, in general, on the state of progress of the interlocking actions of others. No doubt some cases are relatively simple, but any of these complications can enter the detailed analysis.

'Corporate persons' – 'a Church, an Hospital, a Bridge(!) – are discussed in some detail by Hobbes (*Leviathan*, ch. 16), who, however, distinguishes sharply between 'actors' and the 'authors' (authorities, necessarily human) who represent them (see Copp).

Recognizing group action, we can refine the question of whether *Let's* imperatives are really imperatives. To the extent that they have consequences for addressees, they are exactly like joint-action imperatives that might be addressed to the same addressees, together with the actual speaker, by some other person altogether. To this extent they have a clear action reduction for their addressees, subject to conditions concerning corresponding action by the speaker. On the other hand, to the extent that a *Let's* imperative represents a commitment of the speaker to cooperate, it is more like a first-person imperative of the *Let me* variety, whose credentials (though they do not call for a dogmatic decision) we discussed in chapter 1. *Let's* imperatives have both faces.

This said we can leave the verbal question aside.

### DON'T

The word *Don't* it seems, is developing the role of a general negation-particle; we can have,

Don't walk.

Don't go down the mine, Daddy.
Don't you be late.
Don't let's quarrel.
Don't everybody speak at once.
Don't Henry and Mary forget the lunch.

In most of these cases it would be very unnatural to speak *Don't* as two words, *Do not*. Some people object to some of these formulations, in particular (I find) to the last; but any alternative involves circumlocution. In place of *Don't let's*, however, we may have *Let's not*. Note that *Don't* is, pedantically, the negative not of the simple form but of the insistent affirmative with *Do*, which seems to be available in all the same cases, though it is a little unnatural with *you* and with particular third-person subjects. There is no separate emphasizer for *Don't* (see Levenston, 'Imperative Structure in English).

### THE RANGE OF SIMPLE FORMS

The imperative forms we have mentioned so far can be summed up rather incompletely in the diagram.

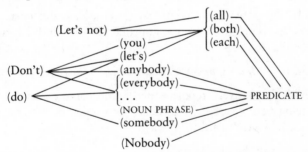

Round brackets indicate optional elements, and the only non-optional one is in fact the PREDICATE on the right of the diagram. I have not indicated possible variations of verb form within the predicate, for example optional *be . . .-ing* and *be* with passive participle, and I have ignored the necessity for certain agreements of person and number. Omitted altogether from the table are tags, vocatives and forms with *let* (other than those with *Let's*). Nevertheless, taking the predicate *play*, the noun-phrase *Henry* and the various pronouns actually listed, the table permits the formation of 46 different imperatives ranging from the plain *Play* through *All play, You play, Let's play, Don't play, Henry play* and *Somebody play* to *Let's not both play, Don't you all play, Do let's each play, Don't Henry play, Do somebody play* and *Nobody play*.

Plain-predicate imperatives generally go into indirect speech as plain infinitives,

> Jones was asked *to be the new chairman*
> Someone told me *to call at the office*
> They said *to go by the coast road*
> You were advised *not to be late.*

(*Don't* becomes *not.*) The main clause, as we noticed in the previous chapter, at least partly specifies the force of the imperative, though some verbs such as *said* are fairly neutral.

Unfortunately there are difficulties in carrying this simple pattern through to other kinds of imperative and of exterior context. If we wish to report the issuing of the imperative,

> Henry and Mary bring the lunch

as spoken by *X* to *Y*, we may say.

> *X* told *Y* that *Henry and Mary should bring the lunch*,

which, with the potentially deontic word *should*, could mistakenly be understood as reporting an opinion that Henry and Mary had a bounden duty, or

> *X* said to *Y* *that Henry and Mary were to bring the lunch*,

which could alternatively report a prediction, or the fact of arrangements' having been made. The difficulty is similar in the case of *Let's* imperatives. If what *X* said to *Y* was,

> Let's go over the accounts,

we seem forced into the similar form,

> *X suggested* to *Y that they should go over the accounts*,

where both *suggested* and *should* could be wrongly interpreted.

In reaction, I suggest recourse to bad grammar again, at least in such cases as call for precision. It happens that there is a sometimes unFowlerish formulation that will meet these cases for us, in which a third-person or first-plural subject is introduced by *for*. In some contexts this is quite at home, for example in,

> It would be a good plan *for Henry and Mary to bring the lunch.*
> It was not necessary *for us to go over the accounts.*

I offer the following increasingly horrible, but unambiguous, further examples:

> He invited for us to have lunch.
> I suggested for you to take the high road and for me to take the low road.
> The sergeant was told for nobody to leave the hall.
> The chairman called out to them for not everybody to speak at once.

Using these twenty-first century forms we can, however, convert our previous diagram to indirect speech almost as a whole

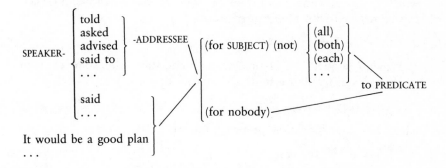

Or the main clause may be in the passive. SPEAKER, ADDRESSEE and SUBJECT may be represented by noun-phrases or pronouns, including *you, everybody* and *somebody* and even, in the case of the first two, *nobody*. But if *all, both* or *each* is included as shown, the SUBJECT must be plural.

Tags, vocatives, emphases, *please* and various politeness are virtually unreportable in grammatical indirect speech and the best that can be done is throw them in and hope for the best. Some of the books call this 'semi-indirect speech' or 'pseudo-quotation',

> The proprietor said would monsier kindly sign the accommodation register.
> They asked the driver to please hurry it along could he?
> He invited me to come, and do bring my charming wife, old boy.

We should remind ourselves, perhaps, that sharp distinction between direct quotation and indirect speech is an Indo-European predilection and that many languages make it only incompletely.

## ALL THE NEGATIONS

It is with some surprise that I notice that there are as many as five different and independent negations applicable to imperatives.

1. The simple negation-word *Don't* is applied indiscriminately to stative predicates or agentive ones. But its force is different in the two cases and we need to split it, conceptually, in two. Let us start with the sense we understand best, the one applicable to states. The stative imperative:

Be here at lunch,

which specifies a certain end-state, the state of your lunchtime presence, can be negated with *Don't* in the form:

Don't be here at lunch,

and then specifies the complementary end-state, the state of your lunchtime absence. If we write the first in the form:

Let *S* be the case,

where *S* is your lunchtime presence, the second is:

Let not-*S* be the case.

I shall call this negation type 1. The reason it is easiest to understand is that *states* (or *states-of-affairs*) are what we ordinarily understand to be expressed by the propositions of ordinary, indicative logic. Negation type 1 is the one closest in spirit to propositional negation.

2. But, applied to an imperative that specifies a more-or-less pure action, such as:

Run,

the word *Don't* changes it from an instruction to carry out that action to an instruction to refrain from doing so:

Don't run.

Since stative and agentive predicates are fairly distinct this does not lead to much actual ambiguity. But cases arise in which we may want one negation rather than the other. The stative imperative:

Be here at lunch;

is understood to mean much the same as the agentive

Take steps to be here at lunch;

but its negation:

Don't be here at lunch;

DOESN'T mean the same as:

Don't take steps to be here at lunch.

And we may sometimes need to negate *Be here at lunch* in this second form rather than in the first. It seems reasonable to regard 'agentive' negation, whether achieved by the simple application of *Don't* to an agentive predicate or in some more complicated way in the case of a stative one, as a unity, and call it negation type 2. Pure agentive predicates (if there are such things) do not have type 1, but stative predicates have both types. Since there is also a possible compound:

*DON'T* take steps *NOT* to be here at lunch,

negations 1 and 2 together give us four basic affirmative-negative forms.

Since most predicates are semantically neither pure agentive nor pure stative, whereas it is clear that use of the simple word *Don't* does not, in practice, lead to much actual ambiguity, some people might be disposed to look for a single, common variety of imperative negation and to make the distinction between my types 1 and 2 in another way. If they succeed, they are welcome; the important thing is to make the distinction. If you take effective action to bring about a certain state of affairs, that state of affairs does, by definition, get brought about. But this does not imply that if you do *not* take the action the state does *not* get brought about. If you are told:

Kill him,

your charter consists both in your performing certain homicidal acts and also (though this is a normal consequence) in your achieving that he ends up dead; but if you are told:

Don't kill him,

although it is fairly clear that it is primarily the acts, not the end-state, that are being denied you – since you are not told to stop him from dying in any other way – it is just possible that what your preceptor *really* wants is that whoever-it-is should be alive, and imagines that *this* will be a consequence of your desisting from action. And if this is what he wants it would be better if he were to say so, that is, to use a formulation that more clearly gives him a negation type 1.

3. Negation type 3 is the sort that is often expressed with the use of emphasizer words, in sentences such as:

Don't *actually* *kill* him,

where it could consistently be added that if, without your agency, he were to fall into the river or walk under a bus it might not be a bad thing. You are not instructed to strive officiously to keep him alive.

Rightly or wrongly, what we say often assumes that there is a 'natural' order of events that will prevail provided nobody, or nobody relevant, interferes. This is not always a clear idea, but we find it, for example, in the distinction between *killing* and *letting die*. There is an extensive recent literature on this distinction, mainly concerned with ethical issues, but which also makes some logical points for us. (See, again, Anselm, *Lambeth Manuscript 59*; and Bennett, 'Whatever the Consequences' and 'Acting and Refraining'; Fitzgerald, 'Acting and Refraining'; Brand, 'The Language of Not Doing'; Dinello, 'On Killing and Letting Die'; Morillo, 'Doing, Refraining, and the Strenuousness of Morality'; Chisholm, 'The Agent as Cause'; Walton, 'Omitting, Refraining and Letting Happen'.)

You can only *kill* someone who would naturally otherwise stay alive; and you can only *let die* someone who would not. It follows that you can't both *kill* and *let die* the same person, at least with the same action or group of actions; and in one sense you can't do neither, since not killing someone presumes his naturally staying alive and not letting him die presumes his naturally dying.

But letting something happen, though not a 'positive' action, is still an action; it may be a matter of conscious decision, and there may be positive things you do as part of it – such as looking in the other direction, pulling out a plug, expressing concurrence or positively *preventing* yourself from interfering. Does this need arguing? Consider the following case:

1. Someone is dying; you can take positive action to let him die, or you can take positive action to save him. But you can also take no positive action either way.

2. You are here, and there is no natural influence that would lead you to be anywhere else. You can, if you wish, go somewhere else; or you can take positive steps not to, such as chaining yourself to your chair, taking a paralytic drug, or more simply just by making a decision to stay. But you can also do neither, namely, just remain or not as the case might be, without troubling your head about a deliberate decision.

3. You are a naturally placid person. You are capable of working yourself up into a state of indignation, or of taking special steps to ensure that you do not. But in most circumstances you just remain placid, without doing either of these things.

One way of putting the point might be to say that there is an ambiguity in the concept of *letting* or *allowing* a state $S$ to obtain; it may be positive or negative, a matter of taking a kind of action or of taking no relevant action at all. Let us enumerate the possibilities.

1. $S$ would be the natural state; you can either (I assume you have the power) *make* it the case that $\bar{S}$; or you can *let* it be the case that $S$; or neither. (You clearly can't do both.)
2. $\bar{S}$ would be the natural state; you can either *make* it the case that $S$; or you can *let* it be the case that $\bar{S}$; or neither. (But not both.)

There are nine joint possibilities, and hence in all $2^9$ or 512 possible specifications, complete, partial or null, that can be built by disjoining them. To introduce some order into our discussion, let me symbolize:

> If it would naturally be the case that $\bar{S}$, take steps to make it the case that $S$

as

> Make $S$

and

> If it would naturally be the case that $S$, take steps to let it be the case that $S$

as,

> Let $S$.

Now the plain state-defined imperative,

> Let it be the case that $S$

can be symbolized,

> Make $S$, Let $S$,

and its negation type 1, namely,

> Let it be the case that $\bar{S}$,

as,

> Make $\bar{S}$, Let $\bar{S}$.

For negation type 2 we need to be able to construct the negations of *Make* and *Let*, that is, corresponding conditionals in which *take steps* is replaced by *don't take steps*. I write these -*Make* and -*Let*; thus,

-Make *S*,

means,

> If it would naturally be the case that *S̄*, don't take steps to make it
> the case that *S*,

which I take to be a negative injunction, different from the positive,

> Let *S̄*,

that is,

> Make sure that the natural order of things, *S̄*, is allowed to run.

The type 2 negation, which we earlier phrased as,

> Don't take steps to bring it about that *S*,

can now be represented more precisely,

> -Make *S*, -Let *S*.

But what we called the type 3 negation,

> Don't take *positive* steps to bring it about that *S*,

is just,

> -Make *S*.

Here, whether you are to let it be the case that *S* if that is what it is
naturally going to be is left open. In other words, this is consistent with
Let *S* or -Let *S*, Make *S̄* or -Make *S̄*.

Negation type 3 does not simply intersect the other two; there is a
complex of possible cases. In a certain sense, however, the only new
distinction that it is necessary to make in analysing this complex is that
between *making* and *letting*, interpreted in this conditional form.

Once again, if there is such a thing as a pure agentive predicate, this
kind of negation does not apply to it.

4. Imperatives are calculated to press, entice or encourage the
addressee to undertake a course of action; but there are locutions whose
role is to negate such pressures, enticements or encouragements. In this
sense I may negate,

> Do so-and-so

by saying,

> You may refrain from doing so-and so

or,

Don't do so-and-so if you don't want to

or

Refrain from doing so-and-so, if you like.

This is not an imperative at all, but a PERMISSIVE (of the kind we have already met in chapter 1), though presumably, if it is itself again negated in the same way, the original imperative results. At the same time it is interesting to note that its normal expression in either the second or third form is as a hypothetical imperative. This is to some extent spurious. As we said earlier, a commander who tells his men

Smoke if you wish

is not COMMANDING them that, if they have a wish to smoke, they must satisfy it. It is much more to the point to regard what he says as a negation of a putative prohibition, the latter being the type 2 negation of a command.

Let us draw a square of opposition:

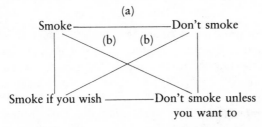

Across the top, in position (a), we have strong type-2 negation. (In the case of stative predicates, *Don't* would give type 1; but in these cases the bottom-row idioms may need reformulation.) Along the diagonals, positions (b), we have the present type 4. On this reckoning, type-2 negation is more analogous to traditional *contrariety* than to *contradiction*. But we are not doing traditional logic.

Type 4 is the 'external' negation commonly recommended by deontic logicians. In fact, as we saw, the nature of the distinction between PERMISSIVES and the corresponding imperatives of top-row forms depends on the variety of imperative under consideration. An INVITATION has both faces, and those who issue permissives often expect, and go close to insisting, that recipients avail themselves of them.

As we noted in chapter 1, there is a complication in application to vicarious – that is, third-person – permissives. If Mrs Smith tells Ernest,

Henry may go to the party

she is uttering the type 4 contradiction of a prohibition. But it is not clear whether the license left by the *may* is given to Henry, or to Ernest; the respective meanings are,

>   (1) Henry go to the party, if *he* likes,

and

>   (2) Henry go to the party, if *you* (Ernest) like.

Type 4 negation, therefore is not necessarily unique. Naturally, addressee–action–reduction resolves the senses.

5 Finally there is a sense in which someone who issues an imperative *commits himself*; and he may alternatively wish *not to commit himself*, and, perhaps, to say so. This is different from explicitly permitting non-compliance. He will say,

>   I do not order you to report to the office

or,

>   I am not giving you advice to the effect that you should buy nickel shares

(whose careful phrasing is necessary because *I do not advise you . . .* might be taken as meaning *I advise you not to . . .*). These look like indicatives, reporting the non-issuing of an imperative; and perhaps, in part, they are. But they also serve to repudiate or withdraw corresponding imperatives, and to this extent they have a function that makes them more than mere reports. Equally, they are not imperatives; though perhaps their negations are, in turn, the imperatives they started off by negating.

This kind of negation has sometimes been called 'illocutionary negations', or something similar (see Searle, *Speech Acts*, p. 32); Hare, 'Meaning and Speech Acts'; Garner, 'Some Doubts About Illocutionary Negation'; Sloman, 'Transformation of Illocutionary Acts'. On the interdefinability (or not) of *permitted* and *obligatory* see von Wright, 'Deontic Logics'; Alchourrón, 'Logic of Norms and Logic of Normative Propositions'. On the general question of embeddability of performatives see Geach, 'Ascriptivism'; Zimmerman, 'Force and Sense'). Negation type 5 is not especially characteristic of imperatives, since non-commitment may need to be indicated in respect of an indicative too, or in respect of locutions of other kinds. But it is important to include it in order to make the point that it is different from negation type 4. The above examples are not examples of explicit permission not to report to the office, or of explicit condoning of non-buying of nickel shares, which could only come from appropriate superiors or advisers respectively. I may refuse to order you to do something in quite other circumstances, namely, precisely *because* I do not have the authority to do so; and refuse to advise you because I do not have the expertise.

When *part* of an imperative or set of imperatives is countermanded by a negation of this kind, there can be difficulties in saying just how far the countermand extends (see Cornides, 'Der Widerruf von Befehlen', and Lewis, 'A Problem about Permission'). The problem is not peculiar to imperatives, but extends also to withdrawal of locutions of other kinds.

Let us put the five kinds of negation together. Representing type 3 by the distinction between *making* and *letting*, we have 32 different affirmative-negative forms associated with a given stative predicate. The following scheme can be used to generate them: *S* is some end-state, and under the numbers 1–5 are phrases in parentheses which may be independently included or omitted to represent the correspondingly numbered negations; or, in case 3, a pair of alternatives.

5                                                4              2
(No commitment as follows:) (Refrain, if you wish from) (not)

$$
\begin{Bmatrix} 3 \\ \text{(making)} \\ \text{(letting)} \end{Bmatrix} \text{it be the case that (not-) } S.
$$

To fix the grammar, rewrite *making* or *letting*, if initial, as *Make* or *Let*, or an initial *not* as *Don't*.

Which is the *true* negation of imperatives? I see no special point in asking the question; but, if it really came to the test – after the manner of competing Chinese religions being debated before the Emperor – strangely, each one of the five would have a case.

## CONJUNCTION

Logicians have sometimes been puzzled to find that so-called 'truth-functional' connectives may be used with imperatives when there are no truths or falsehoods for them to be functions of. The classical statement of this puzzlement is 'Jørgensen's dilemma', so-called by A. Ross ('Imperatives and Logic'; see Jørgensen, 'Imperatives and Logic'). A bold way out of the difficulty is to define 'truth' for imperatives nevertheless, in one of the ways we shall explore in the next chapter, or at least to look around for an alternative concept, not necessarily to be called 'truth', which will do the same job. A wholly more reasonable attitude than either of these would be a readiness to rethink the role of connectives to see what functions they *do* serve when connecting imperatives, and to accept that logicians have only ever thought 'truth-functional' was a good descriptive term because they were wearing indicative blinkers.

The uttering of two sentences *together* – when joined with *and* or other words, or merely apposed, or within some common intonation-pattern – obviously often conveys a meaning different from what would be conveyed by uttering them as if separate and unconnected. I say,

He's here, she's not,

and the implication might be that he treats her badly by not bringing her, or what a pity it is she has these heavy commitments. But in the case of the connective *and* it is an odd fact that we hardly ever join indicatives to imperatives. It would be unusual to the point of bad grammar to say,

It's one o'clock and come and have lunch,
Come back later and he's out at the moment.

(At least in English. I do not know whether there is any other language within which these compounds are formed. The point was noticed by Beardsley, 'Imperative Sentences in Relation to Indicatives'; it is used by Johnson, 'Questions and Requests' to discriminate between questions and the corresponding imperatives of *Tell me . . .* form.) There are just one or two special, idiomatic exceptions; we recognize the possibility of,

I'm the boss here and don't you forget it.

But one style of apparent exception is spurious, namely, when a grammatical imperative is used not as a true imperative at all, but to state a conditional clause,

Give him enough rope and he'll hang himself.
Do that and you'll regret it,

equivalent to the occasional formation with two imperatives,

Marry in haste and repent at leisure.

These translate effortlessly into conditional indicatives; as imperatives they would be anomalous, since they cannot take emphatic *Do*, and statives are regularly natural in them. On the other hand, perhaps oddly, the idiom is no mere foible of English or even of its near neighbours, but extends to every language I have been able to check. I recommend to those interested in universal grammar the task of explaining it. (An attempt is made by Ibañez, 'Über die Beziehungen zwischen Grammatik und Pragmatik . . .'; Bolinger's 'intrinsic consequence' hypothesis, 'The Imperative in English', pp. 340-6, may be relevant.)

When two genuine imperatives are conjoined it must usually be because what they enjoin should be seen as a single task. But there are different ways this might be so. Perhaps they are intended to be carried out together. Or perhaps (a very common case) they are to be performed in sequence but have a common rationale, as in

> Put on your parachute and jump.

(Example from Hall, *What is Value?*, ch. 6.) Some writers (Hare, 'Some Alleged Differences Between Imperatives and Indicatives') have made a lot of the fact that the *order* of performance is indicated by the order of the imperatives in the sentence, and that,

> Jump and put on your parachute

would be quite a different imperative. It has even been suggested that *and* characteristically means and *then* in the case of imperatives, though imperatives are not in fact different in this respect from indicatives; compare,

> She got married and had a baby

with,

> She had a baby and got married.

(On what he calls 'asymmetric conjunction' see Schmerling, 'Asymmetric Conjunction and Rules of Conversation'.)

Order of conjuncts can, it seems, be significant in either mood; we note this in passing. But a much more important point lurks behind this one, and extends to cases in which the order in which the tasks are to be carried out is unimportant. In the case of imperatives – as distinct from indicatives – there are two importantly different kinds of conjunction, the *separable* and the *inseparable*.

The addressee of,

> Walk to work and give up smoking

may have a constitutional aversion to walking to work and refuse to do so. But, if this is so, what should be his or her attitude to giving up smoking? Since they are *two* imperatives, should the second one be carried out independently and on its merits? Or, since they are *one* conjoint imperative, which makes no stipulation concerning preferences among rump possibilities in case it is not going to be carried out as whole, should be question of giving up smoking now be ignored as not separately at issue? We can imagine various lines of reasoning concerning the respective merits of smoking and exercise, but they are not the main point, which is rather: What was the relevant logical force of the imperative? *Is* it to be taken as two independent imperatives, or as a single one with interdependent parts?

It is, no doubt, very common for part of a task to be unperformed or unperformable for any one of a number of kinds of reason, and it would be silly to suggest that people who specify tasks should always foresee all contingencies. Instructees are meant to use 'common sense'; which presumably means that they are supposed to be capable of reading the mind of an imperative issuer to the extent of formulating supplementary instructions for themselves. But to say this is to dodge the logical point again. It is quite possible to formulate unambiguous conjunctions of imperatives, resolving the ambiguities of the plain ones by adding additional words. The specialist can say,

> Walk to work and give up smoking. I mean that you are to do both
> of these things; if you don't, you might as well not do either,

which can be glossed as the three locutions,

> Walk to work *and* give up smoking.
> If you don't walk to work, I don't order you to give up smoking.
> If you don't give up smoking, I don't order you to walk to work.

(The second and third of these are conditional negations type 5.) This is the inseparable sense where the force of the imperative is not to be distributed ovr the conjunction and does not apply to the separate conjuncts. The separable sense is a little easier; it reduces to,

> Whether or not you give up smoking, walk to work.
> Whether or not you walk to work, give up smoking.

The conditional clauses could be held to the redundant, but in practice they are useful to remove residual ambiguity due to the apposition of conjuncts. In logical effect the separable sense is best taken as the fundamental one, subject to care in ordinary-language formulations. The longer, explicit formulation in the case of inseparability is unavoidable where precision is needed.

The distinction between the two senses was probably first noticed by Menger ('A Logic of the Doubtful. . .') for what he called *wishes*. There has been some modern discussion, though it barely makes the main point, by Castañeda, ('A Problem for Utilitarianism') and Westphal ('Utilitarianism and "Conjunctive Acts": . . .').

Generality is like conjunction, and it goes almost without saying that the distinction between separable and inseparable senses applies to the word *all*. If I am told to move all the cars out of the yard and one of them has a flat battery and can't be moved, do I reason that the order can't be carried out and leave them all in? Or do I reason that the order is really separate orders in respect of each car and move all the others? In practice, again, I use 'common sense', relying on what I know to be the probable purpose of the order. But the order *could* have been formulated as a fully separable one,

> For each car, whatever you do about the others, drive it out of the yard,

or as a fully inseparable one,

> Drive *all* the cars out; if any are going to remain in, the order is void for the others.

And there could, of course, be intermediate cases, such as: All the cars are to be driven out, or if not all then at least half, or if not half, *then* don't bother. But the extreme cases are a test of our ability to cope. We shall sometimes, for short, refer to separably general imperatives as *rules*.

On inseparability, in a certain sense, of some PERMISSIONS, (see McLaughlin, 'Further of Derived Obligation').


DISJUNCTION

There are two senses of disjunction too, but they give as relatively little trouble. Before going on to them let us just notice the use of indicatives disjoined to imperatives to indicate consequences of non-compliance, as in,

> Hurry or you'll be late.
> Let's concentrate or we might miss something.

Unlike the spurious imperatives of the previous section that are really conditionals, these do have imperative force. But the indicatives joined to them do have hidden conditionals; the analysis is,

> Hurry. If you *don't* hurry you'll be late.

The special question that arises in the case of disjunctions of imperatives, such as,

> Take her to Knightsbridge or Bond Street,

is whether I am being authorized to make my own choice between the alternatives or whether that choice might still be determined for me by further instructions. If the imperative is interpreted as a *choice-offering* one, a subsequent imperative,

> Don't take her to Bond Street

can be regarded as negating the choice, and I can indignantly object that
I was told earlier that I could take her to Bond Street if I wanted to. But
if it is merely of the weaker *alternative-presenting* kind (so characterized
by Åqvist, 'Choice Offering and Alternative-Presenting Disjunctive
Commands', perhaps following Gombay, 'What *is* Imperative Inference?'), I have no such valid objection; the matter was left open, and it
has now been resolved, that is all.

We already have the conceptual equipment to deal with this
ambiguity. The weaker variety of disjunction, let us say, is a genuine
disjunction in the sense that it does no more nor less than present
alternatives; the stronger should be interpreted as carrying with it
PERMISSIVES that explicate the fact that a choice is being offered. The
choice-offering sense, in our example, can be made explicit by writing it,

> Take her to Knightsbridge or Bond Street; and, take her to
> Knightsbridge if you want to; and, take her to Bond Street if you
> want to.

The weaker has the first clause only. An instruction not to take her to
Bond Street contradicts the express permission of clause 3 of the stronger
form, but is consistent with the weaker one.

It will later be useful to have a technical name for a set of permissions
presenting a choice. I shall call such a set a *heresis*, with the
understanding that they represent non-overlapping possibilities. Many
permissives in fact state hereses, even when they mention only one
member; thus,

> Smoke if you wish

clearly carries with it the implication,

> . . . but you needn't unless you want to,

and is consequently equivalent to the two-member heresis,

> You may smoke.
> You may refrain from smoking.

This is what Ryding, ('The Sense of "Smoking Permitted" . . .') referring
to Tranøy, ('An Important Aspect of Humanism') called a 'free
permission' (see von Wright, 'An Essay in Deontic Logic and the
General Theory of Action', p. 22; Kamp, 'Free Choice Permission';
Scruggs, *A Praxeological Theory for Action-Guiding Discours*). The
word *or*, in permissions, commonly indicates a heresis, though
conjunction is more nearly intended than disjunction (see Loewer,

'Counterfactuals with Disjunctive Antecedents'). But a quantifier sometimes has the same effect; for example in,

Do whatever you like.

A choice-offering imperative, is in effect, an alternative-presenting one coupled with a heresis. In our example,

Take her to Knightsbridge or Bond Street

was the imperative, and the trio,

(You may) take her to Knightsbridge but not Bond Street if you want to.
(You may) take her to Bond Street but not Knightsbridge if you want to.
(You may) take her to both Knightsbridge and Bond Street if you (really) want to.

is a three-way heresis whose addition makes the imperative choice-offering. Hereses are important when we come to consider the properties of mixed sets of imperatives and permissives.

It is not always clear in practice whether a disjunction is choice-offering. This may be because the perpetrator himself is not quite sure. A choice-offering disjunction is one that is presented, as it were, as being the result of a complete analysis of the situation, so that new considerations are unlikely to come along which would lead the issuer of the imperative to want to dictate a further restriction of the choice. But it is sometimes nice to be able to leave things open.

The distinction between choice-offering and alternative-presenting disjunctions resolves 'Ross's paradox', which worried logicians when it was first introduced (by Alf Ross, 'Imperatives and Logic', in 1941), since it suggested that a hallowed law of propositional logic, the deducibility of *Either P or Q* from *P*, was not valid for imperatives. I am told,

Post this letter

and I reason as follows: the order implies,

Post this letter or burn it;

and I must do everything the order implies. But I can carry out the implied order by burning the letter. So I am justified in burning it.

We have not yet considered in what sense an order can be said to imply another one. But, certainly, the second of these two orders is implied by the first *only* when it is taken in its weaker, alternative-presenting sense. And, in this sense, it does not offer the burning of the letter as a live choice.

While we are on disjunction we should notice that an apparent tautology such as,

>    Either do so-and-so or don't

is never as pointless, taken literally, as it is in the parallel indicative case. (The negation, we may assume, is type 1 or type 2.) To start with, if it offers a choice, the permissions so generated are not tautological and do not even have the appearance of pointlessness. But even if it is a mere alternative-presenter, the fact that one or other of the alternatives is enjoined is not an empty fact. That I do not know which of the alternatives is enjoined implies, it is true, that I can not yet take definitive action. But it might be quite reasonable to set about making contingency plans.


IMPERATIVE QUESTIONS

Writers on the grammar or logic of questions often fail to notice that, besides questions whose answers are, logically speaking, indicatives, there are those whose answers are imperatives. Either yes-no questions such as.

>    Shall I bring my wife?

or W-questions (questions formed with interrogative words *who*, *when*, and so on, including, unalphabetically, *how*) such as,

>    Where do I catch the bus?
>    What font shall I use for the headings?

can call for grammatical imperatives, or short replies interpretable as imperatives, as answers. Even *Let's* imperatives may be called for, as in,

>    Where shall we go this afternoon?

Questions of this kind were noticed by Mayo, ('Deliberative Questions: A Criticism') though he regarded them as primarily self-addressed. For discussion see Llewelyn, ('What is a Question?'). The claim by Nesbitt, ('Value-Judgements, Prescriptive Language and Imperatives) that since,

>    What shall I do?

means

What do you command me to do?

such questions are really indicative depends on a reduction we shall discuss in the next chapter. Note, however, that questions of mixed varieties are possible, such as,

Is he here or shall I fetch him?

The correspondence of imperative questions with indicative ones is in general fairly exact, but there is one point at which the two diverge. It concerns the concept of a 'complete answer'.

A question in some sense lays out, for the choice of the addressee, a set of possible answers, from which the addressee is effectively asked to choose one. (For more than this bare sketch of the logic of questions and answers the reader must be referred elsewhere.) A yes-no question has just the two possible answers, codable as *Yes* and *No* (but representing whole answer-sentences). A *W*-question such as,

What is his name?

is answerable with one of the sentences *His name is John, His name is Bill*, . . . – without obvious limit, and hence not capable of enumeration, but nevertheless broadly definable and understood. But in the case of normal indicative questions *just one* of these answers must be singled out; someone who answered this question with,

His name is John or his name is Bill

would be held to have given an *incomplete* answer; and, above all, someone who answered a yes-no indicative question with,

Yes or no

would be held to have given no answer at all.

But now consider imperatives. In answer to the question,

How do I get to Campinas?

I might be told,

Take the Anhanguera or the Bandeirantes.

But if I press that I want precise instructions and should be told which, the reply I get might be,

It doesn't matter. Take whichever you like.

It is not that the two answers are *the same* answer, or necessarily that my informant is ignorant of the right answer and that I should ask someone else. His answer may be quite complete, since there may really be nothing to choose between the two alternatives. Note that the answer is a choice-offering disjunction, not merely an alternative-presenting one; that is, it has a coupled heresis.

Even in the case of a yes-no imperative question there are three possible complete answers, *Yes, No* and *Whichever you like.* In case of this kind, for the questioner to press the addressee to choose further between the alternatives would be to make a different sort of demand, namely, to ask him or her to *make a choice* on behalf of the questioner. Weak-willed people no doubt sometimes do this, but they are not asking imperative questions.

In general, an imperative question is answered not by giving *one* of the answers of the answer-set, but by giving a choice-offering disjunction whose disjuncts are a non-empty subset of the set. An incomplete answer is any answer containing mere alternative-presenting disjunctions, as distinct from choice-offering ones. A question with mixed indicative and imperative answers needs a somewhat elaborated rule, into which we need not enter.

(Belnap, *An Analysis of Questions: Preliminary Report,* para. 3.2.3, noticed another kind of indicative question that seems to admit as answer any non-empty subset of the answer-set, namely, a question such as *What are some examples of prime numbers?* But this is a separate phenomenon, and its imperative analogue would have to be *doubly* disjunctive.)

There is just one kind of indicative question that partly resembles imperatives in this respect, namely, a question that asks for a prediction concerning an unknown fact. Here, as in the imperative case, there may sometimes be nothing to choose between two or more alternatives; since the available evidence may be insufficient to point to one in preference to another or others. We shall notice some other resemblances of imperatives to predictions later.

TIME AND POSSIBILITY

Could the imperative mood really have different 'tenses'? We saw that the grammar books of some languages distinguish a present and a future tense; and also that, independently of language, there is a difference of a kind between *immediate* imperatives, calculated to be carried out more or less without forethought or by reflex action, and *non-immediate* ones in respect of which the addressee may have to plan.

But the actions or states enjoined by an imperative must always be in the future, and that seems to mean that there must be no room for tense distinctions. Imperatives may as well be reckoned as tenseless. Note that the *now* in,

>  Do it now

refers not strictly to the moment of utterance, as it does in the case of indicatives, but to some near future time, without delay; that the *always* in,

>  Do it always

can only mean *always in the future, from some near future time on*; and that,

>  Do it yesterday,

though it does not seem to be actually ungrammatical, is a kind of joke.

The thesis that imperatives always refer to the future has been denied. There is nothing strange or impossible (a Kantian might say) about 'willing' the past or the actual present to be different; and consequently there can be nothing wrong with past tense or strictly present tense imperatives which express this kind of object of the speaker's will. In some languages the subjunctive mood is regularly used to express imperatives, and exists in all tenses. It is true that it is impossible for the addressee of an imperative issued at time to do anything it enjoins in respect of times earlier than some moment slightly later than *t*; but this (it could be said) is a mere physical impossibility and does not put the imperative in any category different from that of imperatives that enjoin other impossibilities such as jumping unaided over a ten-metre wall.

This question has been ably argued elsewhere (Dummett, 'Bringing About the Past'; Bolinger, 'The Imperative in English'). The admission of past-tense imperatives perhaps depends on the illicit equation of imperatives with wishes and /or, perhaps, moral or deontic judgements. (We do make these judgements about the past, in a form such as *He should have . . .*) On the other hand, even if it is conceded that imperatives always refer to the future there remain some difficult borderline cases. Dummett, for example, imagines having a friend involved in an air crash with few survivors, and praying, before the passenger details have been published,

>  Let him have survived!

Even this is not clearly past tense, but (significantly) present-perfect; and it uses the not-typically-imperative *Let* form, and it is addressed, presumably, to Providence or to some magical agency which may be supposed (however unmetaphysically) to be capable of changing the past. But it is the nearest thing to a past-tense imperative that Dummett has been able to propose.

I propose, here, to assume the case proved and, in fact, to speak of *temporal possibility* (and *impossibility*) as especially relevant to imperatives. When an imperative enjoins an action or state that is possible in other respects we shall say that that action or state is *temporally possible* at a given time – we shall usually have in mind the time at which the imperative is issued – provided it is still possible at that time to take steps to carry it out. Generally, an imperative gets more and more difficult to carry out as time goes on until, after a certain time, it is no longer a live option and may be said to have *lapsed*. Note that, according to the definition, even imperatives referring to the future may be temporally impossible to carry out, namely, if there is simply not *enough* time left; and whether there is enough time may sometimes depend on a range of factors. But when the time for the action or state referred to is actually past, or even strictly present, no further factors need be consulted at all.

The concept of temporal possibility is linked, of course, with that of addressee-action-reduction; there must be time to carry out the actions which explicate the imperative content. But it also has some other consequences for a logical theory of imperatives. The first is that we conceive imperatives strictly as what is sometimes called *indexical*. An imperative must be conceived as issued at a specific time – and, actually, in specific other circumstances, whose specification will include details of speaker and addressee – and becomes a different imperative if any of these details is altered. The invitation,

Come to dinner at eight

that my wife might have received from Joan by telephone at 10 am is in certain respects a different one from that her husband George might issue to me in the same words when I run into him in the street at 6 pm, just *because* the actions involved as a consequence of accepting are quite different. (Panic; there is no time left to buy chocolates or flowers.) This does not mean that we cannot, for some purposes, treat them as the same. But when we do we in effect generalize about a family of related imperatives or (equivalently) an imperative abstracted from certain of its circumstantial details. In this respect the logic of imperatives will have to be quite unlike the traditional logic of indicatives, in which we regularly think of a proposition as having a content that is independent of the time at which it is uttered, or of its utterer or utteree. (Though, again, this may be no more than a reflection of the fact that the logic of imperatives is new, and the conceptual abstractional possibilities insufficiently explored.)

Two other consequences are that, in any logical model of imperatives, we shall have to make explicit mention of a *time-scale*; and that imperatives, more than indicatives, are involved with the concepts of physical or causal law and possibility. It would impoverish the logic, to the point of unacceptability, to leave out any of these elements.

## CONDITIONALS

Conditionals, or hypotheticals – I mean the term primarily in its grammatical sense, not that of Kant – with imperative consequent, come in various forms. We have already noticed the use of the phrase *if you want to* (and synonyms) in examples such as,

> Smoke if you wish.
> If you would like, come and have dinner with us this evening.

and also that the main function of the phrase is the not quite literal one of converting an imperative into a permissive (or, as in the second case, giving part-permissive force to an invitation). There are other phrases of this kind that are not quite literal; *please* may be expanded to *if you please* or replaced by *if you would* and similar phrases, and an *if*-clause such as *if I may suggest* or *if it's up to me*, not to mention *if I may be permitted a solecism*, and so on, can qualify a whole illocutionary act, imperative or any other. (On this see Heringer, 'Some Grammatical Correlates of Felicity Conditions and Presupposition', Ch. 4.) The word *want* or *wish* also has another special use in the antecedent of explicit conditionals of the Kantian variety, such as,

> If you want to avoid doing a belly-flopper, curl your toes over the edge and push yourself forward into a somersault.

Conditional *ought*-statements that resemble these conditional imperatives were called 'technical' by Diggs, ('A Technical Ought'; see Greenspan, 'Conditional Oughts and Hypothetical Imperatives'). The antecedent states the aim or end to which the consequent is to be the means. But the statement of the aim or end *avoid doing a belly-flopper* is itself para-imperative so that, in effect, what we have is an imperative conditionalized by something that is itself of imperative form. That *want*, in these cases, is not to be taken literally can be illustrated by the contrast with the case of jokes in which, unexpectedly, it is:

> If you want to visit Paris in August, don't see a travel-agent, see a psychiatrist.

But the simplest and commonest conditional imperative is one in which the antecedent is apparently an unambiguous indicative,

> If the weather's doubtful, call me and make a new arrangement.
> If you run across Jim Bloggs, give him my good wishes.

The consequent, it seems, has imperative force if the antecedent is true; if not, not necessarily. Unfortunately matters are not so simple as this. Compared with the case of indicative-indicative conditionals of the well-known type, there are two vast complicating factors.

The first concerns the possibility – noted by Dummett, ('Truth', p. 150 – that the truth of the antecedent may be actually under the control of the addressee or of some other party to the situation. Sometimes this may not matter; the imperative is, after all, conditional on the antecedent, and if I really want to avoid giving Jim Bloggs your good wishes the taking of steps to make sure not to run across him might be regarded as legitimate within the terms of my instructions. But in even very slightly different cases such as that of,

> If you run across Jim Bloggs, tell him about tomorrow's meeting,

deliberate falsification of the antecedent seems like a kind of logical cheating. If I easily *could* run across Jim Bloggs, then I should let myself do so, and tell him.

An opposite verdict is appropriate in the case of,

> If you stand me up over the Olsen deal don't ever come to *me* for help again.

The implication here is, precisely, that the addressee is enjoined and wished to falsify the antecedent. And the implication may be explicit in a different range of cases, those in which a *second-best* injunction is given,

> Come to the meeting; if you don't, at least send an apology.
> Be good; if you can't be good, be careful.

(The existence of *second-best* imperatives is a relevant consideration in connection with some attempts to reduce imperatives to indicatives, as we shall see in the next chapter.) So we are unable to generalize. It is possible for the utterer of a conditional imperative, if it matters, to avoid ambiguity by making his attitude to falsification of the antecedent explicit. But if he does not do so, the addressee must make his own logic.

The second, and major, complicating factor concerns whether and how the addressee is expected to *know* the truth of the indicative antecedent, and what steps he is expected to take to find out.

It is possible to find cases in which the whole burden of the imperative is in the indicative antecedent. A Professor of Mathematics, going on holiday, tells one of his research students,

> If the hypothesis of linear boundedness is provable, send me a postcard with the word *Eureka* on it.

How many weeks of work the student is expected to put into trying to prove the hypothesis of linear boundedness is unclear; sending the postcard might not take five minutes. (In the story, the student, noting that he had *not* been instructed *not* to send the postcard if the linear boundedness hypothesis was *not* provable, saved himself work and sent the postcard anyway. He failed Mathematics but took his degree in Logic.) But again, we need to do our logic by case-law. In the case of,

> If dough no longer adheres to a cold knife, remove from oven to a cooling-tray

it is obviously part of the injunction that steps be taken to verify the antecedent; yet it is easy to find cases in which unexpected difficulties might loom in the verification-process, virtually leading to the conclusion that the imperative ought to lapse or be radically reinterpreted. I am told,

> If the bridge is up, take the dockland route.

Whether the bridge is up is usually indicated by signs in the streets leading to it, but this time they are out of order and traffic chaos prevents me from getting anywhere near. I *could* find out by abandoning my car and walk several blocks to see, but. . . .

Whatever theory we set up of these imperatives must be sufficiently flexible to allow for the alternative interpretations. But the most important conclusion is that we need to add a codicil to the principle of addressee-action-reduction. The actions of the addressee that form the content of any imperative, besides being aimed directly at effecting what the imperative enjoins, may also need to be directed towards the securing of relevant information. Sometimes, in fact, a very large part of the action that goes towards carrying out a particular imperative may be of this information-gathering character. In the process of spelling out what is enjoined by an imperative we must not forget to spell out to what extent the addressee is expected to ascertain the truth of the antecedents of any contained conditionals, and how he is to go about doing so.

We shall later, in connection with the action-reduction of conditional imperatives in which the concept of knowledge is relevant, need to distinguish between *prospective* conditionals – in the case of which the truth of the conditional is a matter of waiting to see whether a particular contingency is realized – and those for which the means for deciding truth or falsity are at hand and need only be invoked.

A further corollary is that in categorizing imperatives with regard to their logical properties, such as physical possibility, temporal possibility and so on, we must take information-gathering into account. Time can be especially important. It is not much use having time to effect the consequent if there is no time to verify the antecedent first; or, rather, the two things must be seen together, and there must be, at least, a program – that may itself be conditional on the antecedent – that will get the *conditional* imperative satisfied in the time, not merely its detached consequent.

If this were not so, we could effect the most marvellous results. If we were to regard it as temporally possible to carry out an imperative whenever it is temporally possible to carry out its consequent, we could easily, for example, design a perfect betting system. Betting on the fall of a coin, follow the rule:

If the coin is going to fall heads, call 'heads'; if tails, 'tails'.

You win every time.

As a comment on the special logical difficulties that surround the concept of a conditional imperative it is worth noting that we are shy of building them into compounds. We conjoin them, perhaps, without qualm; but we do not negate them, except in the simple sense of negating their consequents, or of withdrawing them as a whole with a negation type 5; and we do not, except at risk of great confusion, disjoin them. It is true that the word *or* gets used, as in,

If there's sleet on the road cut your speed right back or, if it's fine, still watch out for skids on corners.

But the word *or* here points to the presentation of alternatives in the antecedents rather than to the alternativeness of the two conditionals as a whole, and could without much change of meaning be replaced by *and*. In fact we seldom genuinely disjoin conditionals of any kind, as has been argued at length around the question of counterfactuals; (see Lewis, 'Completeness and Decidability of Three Logics of Counterfactual Conditionals'; Nute, 'Counterfactuals'; and McKay and Inwagen, 'Counterfactuals with Disjunctive Antecedents'.

Under what circumstances does a conditional imperative count as having been carried out? There are, of course, strong and weak senses. In the strong sense, it does not count as being carried out unless the consequent has been carried out *because* (perhaps) the antecedent has been found to be true; in the weak sense it has been carried out – or at least has not *failed* to be carried out – if the antecedent has turned out false, or if the consequent has been carried out anyway. Downing, ('Subjunctive Conditionals, Time Order and Causation' and 'Opposite Conditionals and Deontic Logic') invokes this weak sense when he argues, for example, that

> If you come home late, lock the door

and

> If you come home late, don't lock the door

are not imcompatible since you can comply with both by not coming home late. Dummett, ('Truth', p. 151) presupposed this weak sense when he said that when the antecedent is clearly under the addressee's control a conditional imperative reduces, like the 'material conditional' of propositional logic, to a disjunction. To adopt this weak sense in ordinary speech would often, however, be misleading; as we usually speak, compliance and non-compliance are contraries, not contradictories, and there is the third alternative that the antecedent is false and the imperative inapplicable.


IMPERATIVE INFERENCE

Much previous discussion of imperatives by logicians has been aimed at explicating the concept of *imperative inference*, of which there appear at first sight to be uncomplicated examples such as,

> Put all the books on the floor.
> *Nicholas Nickleby* is one of the books.
> Therefore, put *Nicholas Nickleby* on the floor.

In a certain sense the formal logic of these examples is rather easy, and can be set out in well-known ways. But a range of conceptual difficulties awaits us if we push the formal analysis ahead uncritically. The quickest way to see this is to ask ourselves; who would *draw* this conclusion from these premises? If,

> Put all the books on the floor

was an instruction to George by Joan, George might, it is true, correctly deduce that his commission included putting *Nicholas Nickleby* on the floor, and do so; but that would not be good grounds for saying that George deduced the IMPERATIVE

> Put *Nicholas Nickleby* on the floor

from the more general imperative, for George did not receive this imperative and is in no position to give it to himself. It would be acceptable English to say that George was 'implicitly' told to put *Nicholas Nickleby* on the floor, but 'implicit imperatives' may be different from the real thing, and we should be chary of loading them up with the full range of imperative properties. In so far as a process of inference goes on in the mind of George, it might be better represented as his coming to realise that a certain planned ACTION or STATE OF AFFAIRS, the content of the imperative issued by Joan, contains, entails, involves or implies another action or state that is a candidate for his own choice or decision. The containment, entailment, or whatever, is not specifically between imperatives, or even between indicatives, but might as well be represented as one between moodless Harean verbal nouns:

> George's putting all the books on the floor

and

> *Nicholas Nickleby*'s being one of the books

jointly involving,

> George's putting *Nicholas Nickleby* on the floor,

and, given other premisses, other things such as,

> Joan's holding the steps while George climbs on them to reach the top shelf,

which could not be an imperative from Joan to George. Modern logic could be presented just as easily as a theory of the referents of verbal nouns as it could those of indicatives, and it would help our appreciation of our present problem if it were.

It is probably because he appreciated the difficulty of describing such things as just what it is that George *infers* when he places *Nicholas Nickleby* on the floor with the other books that Aristotle produced his doctrine that the conclusion of any 'syllogism dealing with acts to be done' (*Nichomachean Ethics*, 1144a,31) is not a verbally formulable thing at all, but an actual ACTION. But this is not right either. There is a hiatus between the logical process of deciding what is involved in the various forceful para-imperatives relevant to what I do on a given occasion, and what I actually do. At my most rational, I decide what I actually do by a process of evaluating and balancing; most of the time, I react to whim, pressure or drive by a process that is an automatic part of me and which I could not spell out in premisses and conclusions at all. Aristotle realizes this with one half of his mind; he says a lot about how *animals* act, and has a theory that they are mechanical like marionettes (*Movement of Animals*, 701b, 1-33).

But now let us turn to what might have gone on in the mind of Joan, which George, after all, must to some extent read in the process of determining what she says. Joan *intends* George to put all the books on the floor, or so she implies; and that means that she implies that *Nicholas Nickleby*, being one of the books, should be on the floor among them. But it is possible that Joan, for some reason, wishes to read *Nicholas Nickleby*, didn't realize it was among the books, and would not have been prepared to issue the imperative,

Put *Nicholas Nickleby* on the floor

if it had occurred or been put to her. At this stage it is helpful to invoke a distinction made by Bentham (*An Introduction to the Principles of Morals and Legislation* Ch 8; see Stalley, 'Intentions, Beliefs and Imperative Logic'). It is legal principle that a man intends the natural consequences of his acts; but he does not necessarily *primarily* intend them. If I intentionally push you and you fall into the water, it is possible that I should have known you would, and that I must be held responsible; but it does not follow that I intended you to fall into the water. In the same way, Joan may have intended that all the books be on the floor but not intended that *Nicholas Nickleby* be on the floor – either because she did not know *Nicholas Nickleby* was among the books, or because, although she knew, she did not connect. Consequently, despite the validity of the verbal-noun logic, we would misrepresent her if we said, without qualification, that she told George to put *Nicholas Nickleby* on the floor. It was not the IMPERATIVE

Put *Nicholas Nickleby* on the floor

that was implied – except in some specious, invented, secondary sense – by what Joan said, but only: George's putting *Nicholas Nickleby* on the floor.

Even the detachment of the consequent of a conditional imperative with true antecedent doesn't give an imperative that resembles an unconditional one, (see Moritz, 'Imperative Implication and Conditional Imperatives').

None of this necessarily diminishes the responsibility of an imperative-issuer for implications of what he actually says, any more than, in the indicative case, to say that someone 'didn't actually say' *S*, diminishes his responsibility for having said *S* if it follows from what he did say. The cases are parallel. Because, however, it is difficult to discuss imperatives without importing associations of speaker and circumstance, to speak of inference *between imperatives* can be misleading. I propose that we refrain from doing so.

REASONS

This is not quite the whole story about inference. It is common for an imperative to be prefixed by *therefore* or *so*, preceded by *reasons* that are ostensibly premisses of an inference; we have,

> It's lovely in the water, so come on in.
> They close the doors when the performance starts, so don't be late.

Or ostensible premisses are attached afterwards, by way of expansion, as in,

> Don't take him too literally. Politicians say all sorts of things at election time.

But although the conclusions, in these examples, are imperative, the supposed premisses are indicative. This simple fact is at variance with what is usually said about imperative inference. Thus Hare, (*The Language of Morals,*, p. 28) says,

No imperative conclusion can be validly drawn from a set of premisses which does not contain at least one imperative.

And although the inferences in our examples are, perhaps, logically incomplete in the sense that there are other premisses that are taken for granted, there is no reason to suppose that any of those other premisses are imperative. Imperatives would in fact be rather out of place as premisses; in the case of, say,

> It's lovely in the water, so come on in,

to prefix an imperative such as,

> Always take advantage of good swimming conditions

would turn the whole exercise into a piece of bad grammar, like the supposed inference by Joan or George about *Nicholas Nickleby*.

It begins to seem as if, against Hare's principle, although inferences can have imperative premisses or imperative conclusions, they *cannot* have both at once. And in fact even Hare compromised his principle when, later in his book, he claimed that moral statements, namely, statements about what is good or right or wrong, or about what people should or should not do, although they are indicative in character, have imperative consequences. But his second perception was, in one respect, better than his first; the ostensible premisses which support an imperative, though it is solecistic for them to contain imperatives, do frequently contain statements with 'good' or 'should'. We can have,

> Don't cut it like that. You should always point the shears away from you.
> Come for a walk. It would do you good after that heavy lunch.

And if Hare had said that inferences with imperative conclusions must always have PARA-imperative premises of this kind, implicit or expressed, he would not have been on such weak grammatical ground.

The second thing to notice is that our examples are all of ADVICE-imperatives rather than of COMMANDS or REQUESTS. Advice, we said, is accountable; and accountability seems to be of the essence here. The indicative premises represent *rational justifications* of the imperatives, of the kind advice essentially requires and commands and requests do not. It seems to follow, first, that these examples are concerned with a kind of inference that is different from that by which George decides what to do to meet the requirements placed on him by Joan; and, second, that although any variety of imperative can lead to the need for inference of George's kind, only a non-wilful, accountable imperative can occur as a truly imperative conclusion.

One way of dealing with these messy facts is to ignore them as quirks of no concern to the logician. Thus Castañeda, ('There are Command Sh-inferences') proposes, as he says, to set verbal points aside by conflating imperatives with deontics. A 'sh-inference' is any inference involving imperatives and/or 'should'-statements. This enables him to preserve a version of Hare's principle; and all the rest, it can be supposed, is a matter of mood-neutral, 'verbal noun' logic. But something is lost in the process.

To see that the putative 'imperative inferences' of the previous section – first cousins of Aristotle's 'inferences concerning acts to be done', concerned with what is involved or implied in putting a given imperative or para-imperative into practice – are quite different from those that provide justifications of particular, accountable imperatives, we need only see how much more like *induction* or *prediction* the process of justification is. Reasons adduced in support of a proposed action are often partial, often cumulative. We say,

> Take one of the Upper Level subjects. It will interest you much more than another elementary one would. Besides, you'll be going closer to getting the required number of credit points. And you shine at essay writing.

In more complicated cases reasons *against* are adduced too, and a balance struck. Inferences of a 'deductive' kind cannot be partial or cumulative, and cannot be balanced one against another.

But there is an ultimately yet more crucial point than this. The distinction between accountable and non-accountable imperatives, useful as it is, is not sharp; and the 'rational justification' of accountable ones does have parallels, of another and less logical kind, among the others. COMMANDS and DEMANDS, first, are typically backed by sanctions, which may be made explicit in forms which merge with those used for justifications; we have,

> I've got you covered, and I mean business. So don't try anything funny.
> Do take off that stupid plaid shirt. I'm not going to be seen in public with you in that.

The logic is in no ordinary sense that of inference from other imperatives or para-imperatives; yet the indicatives can act, as it were, as vicarious justifications, that do provide the addressee with grounds for compliance. And second, REQUESTS are typically backed by stories of need or worthy purpose, calculated to appeal, as in,

> Could you help with the boxes? I have to get them in, and there's no one else I can ask.

The inference, here, if any, is from the *issuer's* need to the *addressee's* action, of a kind that seems even to defy conflation with that appropriate to COMMANDS and DEMANDS.

Yet the pragmatic likenesses between the different kinds of *backing* imperatives may have – 'justification' is an insufficiently flexible word – is nowhere clearer than when we come to see them all as reasons that can be provided in answer to *Why?* If an addressee queries an imperative its issuer can react by *either*, if it is a command or demand, spelling out a sufficient sanction; *or*, if it is a request, showing it to be of a certain legitimate kind respecting his own interests; *or*, if it is accountable, justifying it. It is true that it can easily be claimed that this apparent correspondence is spurious, and that *Why?* is simply ambiguous as between *What's in it for me?*, *What principle justifies that?* and so forth. But behind the diversity of possible analyses lies a unity of expression that itself, sometimes, is capable of taking over the running. Since all the kinds of backing mentioned are alike partial and cumulative, and since imperatives can be issued that are not clearly of any individual variety, different kinds of answers to *Why?* can be combined, can reinforce, or can need to be balanced. Since there is no way out of this conclusion I propose that we should learn to live with it and, occasionally, try to see the demand for a 'reason' for an imperative not as ambiguous at all, but merely as one than can be variously satisfied. Often enough, the kind of reason given retrospectively determines the variety of the imperative, rather than the other way about.

Imperatives *bring about* their own satisfaction. When X tells Y to do A and Y (as we say) does it, Y has acted *as a result* of the fact that X told him to. (If he does it only accidentally, or would have done it anyway without being told, we hedge at describing him as having carried out the order.) So every imperative has two quite different kinds of relation to a certain set of actions or states: (1) a logical one, namely that it specifies and enjoins it, and (2) a physical, causal, natural-scientific one, namely, that it acts as a factor in getting it realised.

And we forget this at our peril. Their causal role is so central to imperatives that it can nearly be regarded as their sole, even defining, characteristic. At least, without it, they could not have any of the logical characteristics we have so confidently attributed to them.

Seeing the two relations side by side is not, however, quite an easy exercise. In the first place, this is because the logical relation of *specifying* and the natural relation of *causing* normally inhabit different spheres. In fact, according to the way logicians sometimes speak, it is impossible for the two to hold between the same entities, since imperatives, in the sense in which they *specify* anything and can be regarded as *satisfied* or *unsatisfied*, are logical entities and cannot have physical effects. If this is right, my first sentence of this section, above, is a category confusion. (But you understood it, didn't you? And if we make too many distinctions too early we get lost and miss things, as logicians have tended to miss what that sentence said – and some of the other things I shall go on to say.) The sentence should read, say: An act of imperative-utterance is typically a causal factor in the satisfaction of the imperative uttered. That, of course, is inaccurate too; a lot hides behind the word *typically*, and can't be uncovered until some of the other words are explicated. But later.

The second difficulty concerns the word *cause*, which is always tricky where it is *people* that are doing the causing or being caused. (Collingwood explained this rather well in his *An Essay on Meta-physics*, pt. IIIc.) It would be misleading and fruitless to conceive the carrying out of an imperative as an effect that follows mechanically, like the stumbling of someone who is pushed. But when, to give the concept some life and meaning, we use words like *comprehension* and *decision* – not to mention *action* – we are knee-deep in rational psychology, where the words *cause, because, effect, result* (and others) have older meanings that predate physical science. Those meanings are still current and respectable – the addressee, we say, acts *because of*, or *as a result of*, the order – but they need a psychological gloss in terms of understanding, thought, motivation. And since to understand an utterance is to know its meaning, we are back to logic again.

The causal nature of imperatives – at least of COMMANDS – was discussed in some detail by Bohnert, ('The Semiotic Status of Commands') and was also noted by Moser ('Some Remarks about Imperatives'). The case of non-wilful imperatives is complicated by the largely independent arguments for considering *reasons* for an action as causes of it (see Gean, 'Reasons and Causes'; Pears, 'Are Reasons for Actions Causes?'; Macklin, 'Reasons *v.* Causes in Explanation of Action').

My own attempts to swim in this conceptual sea will be presented in later chapters. They are, in effect, two.

1. In order to model a world in which people sometimes act through others, we need to postulate, in those others, a kind of predictability that cannot be equated with physical causal predictability. This is not new, but the need for it is newly underlined by the necessity to make sense of the way we use and speak about imperatives. It is part of the analysis both of how the addressee of a third-person imperative is supposed to motivate the proposed agent, and of how the addressee of any imperative is himself motivated by its issuer.

2. To formulate the dialectic or practical logic of imperatives we shall need to build ourselves a model of the mind of the imperative user or interpreter; not (I hastily add) a model of how our minds *do* or *must* work, but of how, at least, we could build an automation that would make a reasonably intelligent fist of imitating us. This is not new either, but not much has been done on it.

But, as a final topic for this chapter, let me say something about how the *other* kinds of causal influence an imperative act may exert can operate.

You are standing on a cliff, and I say,

Jump!

very loudly. Or perhaps I don't say the word clearly at all, but just make a loud noise that is something like it, or burst a paper bag at the same time. Or perhaps I say it and also give you a little push – or a big push. At the inquest, assuming the true facts reported, all will depend on just *how* big a push I gave you, or how loudly I said the word, and so on. . . . So, can we draw a line between the accompaniments (loud noises, pushes, abruptness of tone) and the essential, semantic content of the word *Jump*, so as to be able to distinguish the rational response to the imperative from the interfering factors? Well, simple English imperatives are commonly just one-syllable verbs (and that is no accident!); and to be imperatives at all they must be spoken 'imperatively', that is, a little abruptly and with a falling intonation – not, for example, as,

Ju-ump?

which would have to be a sort of question. And we are all more or less trained, as part of our language-learning, to be ready with reflex reactions to simple imperatives. And some of us are very suggestible and easily influenced – mechanically and non-rationally, but through the medium of the words and their meanings as much as by 'accompaniments' that can be notionally separated from them. (*Boo!*, in English, is a standard word for frightening people. But in Chinese it is a negative, and its utterance is likely to have the effect that its addressee hastily desists from what he is doing.)

Or suppose you are my trusted family adviser and wish to put me right about my asthma, or my rhododendrons or mining shares. You can give me my advice in a neutral and colourless tone of voice, without gesture or graphic illustration; or you can give it forcefully, earnestly and with the weight of evident or apparent authority; or you can give it, say, 'normally', namely, putting into it the amount of emotion you properly feel yourself or think it demands, smiling when you encourage and frowning a little when you caution. To give it colourlessly – or *over*-forcefully so that I might counter-react – could even be, nearly, to give 'bad' advice couldn't it? Rather give none. Advice, like other imperatives, is calculated to lead to action, and good advice is advice that leads to the *right* action. So it *must* be emotive and forceful when energetic action is required; calm when what is called for is careful thought. Or so a practical man would reason.

Some of this borders on being mistaken, but I do not intend to analyse the mistakes here. For the rest of this book, I shall do as the others do, and assume that a line can be drawn, somehow, between words and their accompaniment. But it can be important to emphasize that the difficulty is not unique to imperatives. Emotive tone and manner of utterance are just as important, and as inseparable, on some occasions when what is uttered is an indicative, or a question, or whatever. Consider the firm assurance that may be necessary to induce belief, the gesture, dramatic tone and hyperbole that is pardonable when what must be conveyed is genuinely extreme in meaning, or urgent; or the matter-of-factness when it is not. Yet the logician still does a useful job with the concept of propositional meaning.

Anyone, in fact, who thinks imperatives are different from this is probably in the grip of a category confusion himself; namely, the one that lumps them in with exclamations as 'interjections', or sees imperatives as allied with other dramatically delivered utterances of whatever grammar. Now that we know that imperatives have a characteristic and highly ramified logic we ought to be proof against this. Emotion and drama may, for all we know, have some kind of logic of their own too; but they can accompany any sort of utterance, and their study needs a different book from this.

# 3

# Three Reductionist Theories

Bertrand Russell once claimed that nearly everything we ever say is imperative (*An Inquiry into Meaning and Truth*, pp. 26-27):

In adult life, all speech ... is, in intention, in the imperative mood. When it seems to be a mere statement, it should be prefaced by the words 'know that'. We know many things, and assert only some of them: those that we assert are those that we desire our hearers to know ...
It follows that when, in adult life, you use a word, you do so, as a rule, not only because what the word 'denotes' is present to sense or imagination, but because you wish your hearer to do something about it ...

He makes an exception only of those utterances, such as involuntary exclamations, in which the language use is unthinking and automatic.

This is not an example of Russell at his philosophical best, but it presents a view to put beside the reductions in the reverse direction that are the main subject of this chapter. Distilled for logical content, it gives us, first, contrasting definitions of imperatives (where it is 'wished that the hearer do something') and indicatives (where 'what is denoted is present to sense or imagination'); and sound, the claim that seriously-intended indicatives are really of the form *Know that ...*

How do we assess claims of this kind? The attempt to divide linguistic utterances systematically into logically different 'moods' is an old one, going back at least to the stoics (see Sextus Empiricus, *Against the Logicians*, II, 70-3), but I am not aware of any good or thorough treatment of the division. In the preceding two chapters we defined our field as we went along, by what amounts to repeated appeals to intuition, but this does not give us a doctrinaire basis on which to start discussing the matter with Russell.

I do not aim, even in this chapter, to provide definitions or a doctrinaire basis, preferring to defend and continue to pursue the method adopted so far. But it does seem possible to propose tests for assessing any formula for reducing all the locutions of one mood, say indicative, to another, say imperative. I shall list four.

1. The first is the *practical interchange* test, which asks how far, and in what circumstances, the proposed translation can replace the original in practice. In applying it we need not be too severe. Certain characteristics such as length or euphony affect eligibility but can be held to be logically irrelevant; as can also, often, the fact that a formulation may be periphrastic or difficult to understand. On the other hand, a supposed substitution must be idle if no one, in any circumstances, would ever choose to make use of it. Philosophers have no special dispensation against being required to make practical sense.

An exacting version of the practical interchange test which has special merit is what we might call the *pleonasm* or *adscitition* test. We are on shaky ground if we say that a simple way of saying something can be 'reduced' to one that expands it by adding extra words or ideas, counselling speakers to waste breath or logicians to waste concepts. It would be better, in these cases, to propose a reduction in the reverse direction.

2. Another good simple test is the *reported speech* test. Could someone who has uttered U be correctly reported as having uttered its proposed substitute V, in the form appropriate to the reporting of utterances of this revised type? If V is a proposed indicative reduction of an imperative U, can someone who utters U really be correctly reported as having *said that* V *is the case*? Once again, we may particularly complain if the reduction, this time in reported speech, is unduly pleonastic or adscititious. But the reported-speech test is really two tests in one. Formulation in reported speech involves choice of an appropriate main verb, *say*, or *ask*, or *order*, or *invite*, or . . . , that goes some way towards classifying the dependent utterance by mood. But it also involves choice of an appropriate reported-speech form of the utterance itself; *that*-clause, or *whether*-clause, or object-and-infinitive, or . . . .

3. Third, there is what might be called the *pragmatic role* test. Differences of logical mood reflect differences of pragmatic function. Indicatives inform hearers as yet uninformed, or display the informed state of the speaker, or admit facts previously unadmitted; interrogatives seek information from someone supposedly better informed, or etc.; imperatives seek or moot specified actions otherwise unlikely to be performed or end-states otherwise unlikely to be realized. The weakness of this as a test is that we are not in a position to give complete characterization of the functions of the various moods, and must be content with case-law. On the other hand, it is clear that the pragmatic

distinctions, though not so simple as have sometimes been thought, are not so complicated that we cannot often reach quite definite verdicts. Note that Sealre ('A Classification of Illocutionary Acts') lists as discriminants 'differences in point (or purpose)', and 'differences in relations to the rest of the discourse'.

4. The fourth test, or range of tests, is, for our purposes, the most important. We already have a fairly clear idea of the diversity of the logic of imperatives, and we have noted a number of points at which it differs from that of indicatives. We are consequently in a reasonable position to mount the *equivalent logic* test. Any proposed translation should preserve, without undue strain or periphrasis, the range of logical properties of the original.

The special importance of the fourth test is that it can be applied not merely to a strong reduction claim but also to various weaker ones. In the cases we shall consider it has often been held that a proposed reduction gives not a literal equivalent but something that can be regarded as equivalent for 'logical' purposes; or that the difference concerns only some 'non-logical' detail such as the force of a special prefix or operator. Our fourth test confronts these weaker formulations on their own ground.

So let us apply the four tests briefly, for practice, to Russell's proposal to reduce all indicatives to imperatives of the form *Know that* . . . We know this formulation chiefly as a translation of an idiom of Arabic, or Biblical Hebrew, where we might read,

> Know, O King, that the armies of your enemies are gathering in the east.

It is not otherwise common in English, but it is intelligible, and consequently seems to pass the practical interchange test. But it hardly survives the stronger, anti-pleonasm version; there seems no point whatever in saying that the empty pair of words *Know that* is 'understood' preceding every simple statement.

It also fails test 2, the reported speech test, even on the weaker version, since there is hardly any sense in saying,

> The messenger told the king to know that the armies . . . ,

and a formulation with *asked* or *advised* as the main verb would be worse, not better.

In applying test 3, the pragmatic role test, we need to ask ourselves just what action or state *Know that* . . . enjoins; and the difficulty is that once the fact the king is supposed to get to know is specified there seems to be nothing else that he is being asked to do. Memorize it?

Persuade himself to believe it? These are ridiculous glosses of what a simple act of information entails. There remains the equivalent logic test, test 4.

In fact, test 4 is less relevant to this case than to the others we shall deal with, since Russell's aim was not the explication of indicative logic. But it is worth noticing that, far from doing anything towards modelling indicative logic in imperative terms, the *Know that* . . . prefix positively obscures it. Is the prefix supposed to be distributive over conjunctions? disjunctions? Does an implication between indicatives become some similar relation between corresponding imperatives? Does the negation of the imperative, *Don't know that* . . . , mean anything at all? I shall not attempt to answer these questions. Russell's reduction fails test 4 handsomely, more completely even than it does tests 1-3.

Russell's aim, perhaps, in saying what he did, was to point out that practical verbal utterances have characteristic purposes and consequences; and he made the claim that they are imperative only because he thought that that was the same thing. But our considerations, for what they are worth, rather favour the project of standing Russell on his head. Someone who said,

> Know that *S*

would do so, typically, in order to impart the information *S* to his hearer, without giving him any instructions as to what he should do about it. If this is so, what he says is not really an imperative and would be less logically misleading if the *Know that* were omitted and the *S* stated alone.

So let us move on to the proposed reductions of imperatives to indicatives that are our main concern. There are three of these, generally quite different in their effect and implications:

1. The *You will* . . . theory, that imperatives are to be regarded as future-tense statements of what will be the case.
2. The *You should* . . . theory, that imperatives are equivalent to moral or deontic statements. This sometimes appears backwards as the assertion that ethical, or moral, or deontic judgements are 'no more than' imperatives.
3. The *I order you to* . . . theory, that says that imperatives may be classified as *performatives* of a certain form. To effect a reduction to indicatives this theory needs to be coupled with one that treats performatives as the indicatives they seem to be, not (as they have sometimes been regarded) as distinct phenomena.

As characteristics of the theories I have in mind, these labels and descriptions are rough and need refining. Adherents moreover often claim not literal equivalence, but equivalence as regards logic, or true meaning, or something else.

I shall state, and discuss, each of the three proposals in turn. But to some extent it could be said that they have a common motivation. Unlike Russell's, these are *conservative* reductions, since those who put them forward feel that the developed logic of indicatives is well understood and fundamental to all kinds of learning, and that the minimum upset to our body of logical theory will be caused if imperatives can be slotted into a place in it. This does not mean, of course, that all who think this should support any one of the reductions in particular, or that those of a different – say, radical or anarchist – philosophical temperament should reject them. In fact, I think all three reductions should be rejected; but the reasons for this conclusion need to be set down.

THE *YOU WILL . . .* THEORY

The view that an imperative such as

Close the door

is logically equivalent to a future-tense indicative, representable in the form,

You will close the door,

is implicit, in one way or another, in all the earlier writings on the logic of imperatives; for example, in Mally, (*Grundgesetze des Sollens*, 1926); Dubislav ('Zur Unbegründbarkeit der Forderungssätze', 1937); Jørgensen, ('Imperatives and Logic', 1937); and Hofstadter and McKinsey, ('On the Logic of Imperatives', 1939). Here *satisfaction* and *dissatisfaction* take the place of *truth* and *falsity*; the imperative is or will be satisfied when and only when the indicative is true, and logical operations are interpreted accordingly. Consequently, all the 'truth-functional' logic of indicatives – which means, in effect, the whole of modern, extensionally-conceived, predicate logic and set theory – can be carried over to imperatives with just a few terminological changes. In particular, in the influential paper of Hofstadter and McKinsey, '*!A*' is written for *Let it be the case that A*, where *A* is a proposition, and a logic is built of what are called *fiats*. Laying down various laws to the effect that the imperative operator distributes through other logical operators – for example, that,

Let it be the case that *A*-and-*B*

is equivalent to,

Let it be the case that *A*, and let it be the case that *B*

– they proceeded to prove a 'triviality metatheorem', to the effect that any logical complex of fiats is equivalent to a single one with the logical operator at the beginning and all the logical complexity confined to what stands under it. (For discussion, see A. Ross, 'Imperatives and Logic'; and Bohnert, 'The Semiotic Status of Commands'). In effect, all that is necessary to construct a logic of fiats is to get a good book on the logic of indicatives and inscribe an exclamation mark on its title-page.

Among writers who have proposed similar or nearly similar logics of imperatives are Leonard ('Interrogatives, Imperatives, Truth, Falsity and Lies'); Castañeda, ('Outline of a Theory on the General Logical Structure of the Language of Action', whose basic logic of both imperatives and deontics rests on an indicative base); Rescher, (*The Logic of Commands*); and Turnbull, ('Imperatives, Logic and Moral Obligation'). There is also a discussion by Aldrich ('Do Commands Express Propositions?'). For an older discussion of difficulties in the identification of imperatives with indicatives see Duncan-Jones, ('Assertions and Commands'). A useful piece of terminology was introduced by Hare, (*The Language of Morals*, p. 17), when he compared,

Your shutting the door in the immediate future, please

and,

Your shutting the door in the immediate future, yes

as respective imperative and indicative formulations. The common part, *Your shutting the door in the immediate future*, is called the PHRASTIC; and the mood-operators (*please* and *yes*) are called NEUSTICS. Hare, ('Meaning and Speech Acts') later made a finer distinction and changed the latter term to TROPICS. Logic, says Hare, is concerned only with the phrastics of utterances, never with their NEUSTICS or TROPICS. Hare did not propose any detailed logic and, for other reasons that we shall come to, is better classified as a *You should . . .* theorist than a *You will . . .* one. But the general idea is clear. Note, incidentally, that Hare formulates his PHRASTICS as verbal nouns.

Thus someone who holds that imperatives can be conceived as indicatives with prefixed exclamation marks, or that indicatives and imperatives can both be represented by verbal nouns with prefixed or attached operators such as *yes* or *please*, is not necessarily on that account a *You will . . .* theorist. It depends on the logical properties that he ascribed to the relevant operators or TROPICS. Moreover, most of the formal treatments give us only sketchy ideas of how we are expected to treat the questions that arise if their theories are treated as fully pragmatic ones. It is possible to say, for example, that satisfaction of an imperative is analogous to truth of an indicative without going on to say that the logic of imperatives proceeds exactly as if they can be truth-functionally compounded. But some logicians are content, even now, to make the strong identification and refer to imperatives as *true* or *false* (see, for example, D. Lewis, *Convention*, p. 150).

Langford in 1942, ('The Notion of Analysis in Moore's Philosophy', p. 333-4) said:

Consider, then, a command of the form 'John, close the door,' and suppose this command actually to be given on a certain occasion. Suppose, further, that on the same occasion someone remarks: 'He will close the door.' When we consider what observations would determine whether or not this command was obeyed and what observations would determine whether or not the corresponding prediction was true, we see that they are indistinguishable, and that in fact the two sentences have the same sense, or express the same idea, namely, that of John's closing the door... Now the sense of an indicative sentence is a proposition, and therefore the sense of an imperative sentence is a proposition. *Hence to give a command is to express a proposition.* [My italics].

A similar claim is that of Gibbons, ('Imperatives and Indicatives') when he distinguished between the *primary meaning* and the *secondary meaning* of an utterance and said that the former is always a proposition; the latter depends (p. 108),

... upon the causal and other relations of the sentence in question to the feelings and attachments of the utterer and to the activities of particular groups within the given group of language-users.

And imperativeness – says Gibbons – is always a matter of secondary meanings, not primary. In an example like Langford's he compares (p. 116),

The class will now dismiss,

addressed to a class by its teacher, with the same sentence uttered as an aside by the headmaster to a visitor.

But now why, if addressed by the teacher to his class, should it not function simultaneously for them as a command, and for the visitor as a prediction? Why, if it comes to that, should it not function also for the class as a prediction? Why indeed, should we not say that, whether or not it functions for anyone as such, it *is* a prediction?

A slightly different, though overlapping, set of arguments for the *You will* . . . reduction is to be found among writers on generative grammar, starting with Chomsky, (*The Logical Structure of Linguistic Theory.* Although not published till 1975, this work was first written in 1955 and is consequently contemporary with Austin's Harvard lectures that formed the basis of *How To Do Things With Words.*) Chomsky wrote (p. 553):

Imperatives are still another form of elliptical sentences. In imperatives, the noun-phrase subject and the auxiliary verb are dropped, leaving only [the main verb phrase] . . . But only a restricted set of [verb phrases] can occur as imperatives. Investigation of the various possibilities serves to determine the restricting class for the transformation $T_{imp}$. Since we have 'give me the record tomorrow' but not 'give me the record yesterday,' we see that the choice of [auxiliary] in the transformed string is not free. For instance, [it] can be 'will' (since we have 'you will give me the record tomorrow' but not 'you will give me the record yesterday') but it cannot be 'have en' (since we have 'you have given me the record yesterday' but not 'you have given me the record tomorrow'). It is simplest to restrict [the auxiliary] to . . . 'will,' 'can,' 'must' etc.
Since we have 'look at yourself,' but not 'look at myself' etc., we see that the noun phrase subject of the string which is carried into an imperative must be *you* . . .

In short, imperatives are to be regarded as having a 'deep structure' (the term used later) of the form *You will* . . . or *You can* . . . or *You must* . . . , and to be generated by a transformation (the $T_{imp}$ mentioned in the extract) that deletes the prefix. Chomsky deals with a number of points of detail, noting, for example, that the occurrence of *do* and *don't* in imperatives is similar to that in questions and proposing, on grounds of simplicity, a dovetailing of the generation procedures.

Katz and Postal, (*An Integrated Theory of Linguistic Descriptions* – see also Postal, 'Underlying and Superficial Linguistic Structure') repeat Chomsky's arguments and add that, since (as they think) the only question-tags that can be attached to imperatives are *will you?* and *won't you?*, the auxiliary must in fact be *will*. Postal also says (p. 254) that this, '. . . provides an explanation of why we understand that imperative sentences refer to the future.' (See also Thorne, 'English Imperative Sentences').

Note, here, that there are two quite different families or arguments at work; linguistic and semantic. Unfortunately, they are arguments for slightly differing theses. What the linguistic arguments try to show is that imperatives ought to be understood as prefixed with the words *You* and *will*, whatever these words mean. But the semantic arguments are to the effect that imperatives are really future-tense indicatives, however these may be expressed. The point is far from academic. English (despite what the older grammar-books say) has no verb-form that is incontestably future in meaning, and uses either the plain present, as in,

He leaves tomorrow;

or one of the auxiliaries *will* and *shall*; or, with special meaning, another auxiliary such as *might* or *could*; or a quasi-auxiliary such as *is going to* or *is about to*. *Will* and *shall* (and *'ll*) cannot be considered as pure future-tense auxiliaries, since (1) they *always*, in statements, carry a guarantee or compulsion along with them, sometimes without any future meaning at all, as in,

No, he's not here. He'll be in the library;

and (2) they often carry overtones of volition or intention, as in,

I'll have another one, please,

which can hardly be called a pure prediction. (See Joos, *The English Verb*, ch. 6, and Ehrman, *The Meanings of the Modals in Present-Day American English*; Boyd and Thorne, 'The Semantics of Modal Verbs'. For present purposes I ignore differences between *will*, *shall* and *'ll*.)

But guarantees, compulsion, intention and volition are all part of the stuff of the imperative situation; and, in consequence, to say that imperative are of the form *You will . . .* may be quite unlike saying that they are future-tense indicatives. I do not want to explore the alternative meanings of *You will . . .* in detail, because they do not affect the main claim, namely, the semantic one. Chomsky, Katz and Postal (it should be clear on reflection) are interested in the semantic claim almost as much, and in the same way, as Langford and Gibbons are, and think their linguistic arguments support it. But, if we want to uncross the wires, we need to recognize *will* for what it is and employ a more neutral formation to represent a pure future tense. In particular, *is going to* is much better; I quote Joos (p. 23): '. . . this is a completely colorless 'future tense' way of speaking. Indeed this seems to be the only uncolored future that English has; . . .'.

And see what a difference the substitution makes; Gibbon's schoolmaster must now make an imperative out of,

The class is now going to dismiss (!)

And if we want to make the case worse, we can throw in a phrase such as *as a matter of fact*; and, for that matter, choose an example not of a command, but of a request or invitation, that is normally issued with less presumption of compliance. Does,

   Pass the mustard

really mean the same as,

   You are, as a matter of fact, going to pass the mustard?

To avoid fussiness, I shall still often say *will* in what follows. In passing, I should remark that an excellent job of demolition was done on Katz and Postal's linguistic arguments by Bolinger, ('The Imperative in English') who incidentally also points out that tags *can't you?*, *would you?* and others can be used with imperatives, destroying the special claims for *will* over other auxiliaries.

   The version of the *You will* . . . reduction that will interest us from this point on, then, is the semantic one, according to which imperatives are to be identified with future-tense indicatives, however expressed. And we can now apply our four tests.

   First, the practical interchange test. From what has just been said, a *pure* future-tense indicative, when the overtones of words like *will* are clearly removed, is not a good practical substitute for an imperative at all, and the plausibility of the earlier examples rested on the fact that they were equivocal. The most the proponents of the theory can claim is that there is a middle ground between imperatives and future-tense indicatives that makes a certain amount of equivocation possible.

   Sometimes even this middle ground vanishes, as we see if we imagine,

   Everybody will leave the hall, sergeant

inappropriately answered with,

   Will they, sir?

The third person is more open to predictions than the second. But we can also find unambiguous second-person cases. Seeing a friend off at the airport, I remark.

   You will be in Madrid by mid-afternoon,

and can be confident that what I say will be taken as a prediction, not an instruction; whereas, if he is my boss and replies,

   You will keep me posted on the Jackson affair while I am away, please,

it is clear that he is instructing me, not predicting.

   I think it is fair to say that the *You will* . . . theory fails the practical interchange test.

   Let us apply the reported-speech test. If Gibbon's school-teacher had uttered an indicative, the event should be describable in the form,

The teacher told the class that it was now going to dismiss.

Could this sentence be taken as meaning that the teacher actually dismissed the class? Its more normal meaning would be that he predicted imminent dismissal without authorizing it. And, even so, we rely on the ambiguity of *told*; alternative main verbs are capable of reporting an imperative only, or an indicative only, and even fail grammatically if we try to press them into the other service. Thus,

They invited us that we were going to come at eight.
I asked him that he was going to sit down.
She requested me that I was going to pass the mustard.

represent failures of imperative main verbs to support indicative-style subordinate clauses, and

Jocelyn informed her to come and have coffee.
The superintendent predicted to the sergeant to clear everyone out of the hall.

are examples of the reverse. If we choose our words carefully we can sometimes construct examples that are ambiguous – say,

I suggested to him their trying Mappin's

– where it is not clear whether he is expected to use his influence with them to get them to Mappin's or merely to note that Mappin's might be where they would be found. But we can hardly embrace such a tenuous ambiguity as an indication of identity. The *You will . . .* theory does not pass the reported-speech test.

Test 3, the pragmatic role test, is hardly worth applying in detail; for, if anything is clear, it is that imperatives and future-tense indicatives typically differ in pragmatic role. And in fact the writers we have quoted all make qualifications that go some way towards setting their claims beyond it. When Langford says that imperative and indicative express the same proposition, or when Gibbons says that they have the same primary meaning, or when Katz and Postal say that they have the same deep structure, each is making a claim consistent with divergences of actual or typical use. Gibbons explicitly allows that there are 'secondary meanings' concerned with pragmatic aspects. So we may leave test 3 aside; the reduction does not even aim to pass it.

The clear, dismal failure of the reduction to pass any of our tests itself begins to set us a problem. The battle is being won too easily; are there shock troops waiting on the flank? Before we apply test 4, let us assume that the reduction-proposal has been stated too strongly, and reformulate it in a way the various authors might be more disposed to maintain.

Perhaps the identification was never intended to be a pragmatic one, even to the extent necessary to pass tests 1 and 2. Is there some way in which we can purge it of pragmatic features, leaving it merely as one about – in some sense to be defined – inner logical structure or, say, semantic reference?

I think that, if we try to do so, we are led back to the logical representations discussed earlier; that is, to the claim that the *formal logic* of imperatives runs exactly parallel with that of indicatives. If it does – and if, in particular, conversion of an imperative to an indicative can be effected by doing no more than affix or delete some kind of operator – it is a short step to saying that there is some semantic entity (a possible action, or event, or state of affairs) that the imperative and the indicative both, in different ways, designate. It would be permissible to restrict the indicatives that may exactly correspond with imperatives to future-tense ones, and perhaps even exclude, say, those in the first person. And, with some such formulation, it seems likely that Langford, Gibbons, and Katz and Postal would all be satisfied. At all events it is methodologically better for us to adopt such a formulation in what follows; for if even the weakest version fails to pass our tests we are home and dry. The weakest formulation, and, therefore, the one with the greatest chance of success is one along the lines of Hare's. This is because the verbal noun that forms Hare's 'phrastic' has been purged even of those properties and associations that attach to traditional propositions or statements. Statements, after all – however much we like to see them as pure logical entities – are typically and potentially associated with a range of pragmatic properties different from those of imperatives; and it is at least in need of proof that imperatives, in so far as they contain or have reference to future-tense statements, have indicative pragmatic potentialities alongside their own. It is also a muddle to suppose that a statement needs, or can have, an 'assertion' operator prefixed to it to give it the pragmatic potentiality which, *qua* statement, it already has. In fact, we can see, lurking behind any formulation that does not, like Hare's, provide us with a mood-neutral, pragmatics-free operand, an older logical prejudice to the effect that logic deals exclusively with propositions and their truth or falsity, namely, with indicatives; and if we were prepared to go along with this prejudice we might as well stop discussing the logic of imperatives altogether. To conceive operands as verbal nouns given us a chance of suspending judgement on the issue. There is one caveat; the verbal nouns must be conceived (unlike, necessarily, Hare's) as future-tense ones and hence as time-indexical, and may need to be conceived as indexical in other ways as well. We shall also require a generic imperative operator – I shall write to *IMP* – that ambiguously represents (assuming this possible) commanding, requesting, advising and the other imperative varieties.

For the purpose of applying test 4, I therefore represent the imperative,

Close the door

in the form,

*IMP* (your future-closing the door)

and in general, the imperative,

*X* do such-and such

as,

*IMP* (*X*'s future-doing such-and-such).

I shall assume that we know how to apply logical operators and connectives to verbal nouns, and in cases of doubt we may decide how to do so by seeing what would happen if we were to apply them to the corresponding indicatives. Further difficulties will be dealt with when we come to them.

Clearly, this proposal stands a better chance of passing our tests than any less carefully formulated one. By definition, the operator *IMP* passes some liberal version of tests 1, 2 and 3. And, in fact, a great part of the material of the previous chapter could be applied, unchanged, to imperatives of this new form. I shall confine comment, in what follows, to several points that cannot. They are, I think, sufficient to dispose of the reduction or, more positively, to show that imperatives raise new, idiosyncratic logical points. There are at least four.

First, the distinction between action-defined and state-defined imperatives. We noticed that state-defined imperatives are usually a little unnatural and invite translation; in effect, that

*IMP* (your future-being here at 9 am)

is the same thing as (in a more literal expression),

*IMP* (your future-taking steps to be here at 9 am).

But although the imperatives may be the same, the indicatives are clearly different. Being here at 9 am and taking steps to be here at 9 am are not the same thing at all. If *taking steps* means *taking adequate steps* the second implies the first; but under no circumstances does the first imply the second. To make them the same we would need to import into *being here at 9 am* the idea that the state so described is to be the result of deliberate addressee-action. This could be done by attaching, say, the adverb *deliberately* to all imperatives as part of their translation. But to treat this adverb as an effective part of the imperative operator would not resolve the difficulty, since it would leave the verbal nouns themselves unequal; and to insist that the theory applies only when the verbal nouns contain this adverb would not only greatly narrow the range of indicatives that may have imperative counterparts but would completely destroy the attraction of the theory, since it would introduce into the indicative logic a concept that complicates it to the point of rendering it obscure. We would do better to analyse *this* kind of indicative by seeing its relation to an imperative.

Second, though there is no difficulty in distinguishing between subject and addressee – the imperative,

> Henry and Mary bring the lunch, John

goes easily into the form,

> John, *IMP* (Henry and Mary's future-bringing the lunch)

with *John* as vocative – the translation completely loses the idea that the addressee is the one who is primarily expected to take the appropriate fulfilling action. We would do better, semantically, to model the imperative in some such form as,

> John, *IMP* (your future-seeing to it that Henry and Mary future-to-that-bring the lunch)

in which is spelt out the sequence of events the imperative foresees. But it is impossible to conceive the qualifications that would need to be made in the indicative counterpart of the imperative logic in any way that does not amount to an elliptical application of imperative logic itself. Once we have accepted the addressee-action-reduction principle for imperatives, the only verbal nouns that are available as operands of the operator *IMP* are those that are already, sufficiently, in addressee-action-reduced form. Otherwise, equivalences and non-equivalences among imperatives will not match those of the corresponding indicatives.

Third, let us consider *permissives*. We conceived these, in chapter 2, as resulting from imperatives by the operation of negation type 4, which must be distinct from a withdrawal or mere annulment of the imperative by a negation type 5. But it is difficult to see how a negation type 4 can be applied to our *IMP*-formulation other than, in some way not yet clear, to the operator *IMP* itself. Certainly, the result must be a locution inconsistent with the unnegated one; and, since consistency is a logical property, one would think the negation should be found in what lies under the operator, namely, in the verbal noun. But there is no kind of negation or other modification of the verbal noun alone that will achieve a permissive, since, by definition, the application of the operator *IMP* to any verbal noun yields not a permissive but a true imperative. And, if we are going to permit logical operators in the prefix, the resultant logic will no longer have an indicative analogue. (There is an indicative analogue of negation type 5, but not of the distinction between negations types 5 and 4.)

Fourth, we have seen that there is, to put it mildly, considerable doubt whether a conditional imperative,

> If so-and-so is the case, do such-and-such

can be truly translated with *IMP* as initial operator; say,

> *IMP* (so-and-so's future-not-being the case or your future-doing such-and-such).

In this, if we license an addressee-action-reduction of the first disjunct, we apparently regard it as the addressee's prerogative to 'satisfy' the whole by making sure *so-and-so* is not the case. It is in general necessary to make it clear that the disjunction is not a choice-offering one, and that the addressee-action is expected to be aimed, conditionally, at satisfying the second disjunct. The alternative of leaving the conditional clause outside the reduction, getting,

> If so-and-so is the case, *IMP* (your future-doing such-and-such),

again transgresses the requirement that all logical processes must concern the operand only. If we adopted it we would be launched on a logical investigation of conditional imperatives independent of the logic of conditional indicatives.

In any case, we noticed that conditional imperatives have, among other functions, the special one of dealing with second-best contingencies as in,

> Come to the meeting; if you don't, at least send an apology.

If the whole of this must go under an *IMP* operator, we get

> *IMP* (your future-coming to the meeting; and either your future-coming to the meeting or your future-sending an apology).

But the truth of the first conjunct makes the conditional that follows vacuous; so that, by indicative logic, the formulation is equivalent simply to,

> *IMP* (your future-coming to the meeting).

There does not seem to be any way in which the reduction can represent second-best imperatives.

On these four points, then, even the weakest of the *You will* . . . theories fails.

Before we leave the question, it is interesting to point out that, although several of our other special points concerning imperative logic can be salvaged for a *You will* . . . theory, this is possibly only if an adjustment is made to it that might not be welcome to some of its adherents. Let us suppose we were to fix the status of the future-tense indicatives as *predictions* by, say, attaching to them some such word as *probably*. We have already noticed that the distinction between choice-offering and (mere) alternative-presenting disjunctions was paralleled by a distinction in the case of corresponding disjunctive predictions, and that the point carries over to the theory of questions. There is also a predictive analogue of permissives in the form

It could be so, for all I am prepared to say, that . . . ,

and there is at least a partial analogue, for predictions, of the procedure of rational justification that may be invoked in support of advice-imperatives. There may also be a partial analogue of the point about separability of conjuncts, since I may be prepared to predict the occurrence of a sequence of events in which the occurrence of some events is probable only conditionally on the occurrence of others. And there are, finally, second-best predictions in the same way as there are second-best imperatives.

The parallelism does not mean that we need alter our verdict. The logic of predictions is not identical with that of imperatives; rather, it is a matter or separate study. And, above all, the logic of predictions, so conceived, is richer and more complex than the logic of 'future-tense indicatives', as these are required to be conceived if a rationale is to be provided for the *You will* . . . reduction.

I shall take it that these fundamental shortcomings demolish the *You will* . . . theory as a contender for our adherence – or even, for that matter, for our tolerance in the 'choose whatever words you will' spirit of some of those who admit that it is inconsistent with the way we actually speak. (See, for example, D. Lewis, 'A Problem about Permission', p. 167). It is true that there is some sense in which the whole discussion of the logic of imperatives could be conducted using nothing but indicatives, by saying what kinds of world satisfy or fail to satisfy them. But that does not mean that imperatives are future-tense indicatives, or share their logic, or that any finished theory of the two can be based on the identification.

## THE *YOU SHOULD* . . . THEORY

So let us turn to the theory that imperatives are really of the form *You should* . . . ; or, of course, X *should* . . . , or one of its approximate equivalents X *ought to* . . . , X *is to* . . . Value-judgemental forms, *The right thing for* X *to do is* . . . , *It would be good if* X . . . , introduce only minimally different, for our purposes irrelevant, considerations. We should also consider 'deontic' formulations such as *It is* X's *duty to* . . . , X *has an obligation to* . . . ; and the deontic claims of other modals and semi-modals such as *must, need to, have to*, and the weaker *might, could, can* and a few others, whose core meanings are different from those of *should* but whose penumbral meanings overlap them. This rather wide range of formulations, and the corresponding range of prudential, moral, legal and social considerations supporting them, partly parallel the varietal distinctions of imperatives made in our first chapter. The *You will* . . . theory lacked this parallelism, and the fact that we find it here suggests that we have a livelier contender for a reduction than our previous one.

The number of writers who equate imperatives with some or all of these forms is very large indeed, and, if it is hard to find an explicit statement of the equivalence, the reason may be that most of them regard it as too obvious to be worth mention. Most of them are, in one way or another, in the tradition of Kant, who says (*Fundamental Principles of the Metaphysics of Ethics*, p. 35).

All imperatives are expressed by the word *ought* [or *shall*] and thereby indicate the relation of an objective law of reason to a will, . . . They say that something would be good to do or to forbear, . . .

The words *ought* and *shall* are the English translator's alternative renderings of the single German word *sollen*. Kant here even equates imperatives and *sollen*-statements alike with the judgement that something is 'good to do'. And although his famous 'categorical imperative' is at least sometimes (for example, on p. 46) stated in a genuinely imperative form,

Act only on that maxim whereby . . .

(German, *Handle nur nach derjenigen Maxime*, . . .'), he speaks of the question of its 'truth' and even talks about 'proving' it, though he doesn't think this is possible. Kant's main dichotomy is not between imperative and indicative, but between practical and pure reason, or between the will and the intellect. We saw that the sphere of pure reason or intellect even encompasses some kinds of imperative, namely, 'rules of skill', though it is practical reason or the will that is concerned with morality.

But modern adherents of what I choose to call for short the *You should* . . . theory are of two kinds, namely, those who say that imperatives are 'no more than' *You should* . . . statements and those who say that *You should* . . . statements are 'no more than' imperatives. Let us consider the second kind first: their motivation is, broadly, the logical-positivist one of explaining away moral or deontic statements by showing that there need be no 'scientific' debate over their truth or falsity. In this vein Carnap wrote (*Philosophy and Logical Syntax*, p. 23, in the passage referred to in chapter 1):

It is easy to see that it is merely a difference of formulation whether we state a norm or a value judgement. A norm or rule has an imperative form, for instance: 'Do not kill!' The corresponding value judgement would be 'Killing is evil' . . . Most philosophers have been deceived by this form into thinking that a value-statement is really an assertive proposition, and must be either true or false . . . But actually a value statement is nothing else than a command in a misleading grammatical form . . .

Value statements belong 'to the realm of metaphysics'. A similar, sometimes more circumspect conflation is found in, for example, Stevenson (*Ethics and Language*, p. 27):

What is the nature of this extrascientific meaning? Let us proceed by analogy, comparing ethical sentences with others that are less perplexing but have a similar use. Interesting analogues can be found in ordinary imperatives. Is there not a ready passage from 'You ought to defend your country' to 'Defend your country'? . . . Both imperative and ethical sentences are used more for encouraging, altering or redirecting people's aims and conduct than for simply describing them. Both differ in this respect from the sentences of science.

Stevenson, admitting that there are also differences, finishes by proposing his famous attitude-plus-imperative reduction; namely,

'This is wrong' means *I disapprove of this; do so as well.*

The imperative apparently concerns only the addressee's adoption of an attitude; but we can perhaps assume that Stevenson intended that the attitude should lead to relevant behaviour. Hare, (*The Language of Morals*) as we noticed, partly resembles Stevenson in thinking that moral statements have a clear imperative component.

Commonly, a term is found to link imperatives, deontics and moral statements and mark them off from others. Carnap's word *norm* (which derives from Wundt) is one of these; Dubislav, ('Zur Unbegründbarkeit der Forderungssätze'), and Rand, ('Logik der Forderungssätze') speak, as in their titles, of *demand-sentences (Forderungssätze)*; Opalek, ('On the Logical-Semantic Structure of Directives', p. 169) says:

The term 'directive' or ('directive statement') is used here in a broad sense, comprising norms, commands, requests, exhortations, suggestions, advice, rules (e.g. of games) and the like.

When Nowell Smith, (*Ethics*, p. 73) referred to words such as *praiseworthy, noteworthy, laudable* and *damnable* as 'gerundive words' he was drawing attention to the fact that they were not merely 'descriptive' but also had implications concerning appropriate attitudes-cum-actions; compare Kanger, ('New Foundations for Ethical Theory'). Broad, ('Some Reflections on Moral-Sense Theories in Ethics', p. 133), referred to the 'interjectional' theory of ethics – compare Acton, ('The Expletive Theory of Morals') – which might serve to remind us that, in traditional grammar books, imperatives are commonly classed, apparently along with optatives and emotives, as interjections. If moral statements are also interjections, we have an even larger conflation; it has been discussed in many places, for example by Barnes, ('Ethics Without Propositions'.

The second kind of modern *You should* . . . theorist has the alternative motive – like that of the *You will* . . . theorist – of explicating imperatives by showing them to be indicatives in disguise. (There is, of course, an irony; if imperatives are of the form *You should* . . . , they are subject to the difficulties that prompt Carnap and others to prefer to see *You should* . . . statements as imperatives – and vice versa! But few writers see both problems at once.) Leonard, 'Interrogatives, Imperatives, Truth, Falsity and Lies', thought that some imperatives were of the *You will* . . . form and some of the *You should* . . . And many writers on deontic logic have also claimed that they were explicating imperatives, though often recognizing some differences; see, again, Castañeda, ('Outline of a Theory on the General Logical Structure of the Language of Action'). Von Wright, the inventor of deontic logic, often includes imperatives in his domain (see discussion in *Norm and Action*, p. 96-102). Yet others, not always proposing a reduction, have spoken as if a normative force, variously described, somehow complemented or contrasted with a future-tense reference. Thus A. Ross, ('Imperatives and Logic'), contrasted a *logic of satisfaction* with a *logic of validity*; Lemmon, ('Deontic Logic and the Logic of Imperatives', p. 52), discussed both *obeyed/disobeyed* and *in force/not in force* as correlates of the indicative *true/false*; Prior, (*Objects of*

*Thought*, p. 65-72) contrasted *obeyedness* with *bindingness*; and Wedeking, (*A Critical Examination of Command Logic*) examined imperative logic under the heads of *satisfaction* and *legitimacy*. The evaluation of an order as *in force* or *not in force* is especially relevant in discussions of chains of command, as in Hanson ('A Logic of Commands').

Perhaps the best evidence of the strength of the *You should . . .* reduction or conflation is to be found in the quantity of ink expended by eminent writers in argument against it. They include, Geach, ('Imperative and Deontic Logic'); Falk, ('Goading and Guilding'); Segerstedt, ('Imperative Propositions and Judgments of Value'); Sellars, ('Imperatives, Intentions and the Logic of "Ought" '; and Toulmin, (*An Examination of the Place of Reason in Ethics*, ch. 4). These people have made many of our critical points for us.

The word *should*, like *will*, has a range of meanings. But in the case of *will* we easily picked out the meaning – plain futurity – that gave the *You will . . .* theory semantic relevance. *Should* is more nebulous.

1. It is used as an educated (though not very educated) substitute for *would* in formal phrases such as,

I should like to apply for the position of . . .

In speech we here often say just *'d*, and the equivalence provides a test to distinguish this use of *should* from others. But the use is mainly a first-person one and unlikely, even in the plural, to be confused with an imperative.

2. It can function as a kind of subjunctive-substitute in *if*-clauses and other subordinate parts of a sentence, as in,

If it should turn up, let me know.

Sometimes we may be unclear, however, whether it has this sense or another. For example,

They insisted we should come

can be glossed,

They insisted we come

(in which *come* is as near a 'true') subjunctive as exists in English), or alternatively as,

They insisted we *ought* to come.

The ambiguity could matter to us, since it might provide a false prop for the *You should . . .* theory. But the gloss in terms of *ought to* tends to reject the subjunctive-substitute sense, though perhaps not as reliably as could be wished.

3. Like all the English modals, *should* can have an epistemic sense, as in,

It should rain later,
That should come to about $15,

or, with *You* subject,

You should be in Madrid by mid-afternoon.

The meaning is approximately *will probably*, or *can reasonably be expected to, if things run true to form.* Hofmann, ('Past Tense Replacement and the Modal System'), contrasted 'epistemic modals' with 'root modals'; the latter term is presumably thought to cover all non-epistemic senses. But we have already set aside the 'guarantee' sense of *will* as not closely relevant to the *You will* . . . theory, and we can surely also set aside epistemic senses of *should* here.

(4. The meanings of *should* in which we are interested are neither the epistemic one, nor any in which it is a dispensable passenger, nor in which it is a grammatical stand-in, but those in which it says something characteristic that cannot be said in any other way. And one of the tests of this – which will at least reject the last two alternatives – is phonological; it ought to be able to *bear stress*. The unstressed *should* in,

You should go to the party

– with, in normal pronunciation, the main stress on *go*, and with the words *You should*, as likely as not, thrown away as a mere *Y'shd* or *Y'sh* – is different in force from the stressed one in,

You *should* go to the *party*.

In the first, *Y'shd* can be seen as a near-empty imperative-modifier; whereas, if the *You should* . . . theory is to be worth taking seriously, it must be a theory of something that can be stressed without completely changing its meaning. What we want is, as it were, the sense of stressed *should* minus the stress. (Again, this is like the sense of *ought to*, which can't be thrown away as *should* can.) Another way of putting this is to say that the sense we want is the one that occurs in the negative *shouldn't*, which always carries stress on its first syllable; so that there is only one negation,

You *should*n't go to the *party*

for two affirmatives, or, in practice, none at all for the throw-away sense. (You can put an extra-heavy stress on *should*n't, but you can't put none at all. And even,

> You should *not* go to the *party*,

with *You should* thrown away, is unlike an imperative.) So a way of picking out the sense we want is to find a way of transforming what we want to say into the negative; here, say, into

> You shouldn't stay away from the party.

Some of these overly verbal points about *should* are highly parochial to English, but we need a focus. For the sake of a name I shall refer to the surviving senses as the *deontic* ones. They are rather diverse and variable, at least so far as the kind of backing or rationale they need or carry is concerned – and also, perhaps, in strength – but the general idea is that the governed action or state-of-affairs is favoured by, or is to be recommended on grounds of, considerations of a moral nature, or of practical utility, and/or is a matter of duty or obligation, operative (generally) on the subject. *You should . . .* statements of this kind are clearly para-imperatives in the broad sense in which we used this term in chapter 1. The question is simply whether they are sufficiently imperative in their force and properties to do duty for the real thing.

Before we get down to detail, we ought to look briefly at the 'approximate synonyms' of *should*; and in particular at those with a slightly different core meaning, such as *must* and *could*. Some of these seem better adapted than *should* to translate some kinds of imperative. Thus *must* is much better for a forceful, threat-backed command, and *could* is better for a casual suggestion. The range of meanings these words can partly parallels the range of *should*; they have epistemic senses, which we must set aside for the same reasons, and they can be throw-away, without stress. On the whole, when they carry stress, their meanings are different from those of *should*, as in,

> You *must* go to the party.
> We *could* try the seafood place.

But we shall need to bear in mind, in discussing *should*, that for the best imperative match a *You should/must/(etc) . . .* theory is a better contender than a *You should . . .* theory, narrowly and linguistically interpreted. Again, this is good method. If (as I forecast) the theory is likely to be rejected, more will be accomplished if it is given its broadest formulation.

Whether the meaning of *should/must/(etc)* can really be spelt out in literal conjunctions and disjunctions of *should, must* and other modals is doubtful. Thus to say that the command,

> Hand over your wallet

means

> You should *or* must (etc.) hand over your wallet

will not do, since this is consistent with the mere,

> You *should* hand over your wallet

and is much too weak. But perhaps we can conceive the compound as a generic imperative modal that yields advice or command or something else according to context in the same way as an imperative does. The cut-up of senses between modal auxiliaries and other modal idioms is, in any case, a highly language-dependent matter; note, for example, that French *Vous devez . . .*, and its counterparts among the other Latins, are broader and can be used for COMMANDS as well as for ADVICE. In effect we need to stretch and squeeze the force of *You should* in much the same way as we conceived that the operator *IMP* shifted the mood of *You will*. We could alternatively suppose, that is to say, that we are dealing with an *IMP (You should . . .)* theory, in which the *IMP* operator is conceived as rectifying the force-mismatch of *should* to the imperative context in which it occurs.

The rest of the sifting can be done as we proceed. Let us apply our four tests.

First, the practical interchange test. And the question, note, is not just whether there exist sentences beginning with deontic *You should* (or approximate synonyms) that can serve as imperatives and vice versa, but whether *all* imperatives are interchangeable with such sentences; and whether the modals in the sentences in question have appropriate deontic senses rather than others, such as throw-away or subjunctive-substitute ones. If we confine ourselves for the moment to *should* itself, the answer is especially simple and clear. In the case of ADVICE, in examples such as,

> You should invest in mining shares,

the *You should . . .* form and the imperative are as interchangeable as could be wished; but in any other case *You should . . .* is completely or faintly inappropriate. A COMMAND or DEMAND can, perhaps, be softened by it, as in,

> You should bring in tea now, please, May;

but this *should* is hardly a deontic one, since hardly emphasizable. A REQUEST in the form,

> You should lend me five dollars

has too keen an edge on it; and an INVITATION

> You should come to my party on the 28th

is a shade offhand. And, on the other hand, *should* has meanings the plain imperative captures less well, as in giving advice of a moral character,

> You shouldn't snap back at him when he criticizes you

(the negative example is deliberate) or, particularly, in laying down an obligation or a duty.

You *must* is just a little better than *You should* in some of these cases; but,

> You must lend me five dollars

is hardly acceptable as a normal REQUEST, and,

> You must come to my party on the 28th

is more than a mere INVITATION, though it may carry one by implication. *You could* is no better in either of these cases. In fact – as we saw – the commonest simple 'indirect' way of expressing an INVITATION or REQUEST is not as a modal indicative at all, but as a modal question, *Would you . . . ?* , *Could you . . . ?* , *Would you like to . . . ?* – and a reduction to question-form would not suit the programs of most of the *You should . . .* theory's proponents. The only kind of second-person indicative prefix that is much usable for a REQUEST is something more elaborate such as,

> You would please me if you would . . . ;

and, for an INVITATION,

> You would be welcome to . . .

If we are prepared to stretch and squeeze our conception of the generic modal *should/must/(etc.)* sufficiently, we can, of course, imagine all these problems of match solved *ad hoc.* In short, the *You should/must/(etc.) . . . theory can be made* to pass test 1, and cannot be faulted formally. There is, however, a cost in naturalness and explanatory power. Let us keep this cost in mind and move on.

If test 2, the reported speech test, works for the *You should . . .* reduction, it ought to be possible to report an imperative using a main verb appropriate to the reporting of an indicative; namely, *tell, inform, say* or something similar. So let us consider,

> He told me I should stand against the wall with my hands up.

He said I should come to dinner.
They informed him he should take the first turning on the right.
Someone suggested they should go for a walk.

And these all sound reasonable as reports of imperatives. But in how many of them does *should* have the deontic sense we selected, rather than the subjunctive-substitute sense? Clearly, in the first example, the *should* is a subjunctive substitute, since stress on *should* would change its meaning, and *should* is not, in any case, an appropriate auxiliary for a COMMAND. The second, if it is an INVITATION, will similarly not stand stress on *should*, or replacement by *ought to*, or even (without change of sense) by *must*. The third passes, apparently because it is ADVICE. And the last is ambiguous as between an imperative suggestion (of going for a walk) and an indicative one (concerning a walk's advisability), perhaps throwing doubt back on the third. In short, although the subjunctive-substitute *should* comes into its own in reported speech, a deontic modal is in order only when it passes in direct speech as well.

If we imagine we have a modified modal *should/must/(etc.)* that can represent any kind of imperative, we can, of course, also suppose that it is available in reported speech. The supposition is not a completely straightforward one, since a conformable main verb needs to be chosen; that is to say, a verb capable of reporting the required range of deontic indicatives. You cannot *confide* to someone that he must stand against the wall with his hands up or (typically) *give him the information* that he ought not to mistreat his dog. And there is a certain oddity about reporting a REQUEST or INVITATION as an indicative at all. Overcoming these difficulties seems to call for another *ad hoc* invention, of a generic main verb that is mood-neutral and force-neutral in respect of what it reports. But one or two existing verbs such as *say* are not too bad, and I pass on.

What (turning to test 3) is the *pragmatic role* of a *You should . . .* statement? Why, adscititiously, do we sometimes choose to prefix these extra words? If the *You should* (or *You must*) is a throw-away, it may do very little apart from softening (or toughening) the plain imperative's edge. But if it is a deontic the answer seems to be that we use it to fix the force of what follows as ADVICE or COMMAND or something else. Then what can be the point of a *You should/must/(etc.)* prefix that, by definition, gives what follows the exact force it has when the prefix is omitted?

What supporters of the reduction seem to want is a formulation that provides the force of an imperative but permits treatment for all other purposes as an indicative. Utterances of the form *You should/must/*

*(etc.)* . . . must be capable of playing the pragmatic role imperatives do – roughly, that they are calculated to get the addressee, perhaps conditionally or subject to qualification, to do or achieve something he would not do or achieve otherwise; but they must also be capable of being true or false and of standing in the usual logical relations to other indicatives. And, surely, further pragmatic features are consequences of this second, logical, requirement. Whatever is true or false can be believed or disbelieved, certain or probable; and its utterance must be able to play the role of imparting information (that is, of causing belief) not otherwise in the addressee's possession (caused), or of displaying such information (belief) on the part of the speaker. And since belief or the possession of information does not strictly imply action, it must be possible in principle to *believe* a *You should/must/(etc.)* . . . imperative without accepting it in the sense of resolving to act on it; or, for that matter, while resolving not to.

Where ADVICE and other non-wilful imperatives are concerned, this is a commonplace. An addressee can reply,

Yes, I agree I should do that; but I'm not going to, because, . . . ;

and an issuer can set another kind of imperative against advice, as in,

You *should* tell the Police; but, I'd say, don't complicate matters.

(Perhaps this even sets one kind of advice against another.) In these cases the *should* loses the practical battle and becomes 'academic', overruled for practical purposes by the explicit imperative. The same subtle distinction is made by the contrast between *should* and *shall* in the first-person questions; namely, between,

When *should* we go?

and,

When *shall* we go?

which might pass as the same question until set in contrast, but then seem to call for indicative and imperative answers respectively.

Add to this that *You should* . . . (though not *You must* . . .) still makes deontic sense said to someone who is clearly not going to comply; and that both *should* and *must* can be used in connection with an action of someone who is already in the process of complying, as in,

I see you're going to marry the girl; and so you should.
He's returning the money, as he must.

Imperatives would be quite out of place in any of these contexts.

The greater interchangeability of modals with non-wilful imperatives than with wilful, can, surely, be directly related to their 'academic' tendencies; because it is precisely in the case of non-wilful imperatives that *justification* can be given, discussed and accepted independently of imperative force. But it should now be clear that even in these areas – for all their occasional success as stand-ins – *You should . . .* and its associates are not as imperatives as imperatives are.

So let us turn to test 4. From the fact that *You should . . .* statements can do duty for imperatives at all, we might deduce that they have *all* the right logical properties. But, although they pass comfortably at some points, they have serious shortcomings. For brevity, I shall do as before and concentrate on the points – three main and a scatter of smaller ones – at which they fail.

First, *You should . . . .* though equally at home with stative and agentive predicates, does not demand, to the extent that imperatives do, the operation of an action-reduction principle – least of all, of an ADDRESSEE-action-reduction principle. A *should*-statement often declares something morally or prudentially desirable without giving any guidance as to whose job it is to do it or to bring it about. The force of,

Children shouldn't die like this

could, it is true, be that the addressee should take personal steps to alleviate the war or famine, but it could also be to the effect that the governments nearer the scene, or the aid agencies, should be acting differently; or none of these. No one suggests that the children themselves, nominated subject of the sentence, can do anything about it. Perhaps, as a cry of frustration, the utterance does no more than complain about the way the world has been ordered by Providence.

If we had accepted the *You should . . .* theory before engaging in the logical discussions of the previous chapter, we might easily have made different decisions on a number of points. Consider, for example, the question of whether there are first-person-plural imperatives. If I say to you,

We should have some exercise before dinner,

what I say is not yet compelling as an imperative actually summoning you to get up from your armchair. Something like,

Come on, then; let's

is necessary for that. And if we had missed this cleavage of *We should . . .* from *Let's . . .* we might have decided either that first-plural imperatives were not real imperatives but deontics, or that they *were* imperatives *because* they were deontics.

Above all, this point drives a wedge between the logic of imperatives and 'deontic logic' as it is usually studied. A deontic propositional operation 'O', if it read as 'It is obligatory that' or (say) 'It should be the case that', makes no distinction between one obligatee and another. Even when its operand is a statement denoting an action of an individual, so that we read

It should be the case that $X$ does such-and-such,

it does not lay the responsibility for action on the subject $X$; and until it is put in context as an individual speech-act it cannot begin to be interpreted as laying any responsibility on the addressee. Our discovery that even *You should* . . . can be interpreted in this non-action-reduced way illustrates that 'deontic logic' – if it is no more than a logic of O and related operators – lacks a whole dimension necessary to the logic of imperatives.

Second, although *You shouldn't* . . . can replace *Don't* to give quite creditable equivalents of negations of types 1, 2 and 3, and *It is not the case that you should* . . . gives a reasonable type 5 negation of *You should* . . . and of any imperative this satisfactorily represents, there are difficulties about a modal rendering of type 4. Certainly, type 4 cannot be formulated in the same way as for imperatives, since,

You should smoke, if you wish

has quite the wrong sense if the *should* is deontic, and is faintly wrong even when it is throw-away. In,

You may smoke (if you wish),

*may* is at home as the permissive correlate of a COMMAND, but not of ADVICE, and does not even cover precisely the same modal territory as *must*. *Needn't and don't have to* negate *must*, but fail to distinguish satisfactorily between type 4 and type 5. In short, the whole question of the varying force of the different modals breaks out again and needs to be rethought for type 4 negation, and the only solution seems to be another *ad hoc* generic modal, a permissive counterpart of *should/must/ (etc.)*. In practice we often switch to imperative idiom for permissives even in the middle of discourse in which the academic *You should* . . . is used for the affirmatives and *You shouldn't* . . . for others negations; as in,

You should practise at least half an hour a day. Vary the time of day if you want to, but it's not a good idea to miss a day or skimp.

But the invention of a generic permissive modal, though it formally solves the problem, is against the spirit of the *You should* . . . reduction;

since, if the object is to reduce imperative to indicative logic, imperative negations should be analysed, directly or indirectly, as indicative ones. There is no way in which an indicative negation could transform one modal auxiliary into another, as distinct from standing in front of it, or after it. (There are not enough slots for *nots*).

In passing, note that the difficulty infects deontic logic, even when it is subjected to its usual restriction; a deontic operator needs two external negations, and there is usually the mechanism for only one. Von Wright, ('Deontic Logics') distinguishes 'positive' permission from permission that is mere absence of prohibition, but only by envisaging alternative axiomatic ways of relating permission to obligation.

The third main mismatch of logical properties concerns time and tense. Retrospective *should*-statements and strictly-present ones occur regularly where the corresponding imperatives would be impossible, as in,

> You should have run up and complained.
> You should be here now, enjoying the fun

– the latter, say, said over the telephone to someone with no chance of arriving before the party is over. The first of these is present perfect (I ignore the traditional contention that *should* is the past of *shall*) and there is no true past, but it clearly refers to past time. In these cases *should have* is usually counterfactual, but it need not be so since we can have,

> Oh, you rang and complained, did you? So you should have.

When a time-general word is used, only content can decide whether it refers to future times only, or to all times. Thus,

> You should always put a small coin in the begging-bowl,

because it states an apparently time-universal rule (but in which, perhaps, *You* is not second-person but impersonal, equivalent to *One* or *People?*) seems to imply that you should have complied yesterday as well as that you should comply tomorrow; but we can imagine circumstances in which this implication is rejected.

Oddly, *You should* . . . statements that it is temporally impossible to satisfy still often raise questions of temporal possibility and satisfiability with respect to *past* times; and it may even be relevant to consider a retrospective addressee-action-reduction. The answer to,

> You should have tripped 'Emergency' and shut down the burners
> before the tanks started to leak

can be,

By the time I knew it had happened the panel was malfunctioning.

But the action-reduction is, as in the case in which the reference is to actions and states temporally possible at the time of speaking, weak in the same respects as indicated earlier.

Besides these three major logical divergences of *You should . . .* from imperatives, note: (1) that there is no strangeness in conjoining an indicative with a *You should . . .*, and that, in consequence, a *You should . . .* formulation cannot stand in for a conditional in the way an imperative can; (2) that although

> You should get married and have a baby

seems both to be non-separable and to prescribe a time-order the apparently equivalent,

> You should get married and you should have a baby

reads much more clearly as a separable conjunction, showing that the reduction does explicate imperative conjunctions; and (3) that although,

> Either come in or don't

tells the hearer not to hover on the doorstep,

> Either you should come in or you shouldn't

is a typical indicative tautology that seems to have no function apart from setting its addressee straight on a point of logic. I call these points minor because they could not be regarded, on their own, as wrecking the reduction. But they add a little bit to the others.

To summarize: If the *You should . . .* theory is to be worth taking seriously at all, it is necessary to set aside the epistemic, throw-away and subjunctive-substitute senses of *should* and to select deontic ones. But it still passes test 1 only of *should* is replaced by an *ad hoc* modal *should/must/(etc.)*, of a kind for which English has no word. It will further not pass test 2 unless we also invent an *ad hoc* main verb capable of reporting indicatives and indicativised imperatives indiscriminately. On a fine point, it fails test 3 because it obscures a distinction – between 'academic' locutions and those that genuinely call for action – that it is sometimes important not to obscure. And, for the same reason, it misses passing test 4 in respect of action-reduction and temporal properties; and, where negation type 4 is concerned, can be made to pass only if another *adhoc* invention is made, namely, of an all-purpose permissive modal.

It can be imagined that a determined reductionist, namely, one for whom formal simplicity was more important than accuracy, might be undeterred by these failures. But that is not quite to the present point. It is true that imperatives and deontic modals touch at many points, just as it is approximately true that France is hexagonal. But the cartographer of imperatives who discovers that their pattern deviates significantly from some pre-desired one should hardly be called on, on those grounds, to suppress his findings.

## THE I ORDER YOU TO ... THEORY

If it were not that the *I order you to* ... theory has so many supporters that it can fairly be described as a new orthodoxy, we could be tempted to dismiss it without ceremony, on the grounds that it is based on a simple logical mistake. Saying you are doing something is not the same, one would think, as doing it, even when the doing is itself a species of saying. But otherwise intelligent philosophers and grammarians can be found who are prepared to make exceptions to this simple thesis; ordering someone to do something, they think, is the same thing as saying you do so; and, when you say you do so, if what you say amounts to a valid order, what you say is true, and the order itself is true too. This thesis can be given a certain plausibility by being analysed, as we shall see, into two half-truths. Unfortunately I find that, rather than adding together into a whole, the half-truths subtract.

The words *I, order* and *you* each (as comparable words did before) do duty for a family; *I* for *We, The Court* and so on; *order* for *request, advise* or any sort of verb denoting the issuing of an imperative; *you* for third-person imperative subjects or agents as well as second. A passive form *You are ordered* ... (or *You are advised* ..., etc) is possible and, in fact, necessary if the reduction is to be applied to imperatives with impersonal issuers, such as most of those in recipes and instruction manuals. Where *Henry* is an imperative subject, the form *I order that Henry* ... or *I order that Henry should* ... might be more appropriate, but what distinction there is need not concern us.

The half-truths in question are: (1) that imperatives are equivalent to *performatives*, and (2) that performatives are equivalent to indicatives. *Performatives*, which we have already met in chapter 1, are locutions such as,

> I promise you I'll be there on Monday.
> I warn you he can be dangerous if you provoke him,
> I declare the nominations closed.

whose utterance in suitable circumstances constitutes not mere description of the acts in question but performance of them; and it is not hard to see that,

I order you to put the cat out

is of this kind. Contention (1), that imperatives are implicitly of this form – though, in one form, it appears as long ago as Husserl, (*Logical Investigations*, vol. 2, pp. 837 and 847) – can be regarded for our purposes as due to the inventor of the performative doctrine, J.L. Austin, who wrote, (in *How To Do Things With Words*, p. 32 1962, but originally Harvard lectures of 1955)

. . . of course, it is both obvious and important that we can on occasion use the utterance 'go' to achieve practically the same as we achieve by the utterance 'I order you to go': and we should say cheerfully in either case, describing subsequently what someone did, that he ordered me to go.

(Though the imperative *Go*, he adds, is inexplicit as between ordering, advising, entreating or what not.) But Austin (p. 6) refused to accept contention (2):

In these examples it seems clear that to utter the sentence (in, of course, the appropriate circumstances) is not to *describe* my doing of what I should be said in so uttering to be doing or to state that I am doing: it is to do it. None of the utterances cited is either true or false: I assert this as obvious and do not argue it. It needs argument no more than that 'damn' is not true or false: it may be that the utterance 'serves to inform you' – but that is quite different. To name the ship *is* to say (in the appropriate circumstances) the words 'I name, &c.'. When I say, before the registrar or alter, &c., 'I do', I am not reporting on a marriage: I am indulging in it.

It follows, then, as Austin sees it, that *I order you to go* is not an assertion that I give the order to go, but the actual giving of that order, and that these are different. Austin does not believe that, implicitly or explicitly, imperatives are indicatives.

But let us confine ourselves first to contention (1). Austin, though he did describe the imperative:

Go

as an implicit performative, claimed no more in the end than that this and the explicit,

I order you to go

are equivalent forms, not that either is in any important way more fundamental. But J.R. Ross, ('On Declarative Sentences') and Sadock,

('Hypersentences') and subsequent others, argued that *all* utterances have implicit performative prefixes that need to be made explicit to establish these utterances' 'deep structure'. Even an utterance of a plain indicative sentence *S* is really an utterance of the form,

I say to you that *S*.

Many of their arguments, which are mainly directed at the indicative case, are not relevant or cogent when applied to imperatives, but three are worth mention. The first, which Ross, (p. 248), credits independently to Bever and Klima, concerns the interpretation of dangling clauses in *since* and other words, as in,

Since you ask me, buy a couple of new tyres.
Come at nine, in case you're in doubt.

What the clause *Since you ask me* explains is *why I tell you* to buy new tyres, but no words to this effect are in the sentence. If it is filled out to read,

Since you ask me, *I tell you* to buy a couple of new tyres,

the clause no longer dangles. We could similarly insert, say, *I suggest that you* in the other example, to get,

I suggest that you come at nine, in case you're in doubt.

In the same vein it can be argued that,

For the last time, go!

can only mean,

For the last time, *I tell you to* go;

and Sadock, (p. 299) gives other examples.

This argument perhaps also supports contention (2), since the inserted words are most naturally interpreted as forming indicative statements.

Second, when a sentence refers more than once to a particular person or thing it is normal to use a pronoun for all but one of the references; we say,

Quincey asked the girl to bring him a plaster,

not,

Quincey asked the girl to bring Quincey a plaster.

We also almost never use proper names or descriptive phrases in reference to ourselves or to our addressees; Quincey would say,

Bring *me*, a plaster,

not (unless he were two years old),

Bring *Quincey* a plaster.

Sadock notices, (p. 304) that the ban on the use of proper names to replace *me* or *you* can be explained by supposing that an understood performative prefix has already made reference to the speaker and addressee. If it is objected that the earlier reference, by means of some phrase such as *I ask you to*, is itself compulsorily by pronoun, it can be replied that this is a special feature of performatives, which are the only constructions in which pronouns occur in a primary sense.

A third consideration can be obtained by adapting what Sadock, citing G. Lakoff, ('A Note on Negation') and Kiparsky ('Fact') says about the use of the word *so* as a pronoun referring to the content of an indicative utterance or thought; we say,

Robert said it looked like rain and Richard said so too;

or, of course,

It looks like rain, and Richard says so too.

Comparison of the examples suggests that the latter has an understood prefix *I say that*. We can similarly refer back to repeated imperatives, usually just with *to*, as in,

The sports writers all said to back Yellow Dream, and the man in the corner shop said to as well,

or, with the same suggestion of a deleted prefix,

Apologize to him; Quincey advises you to also.

In this case the implied prefix is apparently *I advise you to*.

These arguments for an understood prefix are suggestive, but far from knockdown, and there are alternative possible explanations of the various phenomena. The facts by no means fix the form of the supposed prefix, since we can have,

Come round later; Janet wants you to as well,

with the suggestion that the prefix is not a performative one at all, but an *I want you to*. Among general alternative approaches to the postulation of a prefix, Ross considers a 'pragmatic' one according to which (p. 254)

. . . certain elements are present in the context of a speech act, and . . . syntactic processes can refer to such elements. Thus, . . . the context provides an *I* which is 'in the air', so to speak . . .

And grammatical considerations can hardly be called on to discriminate between the hypothesis of something's being 'in the air' and that of the some thing's being 'in the deep structure'. (Ross claims to have identified one that does, but admits that it is very tentative). This being so, the arguments for the existence of a prefix of the form *I order you to* can be construed as no more than arguments to the effect that, when an imperative is issued, there are, 'in the air', ideas of a speaker, an imperative act, and an addressee. Let us turn to contention (2).

Austin's claim that performatives are different in kind from indicatives, and cannot be regarded as true or false statements but only as successful for unsuccessful performances, was an important part of their initial characterization, but has been the subject of extended controversy. It appeared first in his paper 'Other Minds' of 1946, and was supported by Hart, ('The Ascription of Responsibility and Rights'); Harrison, ('Knowing and Promising'); and later Hartnack, ('The Performatory Use of Sentences'); O'Hair ('Performatives and Sentences Verifiable by Their Use'); and Gale, ('Do Performative Utterances have any Constative Function?'). The opposing point of view, according to which a performative is an indicative whose utterance in suitable circumstances automatically makes it true, was supported by Hedenius, ('Performatives'); Lemmon, ('On Sentences Verifiable by their Use'); Åqvist, (*Performatives and Verifiability by the Use of Language*); Danielsson, ('Definitions or "Performative"'); G. Lakoff, ('Linguistics and Natural Logic'); D. Lewis, ('General Semantics'); Cresswell, (*Logics and Languages*, ch. 14); and McGinn, ('Semantics for Non-Indicative Sentences'). For discussion of the controversy see Houston, ('Truth Valuation of Explicit Performatives'), and Price, ('Doing Things Explicitly with Words').

I shall be content here to discuss what I take to be the two main arguments on behalf of the so-called 'descriptive fallacy', that is, contention (2).

The first is, in effect, the same as one in favour of contention (1); if the *Since*-clause in,

Since you ask me, I advise you to buy a couple of new tyres

is to be construed as explaining the *fact* that I advise you, the words *I advise you* must be taken as a statement of that fact. The logical relations indicated by words such as *since* and *in case* must (it is thought) hold between statements.

The second simply points to the many ways in which performatives are linked with indicatives in application. For example, it would be very odd indeed if a question such as,

> Do you advise me to consult Gina?

had to be regarded as having as its yes-answer a non-indicative performative,

> I advise you to consult Gina

and as its no-answer a non-performative indicative,

> I do not advise you to consult Gina.

(I read this here as a type 5 negation. It can also be read as a type 2, equivalent to *I advise you not to* . . . , but this '*not*-exported' form is a linguistic quirk.) It is much more natural to say that both answers are indicative, and that some and only some indicatives are performatives at the same time. Many similar points could be made, about conjunction and disjunction, repetition, indirect speech and so on. They are not, moreover, special to English, but extend to virtually all natural languages.

These arguments are suggestive, but again not knockdown, and there are plenty on the other side. For example, if *I order you to* . . . really gives an indicative, why is it so inappropriate to acknowledge its felicity by saying *That is true* . . . ? The oddity of performative questions is, in any case, something that, in a full logical theory of performatives, it is necessary to accept a budget for. A second grammatical point is that there *is*, in fact, a difference of formulation between a performative and the corresponding present-tense statement, since the verb in the latter is properly put in the continuous rather than plain form, namely, as in *I am ordering you to* . . . , not *I order you to* . . . If I were ordering you to shut down the machine-room and wished to *describe* what I was doing I would say not,

> I *order* you to shut down the machine-room

but,

> I *am ordering* you to shut down the machine-room.

The first form is appropriate to a report of habitual or repeated actions, for example in,

> Whenever they hassle a unionist I order you to shut down the machine-room, don't I?,

but not to a report of a single, concurrent action as in,

You want to know what the whistle means? I'm ordering you to shut down the machine-room, that's what!

The point moreover overlaps the one about direct questions; thus a question of the form *Do you advise me to . . .* ? is more clearly what we called an IMPERATIVE QUESTION, with its three possible answers, than it is an indicative one, and *Are you advising me to . . .* ? is a different question.

Where clauses in *since* and *in case* are concerned, my intuitions tell me that a similar distinction applies. If we compare,

Since you ask me, I advise you not to bother

with

Since you are asking me, I am advising you not to bother,

we may feel that the second can be *clearly* interpreted in the way suggested for the first, but that the first remains in part what it was before the performative was inserted, an imperative with a dangling *since*-clause attached. If this intuition has any basis at all, there is a need, which acceptance of contention (2) would not satisfy, for a semantic account of such clauses.

But the unnaturalness that attends certain grammatical workings-out of Austin's hypothesis is small compared with that associated with the wholehearted acceptance of the doctrine that imperatives themselves have to be regarded as true or false according as they are or are not successfully issued.

When Ross's and Sadock's strong version of contention (1) is teamed up with contention (2), the problem arises of avoiding an infinite regress; for if every locution has a performative prefix, and every performative prefix is an indicative and hence, in principle, another locution, we can go on for ever. In short, it is still necessary to distinguish performatives from 'other' indicatives, and to say that an utterance can have *no more than one* performative prefix. It is also necessary to distinguish, in the case of an indicative *S*, the question of the truth or falsity of the 'explicit'

I say to you that *S*

from that of *S* itself; Thus Cresswell, (*Logics and Languages*, ch. 14), for example, though reducing all other moods to indicative by the postulation of performative prefixes, lays down arbitrarily that, in the case of indicatives themselves, performative prefixes such as *I say to you that* make no difference to truth-value. If this can be done, anything can be done, and the difficulties we run into in making the *I order you to . . .* theory fit the facts of imperative logic can all be resolved by similar fiat. But, since the need to pile up *ad hoc* adjustments is itself an argument against a theory, the exercise of assessing this one along the same lines as the *I will . . .* and *I should . . .* theories seems worth pursuing at least briefly.

It would be possible to apply our tests to the two contentions separately – except that test 4 could hardly give any very definite result in the absence of a developed logic of performatives. But I shall apply them only to the resultant thesis that imperatives are indicatives of the form *I order you to . . .* , and that without wasting too many words.

The practical interchange test seems to work well until we review the points we have just made about the distinction between plain and continuous tenses, the comparable point in the case of questions, and the awkwardness that attaches to application of the words *true* and *false*. If, in place of the performative, a form that is unhesitatingly indicative is substituted, the test works less well.

The reported speech test gives equivocal results also, since,

> The shop-steward *said he* ordered the foreman to shut down the machine-room

is strictly incorrect as a report of the shop-steward's order and represents rather a report of A REPORT of his order; and in any case, as in the case of previous reductions, it is only when a main verb such as *say*, capable of reporting either indicative or imperative, is used that even this degree of ambiguity can be preserved.

And so far as pragmatic role is concerned, although it could be claimed that *I order you to (whatever-it-is)* is calculated to give the hearer information not already in his possession (which, we said, is the most typical role of an indicative) – in this case, information about delivery of an order – it could be held to do this incidentally rather than directly, in the way I give you the information I am sitting in a chair when I sit in a chair in your presence. *I order you to . . .* cannot play the other roles indicatives play, namely, of making an admission of something not previously admitted, or of letting hearers know that state information is in the speaker's possession. When we add that the truth-conditions (if any) of performatives are determined differently from those of typical indicatives, the case begins to look a rather dark grey.

But when we turn to the equivalent logic test, the reduction surely falls apart completely – *unless* we make it work by definition, by letting the logic of imperatives by played out in the embedded predicate, virtually as if the prefix *I order you to* were not there. Otherwise – if the prefix is taken seriously as an indicative with the logical properties indicatives have – type 5 (with perhaps a yet higher type 5) is the only possible negation, conjunctions and disjunctions have properties quite different from those we ascribed to them, and permissives, undertakings and *Let's* forms can be related to imperatives only by relating alternative prefixes to the imperative one. And this brings out a feature of the so-called reduction that makes it, even if valid, a logician's blind alley; namely, that it is not really a reduction at all. If someone did not know what an order was, and needed to be told what meaning to attach to a given one O, it would be no help at all to tell him that it was a locution that, uttered by me to you, meant

I order you to carry out order O,

since he wouldn't understand this any better; O remains embedded in it, unanalysed and unglossed. In some sense its logical properties are there with it, too; but they need to be disinterred before they can be put to use.

It should go without saying that, if we do *not* disinter them, but treat each sentence of the form *I order you to . . .* as if it had logical properties appropriate to its interpretation as an indicative *describing* an order, the properties in question – since, as we said, saying you are doing something is not the same as actually doing it – have minimal relevance to those of the order purportedly described.

I ORDER YOU THAT YOU WILL . . . AND I ORDER YOU THAT YOU SHOULD . . .

The final point made about the *I order you to . . .* theory can be supplemented by pointing out that the O in,

I order you to carry out order O,

since it is unreduced, can itself be made the target of a reduction; for example, along the liner of a *You will . . .* or a *You should . . .* theory. Various more or less specious arguments for one or other reduction can easily be imagined; that the content of the order O is future tense, example or that it has the same kind of force as a deontic. The suggestion is not, however, new. In considering the *You will . . .* and *You should . . .* theories we mooted, in both cases, the possibility, or perhaps necessity, of an imperative prefix *IMP* to supplement the modal one. But proponents of such theories had already made this suggestion. Katz and Postal, (*An Integrated Theory of Linguistic Descriptions*), whom we have already noticed as *You will . . .* theorists, also postulated an imperativizing prefix, to be read roughly (see p. 76) as 'the speaker (asks, demands, insists, etc.) that'; whereas Castañeda, ('Outline of a Theory on the General Logical Structure of the Language of Action') as we already noticed, postulated an operator to get in the other direction, from imperatives to (in his case) deontics.

These proposals call for no more than a comment. A formal prefix, symbolically represented by a letter or abbreviation, is too amorphous an entity for semantic dissection. But the proposal that such a prefix should be read *I order you to* . . . , or something similar, raises again the considerations of the preceding section.

Unfortunately, the *I order you that you will* . . . and the *I order you that you should* . . . theories – which I shall not take the time to characterize in greater detail – though their more elaborate prefixes give promise of greater scope for diversification of logical detail, suffer, considered semantically, from the combined faults of the theories they compound. Our complaint about the *I order you to* . . . theory was mainly that it buried the logical properties of what followed; but our complaints about the *You will* . . . and *You should* . . . theories were that they had the wrong logical properties in the first place, which even an amorphous prefix *IMP*, not construed as burying them, could not rectify.

For what it is worth, a formal prefix *IMP*, with the function, in grammatical or logical theory, of determining mood as imperative, is a semantically much less questionable invention than a spelt-out prefix *I order you to* . . . , that supposedly renders something imperative and indicative at the same time.

Many like-minded philosophers would think that what this chapter shows didn't need showing, and merely exemplifies the 'idiosyncrasy platitude' Moore took from Butler: Everything is itself, nothing is anything else. (See Moore, *Principia Ethica*, flyleaf and p. 206.) Imperatives are not indicatives, they are imperatives. Philosophical reduction-theses are for the uncritical.

For what it is worth, the *You should* . . . theory comes out best of the three. But all three theories seem to say something that is unhelpful and destructive of logical progress, namely, that imperatives ought not to be treated as phenomena requiring study in their own right. The theories encourage us, as it were, to stop looking for anything characteristic or different about imperatives, that might justify natural languages in stubbornly preserving special forms for them.

# 4

# Action-State Semantics

It might or might not be a useful enterprise to build a 'logic of imperatives', in the sense of a set of rules for the manipulation of imperative operators and connectives. But one of its possible benefits, namely, a picture of the things imperatives do and of the relations between them, can be provided in another way, by fitting imperatives into a semantic model. Within such a model we can hope to explicate (1) all the logical properties of imperatives discussed in chapter 2, and (2) what it is for an imperative to be *satisfied*, and what it is for it to be *effective*. Semantic models are artificial constructions, and the definitions and explications achieved within them apply at large only to the extent that the models are sufficiently general and realistic. But that is a qualification that applies to any theory of anything.

What we build is not, of course, a semantics 'of imperatives', to the exclusion of indicatives and locutions of other moods. Semantics is, or should be, of whole languages. But to be capable of dealing usefully with imperatives a semantic system needs to incorporate features usually regarded as specialized, and hence as dispensable in the case of a semantics designed to accommodate indicatives only. The main ones are:

1. a time-scale
2. distinction between actions and states
3. physical and mental causation
4. agency and action-reduction
5. intensionality.

The model will not, on the other hand, contain anything specifically imperatival; the actions and states that may be enjoined by the use of imperatives are drawn from the same stock as those that may be described or predicted by the use of indicatives, though they may need to be put together in differently-shaped bundles. It follows further that a semantic model, at least of this kind, does not provide us with the means to differentiate imperatives according to their *force*; that is, into commands, requests, advice and so on. We shall tackle both these tasks of differentiation in another way later.

One further important consideration is also postponed to a later chapter, not because it would be irrelevant if introduced in this one but because to do so would complicate a picture that is already complicated enough. This is the question of the knowledge and abilities of the issuer, addressee and subject, that may be relevant to the carrying out of the imperative task. For the time being, as it were, the concepts with which we operate are 'objective' ones, that represent the situations that would confront an addressee perfectly informed and possessed of ability – within only 'external' limitations – to avail himself of them. These concepts are meaningful ones and can stand on their own feet; and the model to be built in this chapter is, in any case, general enough to accommodate the envisaged extensions; but the more general concepts will need to be set down and discussed in detail later and the appropriate conclusions drawn.

There are only a few attempts, in the literature, to construct semantic models for imperatives at all, except in the context of theories that reduce them, at short order, to indicatives or deontics and hence find no need to make special attempts to deal with their idiosyncrasies. Apostel, ('Practical Modalities, Practical Inference and Practical Knowledge'), notices the lack; von Wright, ('Deontic Logics') has made a number of partial attempts. Among the more satisfactory treatments is that of Chellas, (*The Logical Form of Imperatives* and 'Imperatives'); but this lacks some of the features of the present one, and can be argued to be insufficiently diversified. A diversified semantics close to the present one – designed, however, to explicate *ability*, not imperatives – is that of Tichý and Oddie, ('Ability & Freedom')

## TIMES, STATES AND CHANGES

Time enters the semantics of imperatives because the issuing of a given imperative may be proper or reasonable at one time but not at another. It will be sufficient for our purpose to assume that time is a sucession of discrete instants

$$\ldots t_{n-1}, t_n, t_{n+1} \ldots,$$

unending and unbeginning. A dense or discontinuous time-scale would complicate the picture without corresponding advantage.

At different instants of time the world is in different *states*, and the difference between its state at $t_n$ and its state at $t_{n+1}$ represents an

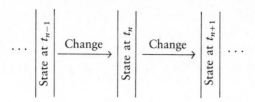

Figure 1

elementary *change* of state, so that we may picture the world at first as in figure 1.

So conceived, elementary changes are not semantically distinct from the pairs of states between which they occur, and we can represent the *world* as the succession of its states alone; or alternatively, if we wish, as the succession of changes alone, given a datum-state for the changes to work on, forward and backwards. This is the way changes are conceived by von Wright, ('Deontic Logics'), and others such as Pratt, ('Semantical Considerations on Floyd-Hoare Logic') and Segerberg, ('Applying Modal Logic'); but we shall shortly have to take changes more seriously as semantically independent entities.

The *meaning* of a given statement can be represented (as usual) as a subset of the set of *possible* worlds so described; namely, as the set of those worlds whose states and changes, at the appropriate times, are or were consistent with the truth of the statement. To say, for example, that Mao swam in the Yangzi is to assert that the world was in certain states, and/or underwent certain changes, during a range of times; and we may identify this statement with the set of those worlds, differing in all conceivable other ways, within which these states and changes occurred. This allocates a meaning to all possible statements, true or false. One and only one of the possible worlds is the actual world, and a statement is true if and only if the subset representing it has this one as a member.

Analogously, the theory of *fiats* of Hofstadter and McKinsey, ('On the Logic of Imperatives'), or the phrastic-neustic logic of Hare, (*The Language of Morals* and 'Meaning and Speech Acts') – independently of whether either is of any use to us as a theory of imperatives – can be modelled by saying that *fiats* (or Harean imperatives) are arbitrary subsets of worlds. Thus

Let it be the case that Mao swam in the Yangzi

picks out, as an 'enjoined' subset, the same subset of worlds as the statement that Mao actually did swim in the Yangzi. The *fiat is satisfied* if and only if the real world is a member of the subset, namely, in the same circumstances as those in which the corresponding statement is true; and the difference between the semantics of the two cases is one of terminology only.

DEEDS AND HAPPENINGS

But the change that takes place when one state of the world is succeeded by another needs to be analysed into component changes, and these fall into two importantly different categories; some just *happen* and some are the result of people's (and perhaps other responsible agents') *doing* things. Physical science has shown us how to break happenings down into elementary happenings, of the sort that can take place in elementary time-intervals. Our next step must be the possibly unpardonable one of assuming that the same breakdown is possible for actions, and that in a given elementary time-interval there may be elementary independent actions, which I shall call *deeds*, attributable to particular agents. Our picture of the world in consequence is seen in figure 2.

That actions can be so divided into elementary deeds is, no doubt, debatable; but I shall treat it simply as a requirement of semantic theory. This means that it is not to the point to take up the general question of whether there are 'basic actions' in, say, the sense in which most writers are agreed there aren't; namely, the sense of Danto ('Freedom and Forbearance' and other writings such as those in his *Analytical Philosophy of Action*). (Several writers – Martin, 'Basic Actions and Simple Actions', Brand, 'Danto on Basic Action', A. Baier, 'The Search for Basic Actions', 'Ways and Means' and 'Intention, Practical Knowledge and Representtion' and Weil and Thalberg, 'The Elements of Basic Action', among others – including Danto himself – have pointed to the difference between saying that an action is 'atomic', in a sense we require here, and saying that it is basic in the sense of not being caused by other actions.) Since the aim of a semantic model is

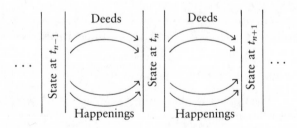

Figure 2

analytical, its fictional components do not need to match reality so long as a match is achieved by the structures that are built out of them. (Compare the analogous case of 'elementary propositions'.) Moreover, we can so define deeds, if we wish, that every possible doer does just one deed at each time; this is just a matter of appropriately enumerting what we take to be deed-types – of regarding instantaneous compound deeds as the components rather than their elements – and of recognizing the possibility of a null-deed. It is perhaps worth saying, in any case, that there are cases in which it is appropriate to allow doing nothing to count as a deed.

Deeds, however, being elementary, will in general be different in character from the actions they make up. Actions (1) may be co-operative, and (2) may have a purpose; but elementary deeds, to the extent that they are designed to enable us to analyse these features of actions, would not fulfil their function unless they were conceived as not having the features themselves. Co-operative action, other than mere 'accidental' co-operation, needs to be achieved by means of interlocking deeds of the individual, co-operators (which may need to include signals from one to another), and if these deeds were joint they would not yet be elementary. Purpose, or the intensional element of action, can be analysed in various ways; but an important way of representing it is by specifying not merely what *is* done by the purposer, but also what he *would do* in each of a range of possible alternative situations (possible worlds). A purposeful action can consequently be analysed as an action that is a function defined on the possible worlds, or on some subset of them; and, within each such world, the action is in principle analysable into elementary deeds. But we shall have no need to see the deeds themselves as functions of worlds.

We also have no need to analyse *happenings*; and we may as well conceive all the happenings at a given time as amalgamated, making up one big happening. (It would be possible, formally, to regard happenings as deeds of a special additional doer, Fate or the Good Lord; but it is not clear that this would result in any simplification.) But we cannot amalgamate all the deeds, or the happenings with any of the deeds, since we need to distinguish the deeds of different doers.

The elementary referents of a semantic system involving time should also be required to be logically independent as between one time and another. Thus from a fact about certain states or deeds or happenings at given times it should not be *logically* possible to deduce anything about states or deeds or happenings at given different times. And we might also require that states should be independent of happenings and of deeds of any doers. This is a big requirement, and to state it precisely we need to introduce the notion of the set $S$ of possible states the world can assume at any time, the set $D$ of possible deeds of any doer, and the set $P$ of doers. Let us imagine all the happenings that take place at a given time amalgamated as one big happening, and let $H$ be the set of such possible big happenings at any time at all. Now let us imagine that we have a complete specification of the world for the whole of time, namely that, for every time, we are given (1) a member of the set of states $S$, representing the state the world is in at that time, (2) a member of $H$, namely, the big happening that happens starting at that time, and (3) for each member of $P$, a member of $D$, namely, for each doer the deed he does starting at that time. Our requirement can now be put in the form: All such specifications are logically possible. That is to say, the set of all such specifications represents the set, which we shall call $W$, of logically possible worlds, of which the real world is one member. In symbols,

$$W = (S \times H \times D^P)^T.$$

That the state of the world at any time is logically independent of its state at other times (though not, of course, independent in any but a pure logical sense) seems to me to be readily enough acceptable; and perhaps, also, that individual deeds, even at a given time, are independent of one another and of happenings. But something needs to be said in defence of the stipulation that deeds are independent of states. This is because actions and states are often defined in terms of one another; I cannot, for example, have raised my arm unless it was first down and then up. The sequence of states, although it does not alone constitute the action, is a necessary condition of it. In other cases the initial state alone, or the final state alone, is a necessary condition. Similarly, actions or happenings sometimes seem to be a necessary condition of states; I cannot be first in one place and then in another without, however magically and inexplicably, having moved or been transported there. But to recognize either of these necessary conditions would apparently be to declare that some members of $W$ are not logically possible. (It will later – in chapter 6 – be necessary to explore the dependence of deeds on doers; that is, the extent to which it is necessary or desirable to consider some deeds as possible to some doers but impossible to others.)

In reply, two things should be said: first, that the concept of logical possibility is not as important as it is sometimes thought to be, and will here in any case shortly be supplemented with the more restrictive concept of physical possibility; second, that, once again, provided the structures that are built out of the elements match reality, it does not matter very much whether the elements themselves do so. Thus it does no harm to recognize that some macroscopic actions, such as raising an arm, require to be defined partly in terms of initial and final states; and the conceptual separation of deeds from states facilitates just this recognition. Similarly in the converse cases. On the other hand, we should perhaps beware, conceptually, of pseudo-states such as the state of something's *having happened* or *having been done*, or *being about to happen* or be done, which are not analysable into elementary states at all, but into happenings and deeds; and perhaps also of pseudo-deeds or happenings that are in reality nothing but sequences of states.

Despite all this, an intransigent reader who insists that states *are* logically related, in some cases, to deeds and happenings may, if he wishes, assume what he takes to be logically impossible combinations expunged from our specifications, so that W is the consistent subset of the W originally defined. Nothing else will hang on this decision.

So let us sum up to date. Worlds W are two-way-infinite sequences of timed states S, deeds D of doers P, and (big) happenings H. In each world there is just one state, one deed of each doer, and one happening, at each time. We regard all such sequences as logically possible. And now let us turn it backwards; timed states, happenings and deeds of doers can be defined as subsets of worlds. Consider, for example, those worlds in which state *s* occurs at time *t*; since they differ in all other possible ways they can be regarded as *defining* the occurrence of state *s* at time *t*. It follows that the content of the statement,

The world is in state *s* at time *t*

– or of the *fiat*,

Let the world be in state *s* at time *t* –

can be represented as this subset, say W', of the set of worlds. Similarly deeds and happenings can be represented as sets of worlds. The deed-fiat,

Let it be the case that *p* does *d* at time *t*

and the happening-fiat,

Let it be the case that *h* happens at time *t*

have sets of worlds as their contents, namely, all those worlds, respectively, in which *p* does *d* at time *t* and in which *h* happens at time *t*. But furthermore, we can also represent *any combination* of states, deeds and happenings as sets of worlds, namely, those worlds within which the combination occurs. We can also imagine that the analysis of the possible states and happenings is pushed into detail, so that sets of states and sets of happenings represent states of, and happenings to, individual objects and regions; though it will not in fact be necessary for us to pursue the analysis in this direction. Consequently we have at hand the means for a very powerful generalization about the contents of, at least, statements and fiats: they are all subsets of the set $W$ of worlds. We have also, by bringing agents $P$ into our model, paved the way for an analysis of imperatives of a more general kind.

It would be possible, for some purposes, to conceive the world less lavishly, either as a *world of states* or, say, a *world of events*, where events are deeds plus happenings. Neither of these more restricted conceptions would be adequate for the representation of imperatives, but the point should be made, perhaps, that most logical models are built on one or other of them. For many purposes we are satisfied to think that the world can be fully described by giving a catalogue of its successive states, that is, by an allocation of a member of $S$ to each time; for others, by giving a description of what goes on in it, namely, by a similar allocation to each time, of a member of $H$ and perhaps also, for each member of $P$, a member of $D$. But, unless the concept of a state is somehow expanded to include, explicitly or implicitly, that of an event, or vice versa – which, in either case, blurs an important distinction – both accounts are deficient. If $W_s$ is the set of worlds of states, and $W_e$ the set of worlds of events, our set $W$ is the Cartesian product, $W_s \times W_e$, of these; or (if you wish to assume that events and states are partly logically related) a subset of it.

CAUSE AND CHOICE

Now let us turn to physical necessity, whose incorporation in the model is increasingly seen to be necessary to relate states to deeds and happenings, and because the reasonableness of an imperative depends strongly on the existence of a physical (not merely logical) means of carrying it out. Its effect is to narrow the range of possible worlds from $W$ to $W_{phys}$, the set of *physically possible worlds*. $W_{phys}$ is the set of all worlds that are consistent with the laws of nature and is the subset of $W$ that represents a statement of those laws. The concept of a 'law of nature' is in practice a little loose, and some people may prefer to think of $W_{phys}$ as a relative concept that depends on our having some particular set of laws in mind. However that may be, physically possible worlds are a subset of the logically possible worlds, and the real world is a member of both sets.

In a discrete-time system, laws of nature can probably all be represented as causal ones; though in scientific practice they are not. (Compare 'conservation' laws such as the law of conservation of energy.) Our model is general enough to include both causal laws and others, though we shall have to make a distinction in a moment between 'physical' causation and other kinds.

Within the set $W_{phys}$, do we still need to distinguish between states, happenings and deeds? We would normally want to say that state-changes are *fully* determined by the happenings and deeds that link them; that is, that the state of the world at time $t+1$ is determined by the state at time $t$ plus the happenings and deeds that happen and are done at $t$; and also that happenings (though perhaps not deeds) are determined by preceding states. (The reverse time-direction is more problematical, since different states at $t$ and/or happenings and deeds in the interval may lead to the same state at $t+1$.) But we are also quite content, sometimes, to postulate that certain events are random and unpredictable, or perhaps predictable only statistically. Even physicists speak this way, for example, about the fission of individual atomic nuclei. Our prejudices regarding physical determinism are not firm.

Much stronger claims are sometimes made. The most famous is that of Laplacian determinism. Laplace, (*Essai philosophique sur les probabilités*) asserted that, if we knew the complete state of the world at any one instant, the laws of nature would allow us to predict its state at any other, earlier or later, and in fact to give a complete past and future history of the world. This is equivalent to saying that there are exactly as many worlds in $W_{phys}$ as there are possible states $S$ at any given time, one world for each state. This is a reasonable claim only if we assume both that the states are fully described, so that $S$ is as large as possible, and also that the laws of nature are fully stated, so that $W_{phys}$ is as small as possible. In practice, of course, only the sanguine expect completely reliable predictions about anything much; and there are also theoretical complications, such as, in physics, the question of what 'complete information' is in a world subject to the uncertainty principle. Nevertheless it is probably fair to say that Laplacian determinism is still an approximate representation of the creed of orthodox science. It has the consequence not only that all *happenings* are determined directly by the states from which they arise, but also all the *deeds of all doers*.

Laplacian determinism is sometimes taken to imply that no agent ever has a *choice* of what he does. It need not be taken as implying this, and if it does so it is inconsistent with the presuppositions of any issuer of imperatives, since the characteristic purpose of imperatives is to influence choice. It is futile to tell or ask anyone to do something it is not possible for him to do, and equally futile to tell him to do something he cannot help doing. It does not help us in this dilemma to fall back on the fact that we do not know the complete state of the world or all the laws of nature, for the difficulty is raised as much by the thesis that actions are predictable in theory as it would be by the thesis that they are predictable in practice. It is made even worse when we take into account the fact that the utterance of the imperative may itself be one of the causal factors in its satisfaction, and that the utterance is an action of the utterer and subject to whatever laws of nature are applicable to actions. I propose, however, to sidestep these difficulties. In so far as our interest is in the assumptions necessary for the building of the logic of imperatives, Laplacian determinism is too strong for our purpose, and has no interest for us. In its place, and in order to make simple sense of choice and choosing, we need a weaker one; or, actually, two.

Actions, in short, are in a proper sense the result of free choice, and the list of 'laws of nature' appropriate to the recognition of this freedom may be shorter than the one envisaged by Laplace and the physicist. In fact we need two lists. In the first place there is a sense in which elementary deeds can be regarded as completely open to the free choice of an agent; and List One will therefore contain no laws determining or restricting deeds. According to this way of thinking, a *forced* action is not really an action; in the case of an action that *appears* to be forced, what happens is either that the agent complies (possibly reluctantly, but still deliberately) with some persuasive force such as a threat, or that, if he really has no alternative, what he 'does' is not one of his actions at all, but a happening, or an action of the forcing agent. What he 'does' himself, in this case, is irrelevant, because it is ineffectual. The physical restrictions on choice are sufficiently represented, in List One, by the laws affecting states and happenings, since these independently imply that, from appropriate starting states, there are states that cannot be achieved, and happenings that cannot be engineered, by any deed.

List Two is longer and contains laws of a different kind, namely, what might be called 'principles of choice'. Free actions can be influenced and are, to that extent, at least partially predictable. To issue an imperative is, in general, to attempt to influence free action, and an imperative may also require that its addressee influence the free actions of others. We have no detailed theory of these influences, which represent what an agent 'is likely' or 'might be expected' to do. For theoretical simplicity let us assume that the state of the world at a given time determinately restricts the deeds a doer *will* choose to do (without restricting those he *can*).

The kind of determinism implied by the first (shorter) list has often been recommended by writers on freewill; note, in particular, the famous paper by Hobart, ('Free Will as Involving Determination and Inconceivable Without it'). In order to make sense of the concept of action we need to be able to assume that the world is predictably influenced – at least to a practical degree – by elementary deeds, and that the sequence of states and happenings is similarly practically determinate except in so far as the deeds of ourselves and other doers are interposed; and these requirements are as important as the negative one that the laws do not touch the concept of action itself. For a statement of the view of cause that underlies the alternative List Two, see Collingwood, (*An Essay on Metaphysics*, pt III) who remarks that the sense of *cause* in which one person causes another to do something is its primitive one, and that *cause* here means *provide with a motive*. Thus for effective action we also need to be able to assume that we know, within limits, what other doers will do, and this knowledge is not in contradiction with the fact that they will be doing it freely. In this connection note the distinction of Chisholm, ('The Agent as Cause') between 'agent causation' and 'event causation'.

It should be remarked that the present distinction between two sets of laws – natural laws and 'laws of choice' – could, subject to a certain kind of interpretation, be replaced by one between laws whose variation would make the world very different, and mere 'minor variation' possibilities. To do this would bring the analysis closer to the style proposed (in other connections) by Lewis, (*Counterfactuals*), and others such as Stalnaker, ('Possible Worlds'), who have taken it up. But it is necessary, here, for realism, to be relatively specific about the nature of the two sets of laws.

I shall take $W_{phys}$ to be the subset of worlds left possible by List One. The model can accommodate various more or less determinist possibilities. One rather clean and simple set of assumed properties would be the following: (1) given a state $s$ and a time $t$, there is just one big happening $h$ such that at least one member of $W_{phys}$ is in $s$ at $t$ and has $h$ at $t$; and (2) given a state $s$ and a time $t$, and an allocation of a deed to each doer, there is just one state $s'$ such that at least one member of $W_{phys}$ is in state $s$ at $t$, is such that doers do the deeds allocated at $t$, and is in state $s'$ at $t+1$. In short, states determine succeeding happenings; states and deeds together determine succeeding states; but nothing determines succeeding deeds. (No stipulation is made about determination backwards in time; nothing of interest hangs on it.) Here, happenings become passengers in our conceptual scheme and, in a certain sense, states also, since, given just one 'initial' state, all subsequent states and happenings are determined by deeds. But this degeneracy would disappear if the postulated properties were relaxed to become, say, statistical.

The effect of List Two, which contains laws about how free agents choose, is to narrow the range of each doer's deeds and hence from $W_{phys}$ a subset I shall call $W_{choosable}$ (The name is not quite right, but a further development will improve its match. In any case I here mean by *chooseable* not so much *capable of being chosen*, since all members of $W_{phys}$ are that, but *suitable for choice*; rather on the analogy of *desirable*.) Choosability is a matter not so much of what agents *could* or *could not* do, as of what they *would* or *would not*. A doer's choosable deeds, at any time, are the ones that are left after we have eliminated those that he can be relied on not to do.

<br>

## TEMPORAL POSSIBILITY

There is a special sense of the word *possible* with which physical possibility is easily confused, and with which the concepts *logically possible, physically possible* and *choosable* interact. We often regard something as impossible because it is *too late* to do it of bring it about, although there might have been no difficulty if appropriate steps had been taken earlier. In this sense,

It is possible to get the letter to him by the 31st

means

It is *not too late* to get the letter to him by the 31st,

and the word *possible* is indexical, since the truth or falsity of the statement depends on the time of its utterance. The indexicality may be removed by making a time explicit, as in, say,

It was possible on the 29th to get the letter to him by the 31st,

in which case it becomes simply a relative concept, relative to the time mentioned. It may also be relative to other circumstances; in general, to the state of the world at the time in question or, still more generally, to the world's past history. (But one other apparent relativity, namely, to agents, is a confusion. It seems at first to be the case that there are things that are possible, in the relevant sense, for some people at a given time but not for others, such as being in China in the succeeding five minutes. But although $X$'s being in China may be possible and $Y$'s not, these are different events.)

Let us call a state, happening or action *temporally possible* if it might yet come about or be done; or, in general, *temporally possible* in world $w$ at time $t$ if the history of world $w$ up to time $t$ is not, was not or will not be such as to exclude it. It has sometimes seemed to philosophers odd to regard divergent futures as equally possible in a world which, in fact, realises just one of those futures, but this is one of the ways in which we do use the word *possible*, and it requires recognition. But temporal possibility is, in a sense, a gloss added to other kinds, and we can immediately distinguish three clear subsenses, corresponding with the three senses of possibility we have already introduced; namely, we distinguish *temporal logical possibility* from *temporal physical possibility* and *temporal choosability*. To notate them I shall use the same symbols as before, but add argument-symbols for the world and the time to which the temporal concepts are relative. Thus $W(w, t)$, the set of *temporally logically possible worlds* relative to world $w$ at time $t$, is that subset of $W$ whose members are exactly like $w$ before $t$ and in respect of their state at $t$, but which vary in all conceivable ways thereafter. And $W_{phys}(w, t)$, the set of *temporally physically possible worlds* relative to $w$ at $t$, is just that set of worlds that are members of both $W(w, t)$ and $W_{phys}$. The set $W_{phys}(w, t)$ is smaller than $W(w, t)$ since there are various future states and happenings that are logically possible but that it is too late (in $w$ at $t$) for anyone to take steps to bring about, not to mention logically possible actions which no one will be able to perform since they have such states as their necessary conditions. The set $W_{choosable}(w, t)$ of *temporally choosable worlds* relative to $w$ at $t$ is similarly the intersection of the sets $W(w, t)$ and $W_{choosable}$ and represents that subset of $W_{phys}(w, t)$ which omits, at and after $t$, those worlds in which there are deeds that the relevant doers can be relied on not to do.

According to the principle of determinism that went into our definition of $W_{phys}$, a world that is presently like the real world can differ from it in the future only in so far as (and after) it contains different deeds. Consequently the only feature of $w$ that is relevant to the definition of $W_{phys}(w, t)$ and $W_{choosable}(w, t)$ is its state at $t$; and the temporally physically possible worlds, given this state, are those that result from the various deeds that doers can, if they choose, do from $t$ on. Some of those deeds, however, are deeds that their doers can be relied on not to do; and if we drop worlds containing these, those that are left are the temporally choosable.

One further definition and then we are done. We sometimes want to discriminate the things a particular agent or group of agents *could* do, while allowing that they are constricted by what *other* agents *would* do. This gives us a kind of possibility that is a cross, relative to a particular agent or group, between temporal physical possibility and temporal choosability. I think it deserves a special name, and I shall call it *active possibility*. The set $W_{active}(w, p, t)$ of *actively possible worlds*, (for $p$ in $w$ at $t$, is that subset of $W_{phys}(w, t)$ in which the deeds of *doers other than $p$* are constrained to be choosable. The generalization to the case in which the single agent $p$ is replaced by a group $P'$ is immediate.

Armed with the concept of active possibility we are close to being ready to specify the circumstances under which it can be reasonable to issue a given imperative to a given prospective agent or agents.

### FORMAL RULES

The sets of worlds so far defined are related as in figure 3.

It would be possible to set down precisely the logical assumptions that must be made about the various world-sets and, by consequence, the concepts of possibility as they apply to deeds, states and complexes of them. Most of them follow from what has already been said, but a few ought to be laid down in addition. For example, note that as time passes, the crystallization of temporal possibilities shrinks the relevant sets of worlds, so that if $t'$ is later than $t$, $W(w, t')$ is properly contained in $W(w, t)$; and similarly for the other sets with time as argument. Note also that the world $w$ is a member of $W_{choosable}(w, t)$, which is at the left of the above diagram; and hence also a member of all the others. But the real world need be a member only of those in the bottom row. Similar remarks could be multiplied, but no particularly controversial or interesting results emerge.

Deeds, happenings, states and complexes of them are called logically possible, physically possible, choosable, temporally logically possible relative to $w$ at $t, \ldots$, if they are components of possible worlds of the respective categories. They are, of course, *actual* if and only if they are components of the real world.

There are also derived modal concepts. In particular, a deed, happening, state or complex of them is *logically necessary* if it is a component of *all logically possible* worlds, and similarly *physically necessary* if . . . (and so on). There is no obvious apodeictic correlate of the term *choosable*, but I shall say *choosably inevitable*. Deeds, states, . . . that are *past* at a given time in a given world are *temporally necessary* relative to that world and time, in all subsenses. This piece of nomenclature is inept but consistent, and should need only a brief apology.

$$W_{choosable}(w, t) \xrightarrow{\ C\ } W_{active}(w, p, t) \xrightarrow{\ C\ } W_{phys}(w, t) \xrightarrow{\ C\ } W(w, t)$$

$$W_{choosable} \qquad\qquad\qquad C \qquad\qquad\qquad W_{phys} \qquad C \quad W$$

The sign 'C' indicates proper containment.

Figure 3

### THE CONTENT OF IMPERATIVES

It is Intermission, and we should lower the safety curtain and repeat that model-building is to some extent an arbitrary exercise, calculated to depict main features, but not necessarily details, of reality. Since we now turn to the representation of imperatives, a particular caution should be repeated concerning the special assumptions that went into the concept of an elementary deed. We easily understand that extensive tasks, such as, say, mounting a military campaign to drive the Germans out of North Africa, must be modelled as a vast complex of deeds, conditional on states, happenings and the deeds of others. But it may not be so easy to keep in mind that a complexity similar in kind, different only in scope, generally attends even very simple tasks such as closing a door. When it matters, this 'elementary' action also needs to be analysed as a program of conditional elementary deeds, varied to meet a range of possible circumstances. Imperatives that enjoin pure, simple deeds are at best a limiting case, of little practical importance. In effect, every imperative is complex.

Fortunately for the logic, full generality is nearly as easily achieved as full particularity. We can represent the basic content of any imperative $i$ as the set $W_i$ of worlds within any one of which it would count as having been carried out. The case of a single deed is included in this, since the members of $W_i$ may differ in all possible ways except in having in common the doing of that deed. But state-defined and happening-defined imperatives and those that enjoin complex and general actions and states-of-affairs can be represented equally well. Provided it is possible to give a clear, extended account of what an imperative means – which I take to be equivalent to saying precisely under what circumstances it would count as having been carried out – it can be represented as a set of worlds. The possibilities are all included.

To be so expressible, an imperative needs only a certain logical definiteness. This is really, of course, a matter of definition: the kind of definiteness it needs is that kind that makes possible an expression as a set of possible worlds. But it may be worth while spelling out a little what is excluded. First, all language is more or less vague; but no apology is needed for not building vagueness into a logical model. Second, there may be various kinds of periphrastic or circular specification that defeat depiction. The imperative analogue of the liar paradox,

Disobey this order!,

does not merely specify a logically impossible task or generate the null-set of worlds; it does not, in any clear sense, specify a 'task' at all, any more than,

This statement is false'

specifies an identifiable truth or falsehood.

But third, it must be made very clear what is meant, in the definition, by saying that an imperative is 'carried out'; because the definition of *satisfaction* is a main concern of this chapter, and it is important to distinguish stronger and weaker senses of that word. Most logicians will understand if I say that the set $W_i$ is meant to be the set of worlds in which $i$ is satisfied *extensionally*. In more detail, as follows: let us suppose we take the exact words of the imperative, and transform them into indicative mood as a description of an act, or state, or happening, or complex of these things; and let us transport ourselves to a sufficiently distant future time and put this description in the past tense. (If necessary – to deal with a possible objection – let us postulate that there is, by definition, an 'infinite' future time, at which even time-universal imperatives can be regarded as having been definitively satisfied or dissatisfied.) Now the worlds which *extensionally satisfy* the imperative are just those of which the description is true. The imperative,

Drive the Germans out of North Africa

is extensionally satisfied in just those worlds in which it will later be true to say that the addressee (at a relative time implied by the imperative) drove the Germans out of North Africa. The imperative,

Everybody leave the room

is extensionally satisfied in those worlds in which it will be true that everybody (whoever is meant) left the room. No feature of those worlds is relevant apart from the bare truth of the description. The point is particularly clear in the case of a state-defined imperative; thus,

Be here at 9 on Monday

is extensionally satisfied if it is later possible to say truly that he (or she, or whoever) was there on 9 on Monday, however that came about. No question, yet, of any action-reduction, of whether any acts or outcomes were deliberate, of choosability, even of physical possibility. The imperative,

Break the law of gravity

is extensionally satisfied, in the appropriate logical sense, in those (logically possible) worlds in which the addressee duly breaks the law of gravity.

I labour this explanation because it is important to separate the basic or (as we may now call it) extensional content of an imperative from the plethora of implied actions, purposes, necessary conditions and felicity conditions it carries with it. The latter will be our main concern for the remainder of this chapter, since they are what give imperatives their different logic. But an imperative need generally figure on our definitions only in the shape of a world-set $W_i$.

For just a few purposes an extended concept of extensional satisfaction is needed. Some of the worlds in which the imperative $i$ is *not* extensionally satisfied may come nearer to satisfying it than others; and this distinction may need to be marked. As well as the set $W_i$ of worlds in which $i$ is fully satisfied there may be a set $W_i^2$ in which it has 'second-best' satisfaction, another set $W_i^3$ in which it has 'third-best', and so on, theoretically without limit. In the example we used earlier,

Attend the meeting; or, at least, send an apology,

'best' satisfaction is achieved by attending the meeting, 'second-best' by sending an apology instead. When there is question of alternative satisfactions of this kind the term *extensional satisfaction* needs to be used in this extended way.

YOU WILL ... AND YOU SHOULD ...

For the sake of contrast, let us sketch how imperatives would be incorporated in our model if we were to adopt the *You will* ... or the *You should* ... reduction of chapter 3.

In effect, the *You will* ... reduction, if we purge it of the ambiguity of *will* and the explicit temporal and personal indexicality, and treat it as a semantic thesis to the effect that none of the logical properties of imperatives are different from those of the corresponding indicatives, becomes equivalent to the thesis that extensional content and extensional satisfaction are the only logical concepts we need. All imperatives are *fiats*, constructible from indicatives by means of an operator such as *IMP* or *Let it be the case that*. An imperative is satisfied, in all senses of that word, when the real world is a member of the set that defines its extensional content; thus,

$$w \varepsilon W_i.$$

It follows that the (one and only) negation $\bar{i}$ of an imperative $i$ is satisfied when and only when $w$ is *not* a member of $W_i$ that the (one and only) conjunction $i \,\&\, j$ of imperatives $i$ and $j$ is satisfied when $w$ is a member of both $W_i$ and $W_j$, that is, of their intersection $W_i \cap W_j$. And so on.

A few of the special imperative properties discussed in chapter 2 could be modelled, for this logic, more or less *ad hoc*; restriction to future time, for example, relative to an assumed time of utterance, or availability of second-best alternatives (by the extended definition). But for most of them the definition lacks the necessary richness. That there is nothing 'positively' wrong with this logic might be argued from the fact that it can be represented as a capsule within our own. But the rest of the chapter will display its limitations.

So far as the *You should* . . . theory is concerned, I shall discuss here only one of the various styles of semantic interpretation that have been proposed on 'deontic logic'. (See Kripke, 'Semantic Analysis of Modal Logic I, Normal Propositional Logics', p. 95; W.H. Hanson, 'Semantics for Deontic Logic'; Cresswell, 'Some Further Semantics for Deontic Logic'.) According to this, the basic judgment to be made about an imperative – conceived as equivalent to a deontic proposition – concerns its conformity or otherwise to some big imperative or plan, such as natural, human or divine law or, perhaps, the rules of a game or a club. The worlds in which this big imperative is extensionally satisfied are the 'good' worlds, $W_{good}$; and an ordinary imperative $i$ is 'good' or 'right' or 'in force' or 'valid' (whichever word we like to choose) if and only if it is implied by the big one; thus,

$$W_{good} \subseteq W_i$$

We can, if we wish, express this condition backwards by saying that if what $i$ specifies is *not* done, a 'bad' world will result, or (say) that something terrible will ensue; and the theory is therefore equivalent to (the simplest version of) the 'sanction' theory of deontic logic of Anderson, or Japanese-Korean theory. (In Japanese and Korean a mild imperative or deontic *Do D* is commonly expressed by an idiom that translates approximately *If you don't do D, it won't do*. For Anderson's simplest formulation of the 'sanction' theory see his, 'The Formal Analysis of Normative Systems'. Later formulations remedied some of the deficiencies of the earlier by substituting alternative definitions of entailments; see Anderson, 'Some Nasty Problems in the Formal Logic of Ethics'. For a relative or consequential concept of 'obligatory' formally equivalent to a 'sanction' theory see Angstl, 'On the Logic of Norms: A Natural Deontics'.) There are also models in which worlds are regarded not merely as 'good' or 'bad' but as capable of being ranged on a scale of 'goodness'. These take their starting-point from logics of 'better' such as those of Halldén, (*On the Logic of 'Better'*); and Åqvist, ('Deontic Logic Based on a Logic of "Better"'), and 'A Binary Primitive in Deontic Logic'); and Åqvist has sketched a model for such a graded system of worlds as a means towards resolving the 'good Samaritan' paradox – see his 'Good Samaritans, Contrary-to-Duty Imperatives and Epistemic Obligations'. (But I do not think anyone has tackled the problem of felicific arithmetic that would apply to an imperative with its own scale of degrees of satisfaction.)

The imperative logic erected on the concept of 'good' and 'bad' worlds is richer than that of pure extensional satisfaction since it recognises an 'indifferent' category between 'good' and 'bad' imperatives – when the sets $W_i$ and $W_{good}$ merely overlap – and hence a negation type 4. In some versions it is also combined with a logic of necessity and possibility to make some of the points about imperative propriety or felicity. So long as they are not regarded as presenting the whole truth about imperatives, these definitions are not 'positively' wrong either, and the model can accommodate them. But they are a side-issue to our main theme.

STRATEGIES

No imperatives counts as wholeheartedly satisfied if it is possible to say of it *He wouldn't have done it if it hadn't been for so-and-so, or It only came about by accident, or It would have come about anyway, what he did was irrelevant to it (or impeded it)*. Conversely, even when extensional satisfaction is lacking, we sometimes want to say *Yes, but it wasn't his fault*, or *He did everything he could*. Full or wholehearted satisfaction perhaps includes extensional, but what it adds is sometimes seen as the more important component.

The extra ingredients are, first, an element of intension; and second, the expression of this in terms of action. We also need to make clear the differing roles and necessary contributions of the addressee and of other people (who, in the case of a third-person imperative, include the subject(s), in both the intension and in the action taken. The easiest way to approach this cluster of supplements is through the concept of a *strategy*.

A *strategy* can be defined formally as an allocation of deeds, one for each time and for each appropriate context at that time. In order to make the concept of a *context* precise, let us define a *history*, of any world at any time $t$, as a full account of the past states, deeds and happenings of that world, up to and including its state at $t$. Expressed as a set of worlds, this is actually the same set as $W(w, t)$, the set of temporally logically possible worlds in $w$ at $t$ – we simply see it, as it were, from a different point of view. Now if $J_t$ is the set of possible histories at $t$, a *strategy at time t* is an allocation of a deed to each history at each time from $t$ on; that is, an allocation of a deed to each $j_{t'}$.

where $j_t{}'$ ε $J_{t'}$, *for each* $t' \geq t$ Let the set of possible strategies at time $t$ be $Q_t$, and the set of possible *worlds* in which the deeds of $p$ are among those specified by a given such strategy $q_t$ (where $q_t$ ε $Q_t$) be

$$W_{strat}(p, q_t).$$

So defined, a strategy is overspecified. Although it is right and proper that a strategy should be defined so as to allocate deeds to various counterfactual histories (to express what $p$ *would do if* these happened or had happened, and hence give strategies the necessary intensional element), it is generally assumed, when a strategy is specified, that it is going to be *followed*, and this restricts the histories that will need to be taken into account at future times. But it is easiest to ignore this point so far as the definition is concerned and make allowance, where necessary, as we proceed.

For certain purposes, however, the predictably counter-factual worlds are also irrelevant. We may wish to ignore temporally physically impossible worlds, confining consideration to those of the intersection (in respect of the following by $p$ in world $w$, starting at $t$, of strategy $q_t$)

$$W_{strat}(p, q_t) \cap W_{phys}(w, t).$$

And if the strategy is conceived as a strategy of $p$ alone, we may also wish to ignore worlds in which agents other than $p$ do deeds which in fact they would not do. Although, in discussing the strategies open to $p$ it would not be realistic to limit consideration to those actually choosable by $p$, we need not consider any worlds containing non-choosable deeds of others. This means that we limit consideration to *active* possibilities for $p$ at $t$, namely to the intersection,

$$W_{strat}(p, q_t) \cap W_{active}(w, p, t).$$

In deciding on a strategy, p may assume that, if he chooses and follows $q_t$, the outcome will be a world that is a member of this set.

Where the single agent $p$ is replaced by a group, $P'$, a strategy for the group is simply a group of individual strategies, one for each member. This apparently atomistic assumption is less so that it at first seems, since we can readily suppose, if we wish, that the strategies are prechosen in concert, and also that the individual actions interlock and are complementary. The set of worlds in which the group strategy is followed is the intersection of the sets for the individual strategies. There are subtleties here; for example, in the question to what degree and for what purposes each group-member should presume choosability of the actions of the others. But there are no fundamental difficulties.

We are interested mainly in strategies that have as their object the satisfaction of imperatives. Let us suppose that $p$ has just been issued with an imperative $i$, and wants to choose a strategy that will satisfy it; and, for reasons we shall come to in the next chapter, let us confine ourselves to imperatives of simple forms, without, in particular, separably conjunctive or instantial parts. If all the outcomes of a choice $q_t$ satisfy $i$, namely, if,

$$\{ W_{strat}(p, q_t) \cap W_{active}(w, p, t) \} \underline{\subset} W_i,$$

$q_t$ is adequate to achieve extensional satisfaction of $i$ and can be called an $i$-strategy.

A sufficient, and the simplest, condition of *wholehearted satisfaction* of an imperative $i$ addressed to $p$ in $w$ at $t$ is the following: $p$ chooses and follows an $i$-strategy.

## PARTIAL STRATEGIES

But, in practice, no one ever chooses or is allocated a strategy in the minute detail that specifies every deed; and certainly not to the end of time. Some deed-choices are left open, some merely restricted. If all are left open we have a null-strategy, or no strategy at all; but in intermediate cases masterful inactivity, or simply doing whatever you feel like or getting on with something else, may often be the best or only course for stretches of time while events unfold. A partial allocation of deeds is a *partial strategy*; and in practice, all strategies are partial. At the very least, then, for practical purposes, we need to see strategies as disjunctions of complete strategies, $Q_t' \underline{\subset} Q_t$, and the world-set $W_{strat}(p, q_t)$ as replaced by $W_{strat}(p, Q_t')$, which is the join of the world-sets for the individual members.

But another idea is important here. In many or most practical cases there is no way of *ensuring* that a given sequence of deeds will secure the end enjoined by an imperative $i$; that is, there are no $i$-strategies, as we have defined them, at all. But it does not follow from this that nothing can, or need, be done. Under these circumstances the addressees of an imperative would be expected, at least, to act in such a way as to keep extensional satisfaction within the bounds of possibility. This means that he must not do any deed $d$ that would *infringe* – that is, that would ensure dissatisfaction of – the imperative. It is only if there is neither any $i$-strategy nor any deed that will make impossible $i$'s extensional satisfaction that he has no choice to make. Usually this happens only when $i$ has lapsed. But in such a circumstance we may as well say that $i$ has no effect and does not prohibit any deeds, that is, leaves all deeds open.

A *partial i*-strategy for $p$ in $w$ at $t$ is consequently a choice, not of an individual deed $d$, but of a subset $D'$ of deeds, for each $t' \geq t$ and for each, $j_t$, with the following properties:

1. if there are *i*-strategies for $p$ in $w$ at $t'$ given $j_t'$, $D'$ is contained in the set of deeds defined by them;
2. if there are no *i*-strategies, but there are deeds $D''$ that are not deeds of $p$ at $t'$ in any $W_i$ $D'$ excludes these deeds, that is, $D' = D - D''$;
3. (vacuously) if there are neither *i*-strategies nor any deeds $D''$ as in (2), $D'$ is unrestricted.

The weakest partial *i*-strategy of the addressee or the joint addressees, or the set of such strategies for the various addresses severally, in a given world at a given time, is the *addressee-action-reduction* of $i$ in that world at that time.

WHOLEHEARTED SATISFACTION

The sufficient condition of wholehearted satisfaction set down a page or so ago is too strong to be a necessary condition, and we shall consider weaker formulations in a moment. But let us pause and look at its implications. First, the *choosing* of a strategy. For us to be able to say that $p$ wholeheartedly satisfies $i$ it is obviously not enough that $p$'s deeds be in fact the relevant ones of an *i*-strategy, since he could choose to do those deeds for the wrong reasons or have been forced into them by others, and not much more than extensional satisfaction would have been achieved. In effect, we must assume that each doer *has* a strategy (at least partial, possibly null) at each time; and this intensional notion needs to become part of our conceptual apparatus. Since people do not always do what they intend to do, it is not necessary to assume that $p$'s actual deed at $t$ furthers his chosen strategy at $t$. But to say that he *follows* his strategy will have this implication.

To say that $p$ follows a strategy $q_t$ must, however, also mean more than just that his future deeds are among those that $q_t$ allocates; because, if the idea of *having* a strategy is to make sense, he must have strategies at future times as well as at $t$, and these cannot (by definition) be $q_t$, though they may be consistent with it. Consistency of strategies as between one time and another is, however, easy to define, since the progress of time merely narrows the range of open possibilities. If $t'$ is later than $t$ and $p$ has $q_t$ at $t$ and $q'_{t'}$ at $t'$ his later strategy is consistent with his earlier if and only if

$W_{strat}(p, q_t) \subseteq W_{strat}(p, q'_{t'})$.

*Following* a strategy therefore has two parts to it: (1) having consistent future strategies, and (2) doing, at each time, the deed allocated by the strategy current at that time, for the true history at that time. Strategies progressively shrink, in a way determined by the unfolding of events – that is, by the deed done and the deeds of others – which determine a new history that in turn determines what branches of the strategy-tree remain.

But the concept of a simple strategy, planned in detail to the end of time, is, as we said, unrealistic. So the first weakening of the criterion must be one that accommodate partial strategies. It is a sufficient condition of wholehearted satisfaction of $i$ (by $p$ in $w$, starting at $t$) that $p$ choose and follow a *partial* $i$-strategy, namely, a strategy $Q'_t$ such that,

$$\{ W_{strat}(p, Q^i_t) \cap W_{active}(w, p, t) \} \subseteq W_i$$

Future strategies must again progressively shrink, and a deed must be done, at each time, from among those specified by the strategy for the true history at that time. The weakening has two important consequences. The first is that it allows $p$ to have other aims and purposes than the satisfaction of $i$ alone. For example, if he subsequently receives and decides to carry out a second imperative $j$ – and provided its satisfaction can be achieved without prejudice to his plan to satisfy $i$ – he may shrink his strategy in such a way that its outcomes will be contained not merely within $W_i$, but within $W_i \cap W_j$; and so on as he develops new aims and purposes again, so long as they are consistent with his plans to satisfy the old ones. With this improvement in the definition we no longer need to suppose that the agent's life revolves round the satisfaction of $i$ alone.

The emendation that replaces the requirement of a complete $i$-strategy by that of a partial one incidentally takes care of what happens when an imperative has *lapsed*; that is, when either it has not been satisfied and it is too late to do anything about it, or it *has* been satisfied and nothing more remains to be done. So far as the particular imperative is concerned, all the subsequent strategies may as well be null ones. According to our definition of (complete) $i$-strategy, these are $i$-strategies only if $i$ has been satisfied; but, in framing a definition of *partial strategy*, we allowed that any strategy is a partial $i$-strategy if $i$ has lapsed. In passing let us note that a definition of *lapsing* is most easily provided by putting this point back-to-front: An imperative $i$ is said to have *lapsed* (for $p$ in $w$ at $t$) if all strategies are (complete or partial) $i$-strategies. The definition takes in actively necessary and actively impossible imperatives as special cases, but anyone who cares may exclude these *ad hoc*.

However, the criterion is still to strong. What if there are two routes to the satisfaction of *i*, and *p*, having chosen the first, changes his mind (perhaps, to satisfy *j* as well) in time to prefer the second? Or what if, having chosen an *i*-strategy or partial *i*-strategy specified in great detail, he finds (perhaps, with the unfolding of events) that this is unnecessary and may be relaxed to one that is more open? In either case, the progressive strategies no longer shrink. But does this matter?

The appropriate weaker formulation is as follows: At any time from *t* on, *p* should have and act in accordance with a partial *i*-strategy. I think this is now final.

Perhaps, in practice, we disapprove of over-frequent changes of mind made without good reason. But whether this disapproval should be regarded as logically based is not clear; and, in any case, there is no limit to the number of times good reasons for a change may present themselves. And, in this case, we praise adaptability.

Oddly, from the fact that *p* acts at each time from *t* on in accordance with an *i*-strategy, it does not follow that the sequence of his deeds is a sequence within an *i*-strategy available at *t*. This is because whether later deeds fall within *i*-strategies may be conditional on events (deeds of others) not temporally inevitable at *t*. The relaxation of the criterion is, consequently, real and significant. I restate it in full as follows.

A person *p* in receipt of an imperative *i* in world *w* at time *t* wholeheartedly satisfies *i* if, at all times $t' \geq t$, he adopts a partial strategy $Q_{t'}$ such that

$$\{ W_{strat}(p, Q_{t'}) \cap W_{active}(w, p, t') \} \subseteq W_i.$$

and does one of the deeds allocated by this $Q_{t'}$ for the true history at $t'$.


## POINTFULNESS

Not every imperative is satisfiable. An imperative may enjoin a *logical impossibility*, namely, if $W_i$ is empty; or what it enjoins may be *physically impossible* (against laws of nature), *temporally logically impossible* (partly or wholly in the past), *temporally physically impossible* (not possible in the time), or *actively impossible* (other people won't co-operate). All these go easily into symbols. The last is the most important, and is definable,

$$W_i \cap W_{active}(w, p, t) = 0.$$

(Several of the concepts are, of course, relative to a world and a time, and this one is also relative to an agent). And if the content of *i* is not an active possibility, even extensional satisfaction is not possible, much less wholehearted. There are no *i*-strategies.

An impossible imperative could aptly be called *pointless*; in fact, *logically pointless* or *physically pointless* or . . . But impossibility is not the only source of pointlessness; necessity will do as well. If what *i* enjoins is *logically necessary* (so that $W_i = W$), nothing that could ever happen or be done has any relevance to its satisfaction; and even if it is *actively necessary* all actively possible strategies are *i*-strategies. An imperative *i* is actively necessary (for *p* in *w* at *t*) if it is extensionally satisfied in all actively possible worlds; thus

$$W_{active}(w, p, t) \subseteq W_i.$$

But it is important to distinguish *pointlessness* (of whatever kind) of an imperative from mere non-availability, or over-availability, of strategies at a particular time. This is because the availability of strategies changes with events. An *i*-strategy is a strategy that guarantees the satisfaction of *i*; but, although there may be no way *now* in which I can act to guarantee a given result, later events may provide me with one. This even suggests a further weakening of the wholehearted satisfaction criterion; *i* might be regarded as whole-heartedly satisfied by *p* if, although no *i*-strategy is available at *t*, *p* adopts and follows a partial *i*-strategy as soon as one becomes available later. But there are difficulties.

The trouble is that the fact that a partial *i*-strategy *may* become available later is, at least sometimes, in principle, predictable; and earlier deeds can influence the possibility. Thus it would be possible for *p* to adopt second-order goals or strategies in respect of this possibility. In one extreme case he could, perhaps, even act, without actually making satisfaction of *i* impossible, to close off almost every possibility that an *i*-strategy will later eventuate, leaving only (say) one very improbable one alive. Or he may keep his options, and his eyes, open. But we cannot counsel the recipient of *i* always to keep *i*-options open either, since sometimes the options may be mutually incompatible and he may keep a given one open only by closing others.

Human beings being human, not much of this often gets worked out in detail. Chances get missed, hunches are followed that may or may not be sound, and what is done is sometimes done for the wrong reasons. Agents trust unwisely that awkward eventualities will not arise, rely uncertainly on the good sense of those who may lack it, postpone decisions until in a mood to make them and then find it is too late. Up to a point these strategical imperfections may be rationally excused on grounds we have not incorporated in our model, those of lack of knowledge and consequent necessity for guesswork; but that cannot be the whole story. In short, in matters of practical complexity true wholehearted satisfaction of imperatives is at best the exception and is not demanded or expected. And anyway, when we plumb some of the finer points of the model it becomes clear that wholehearted satisfaction is a theoretical, unpractical concept just as extensional is. It can nevertheless be preferred for logical study in view of the richness and range of the considerations it incorporates.

We laid down one specific limitation on the imperatives to which the model applies, namely, that they must not have separably conjunctive or instantial parts; this restriction will be explained in the next chapter. There are also one or two others. It is here supposed, for example, that the addressee or addressees of the imperative get total responsibility for its execution; but, in practice, the responsibility must sometimes be regarded as shared with others who are not addressees at all, but who may be informed of the imperative or may be used by addressees as means. For that matter, these may sometimes be regarded as having some independent discretion, or can be regarded as being in independent communication with the issuer. There are also imperatives which, though it is not impossible that they may be satisfied as a result of effort on the part of the addressee, are virtually impossible to satisfy wholeheartedly, by some strategy that can be guaranteed to succeed. Thus Margolis, ('Actions and Ways of Failing'), distinguishes what he calls 'supervenient' contingencies such as that enjoined in,

> Write a great poem.

We shall also return to some features of these in a subsequent chapter.

Note, finally, the interesting phenomenon of 'burning one's boats', namely, making one's own pursuit of a certain course of action physically necessary. We also sometimes give ourselves a 'set' that, in suitable circumstances, makes our own future deeds choosably inevitable, or narrows their range so that the remaining alternatives are all *i*-strategies. One can even imagine doing this mediately through other people.

EFFECTIVENESS

An imperative is *effective* if it brings about what it enjoins. Up to the present we have been looking at strategies from the point of view of the addressee of an imperative, but it is now appropriate, as it were, to take a step back and enlarge our field of view. Let us suppose the imperative *i issued* to $p$ by $p''$ in the shape of an utterance $u$ that takes place or becomes effective at time $t-1$, and that the state of the world $w$ in which $p$ finds himself at $t$ reflects this utterance in the sense that it has been partly causally conditioned by it. When we look at the situation from the point of view of $p''$, what additional logical conditions of pointfulness, felicity, and so on, are brought in?

Some of the *causal* features of the utterance $u$ move outside the ordinary bounds of logic in the sense that they involve not only the content ($i$, or $W_i$) of $u$ but also concomitants such as whether it is made clearly or obscurely, forcefully or timidly, with or without overtones of threat or enticement. But the content is also involved.

We can regard the utterance $u$ as *effective* in world $w$ at time $t-1$ if and only if the satisfaction of the imperative $i$ it expresses is *choosably inevitable* at $t$, namely, if and only if

$$W_{choosable}(w, t) \subseteq W_i.$$

Oddly, this now does not involve the addressee $p$ at all, though it naturally makes a difference to the state of $w$ at $t$ that $i$ was uttered to $p$ rather than to someone else. For $p$ chooses among the things he *could* do; but for the utterer $p''$ the considerations are only what $p$, along with others *will* do, and he may consider them equally as instruments.

The utterer $p''$ is, of course, in a position to help or hinder the satisfaction of $i$ by $p$. There are various interesting possibilities, such as that $p''$ will deliberately frustrate the carrying out of his own imperative, or that he expects and allows that he will himself be used by $p$ as an instrument in its satisfaction. But it seems possible to insulate the logic of the imperative itself from these complications. The importance of the other actions of $p''$ resides in the fact that they can be taken to include the concomitant features of the imperative utterance. If we wish to take these into account but do not regard them strictly as part of the logic, we can discuss, at least, their causal properties within our model.

Seen from the point of view of $p''$ there is a new range of pointfulness conditions governing, this time, the *utterance $u$* of the imperative $i$; that is to say, there are new questions of logical pointfulness, physical pointfulness, . . . of a given *style of utterance* of $i$ at $t-1$. And we may interpret this term *style of utterance* broadly or narrowly, as we wish. If we interpret it broadly, the 'concomitants' find their way into the logical treatment after all.

The object of our semantic model is to provide a setting within which logical points such as those of chapter 2 can be played out. In most cases the way the various points actually made in chapter 2 are elucidated is obvious enough, and will be left to the reader. But a few seem to call for extra comment.

1. The modelling of negations of types 1 and 2 can be left to look after itself, and type 5 is less a semantic than a pragmatic matter and will occupy us later. But types 3 and 4 call for some special comments. Let us start with type 4, which is most obviously dealt with by making separate provision, within the model, for *permissives*. The extensional content of a permissive $m$ can be conceived as a world-set $W_m$, obtained from it in exactly the same way as $W_i$ as obtained from $i$; and the various kinds of pointfulness are defined analogously. But, in relation to an actively pointful permission, the interesting property of a strategy is not so much whether it (extensionally or wholeheartedly) *satisfies* it as whether it (extensionally or wholeheartedly) *takes advantage of* it, namely, whether the world-sets overlap; thus

$$W_{strat}(p, Q'_t) \cap W_{active}(w, p, t) \cap W_m \neq 0.$$

In the case of the relations between imperatives and permissives, *active possibilities* are of more practical importance than mere *logical possibilities*, and a permission may, for example, be actively empty if the active possibilities it seems to open up are otherwise pre-empted. We used permissives above to explicate *choice-offering* disjunctions of imperatives, and these need no further comment here. The possible conflicts of permissives with imperatives, and the role permissives may play in connection with conflicts between imperatives, will be discussed later.

Negation type 3 depends on the concept of a 'normal' or 'natural' course of events. It is not clear exactly what this is, and we should, perhaps, recognize that the concept is not and has never been a precise one. But a certain amount of what we have said provides some clues. In the first place, we have distinguished, for other reasons, between what people *can* do or not do, and what they *can be relied on* to do or not do; and, although we regard the latter kind of judgement about a person as one about quite determinate features of his behaviour, it is clear that in practice the addition of a saving phrase such as 'in the normal course of events' would be proper and realistic. People, in other words, though it may be useful and essential to us to predict their actions and act on those predictions, can fail and surprise us, and it is often this kind of conformity to or deviation from expected behaviour that is referred to.

But the same kind of point applies to predictions about inanimate objects. In the absence of Laplacian knowledge of what the future of the world will be, we rely on predictions based on imperfect generalizations; in the 'normal course of events' unsupported objects fall, my car will convey me to work, and there will be no earthquake today in Sydney. We could pin this concept down with a model by supposing we had a list of the imperfect generalizations on which these judgements depend, and defining, with their use, a set of 'normal' worlds.

Where my own actions are concerned, something different is necessary; I have conservative courses of action, but there are also deviations from them that I sometimes make by dint of effort. The concept of a 'positive' action, even of a 'negative' kind, is clearer. This, too, could be modelled *ad hoc* by postulating this kind of distinction between my available deeds. But it also has close connections with the fact that actions, as we understand them, are more intensional than this model allows. Again, we shall make some further progress towards a satisfactory account in a later chapter.

2. Where there is an explicit *second-best* alternative to an imperative, we normally suppose that, when something impedes the satisfaction of the first alternative, the second-best takes on whatever force the first originally had. But there can be a real question whether the addressee should not sometimes 'go for broke' for the first alternative and sacrifice chances of achieving the second if he fails, or whether he should 'play safe' and achieve the second at all costs. This is a matter of relative values, and logic can only lay out the alternatives. But it is worth pointing out that they may be complicated.

The extended definition of extensional satisfaction that allows for second-best alternatives is here also intended to provide the means of distinguishing separable from inseparable conjunctions. The question whether the force of a conjunctive imperative *i-and-j* extends to the conjuncts *i* and *j* individually is really the question of what is supposed to be done if *i* and *j* are not, together, going to be satisfied. Is the satisfaction of *i* without *j* a second-best alternative? Or of *j* without *i*? Or of neither? Or is the choice indifferent between some of these? The assumption that a given conjunction is a separable one is to the effect that satisfaction of *i* without *j*, or of *j* without *i*, is better than satisfaction of neither. This means that the extended definition permits its explication within the model.

3. As we have seen, there are many complications in the logic of group action. Most of them, however, arise from the uncertainty a

given member of the group may have about the actions – whether in supposed conformity with a group strategy, or outside it – of the other members. Where there is no such uncertainty the remaining problem – that of explicating *joint* as distinct from *several* responsibility of the members – is open to essentially the same treatment as that of explicating the two conjunctions. The question at issue, that is, is one of which alternative is second-best or third-best or . . . if the best is rendered unattainable by the delinquency of one or more members. *Several* responsibility functions like separable conjunction, so that, if one member is delinquent, second-best satisfaction is achieved by the continuing appropriate action of others. *Joint* responsibility is consistent with the possibility that the others can do nothing to retrieve the situation and may as well not bother. (But responsibility also raises other issues.)

The special case in which a third-person subject is a member of an addressee group seems to be one in which the subject has the main responsibility for action. If he acts, and the others do nothing, all is well; if he does not act, there may or may not be a second-best alternative of the others' doing something about it. There is a different kind of asymmetry in the case of a *Let's* imperative, where, if the issuer does not take the relevant action, the addressee(s) could be held to be absolved.

4. In the case of conditional imperatives, a formulation in terms of choice of strategies virtually forces a decision whether to count falsification of the antecedent as satisfaction. Conditionals are quite basic to the expression of strategies, since deeds are conditional on histories. But these, because the antecedents are past and no longer contingent, raise no problems – except for problems in connection with the agents' knowledge, or lack of it, of the truth of antecedents, to which we shall also come later.

# 5

# The Consistency of a Set of Imperatives

Such as the rules of a club, or a game, the instructions that come with a calculator or a washing machine, guidelines for salesmen or party speakers, service regulations, the precepts of a moral code or code of laws – or any combination of these. At will, we can spread the net wider; for it can make sense to speak, say, of an intention as consistent or inconsistent with, say, personal interests or wishes. It would be a mistake to generalize about all these possibilities at once, and not everything I say applies to all of them. But a large part of what needs to be said about the logical relations between members of a set can be said generally about virtually all imperatives and para-imperatives. In this chapter I shall accept the risk of conflating forms that are too diverse, in an effort to avoid the converse risk of narrowness; and, since I cannot keep saying 'imperatives, para-imperatives, rules, goals, promises, . . .', I shall often say just 'imperatives'. I shall, however, be more concerned than in previous chapters with *rules*, in the special sense of imperatives of separably general form.

Among logical relations I shall concentrate on *consistency*, which, although it is only one among a number of logical properties and relations that are in need of explication, is in some respects central. And the question of whether a given set of imperatives is consistent is at first sight simple enough; either the members of the set together enjoin a possible state-of-affairs, or they do not. But that assessment only echoes the *You will . . .* theory. We need to gloss 'possible state-of-affairs' in terms of the different kinds of possibility discussed in the previous chapter; to take into account the fact that the outcome of a strategy is, in general, contingent on actions and happenings not under the agent's control; to incorporate the consequences of the fact that whether a given aim is achievable may be affected negatively or *positively* by what parallel aims are undertaken; above all to add permissives to the set;

and to add indicatives, in so far as they contribute to the meanings of the central concepts of temporal physical and active possibility and temporal choosability. The difficulties that are met when we take all these things into account simultaneously are such that I do not think the problem of giving criteria of consistency for imperatives has so far been solved.

The 'solution' offered in this chapter proceeds, first, in talking about something else, namely, *quandaries*, or situations in which an agent cannot act without infringing at least one of a given set of imperatives; and *antagonisms*, where two or more imperatives cannot all be carried out, although there is no quandary; and *obstructed permissions*, permissions restricted by other imperatives in such a way that an agent is unable to take advantage of them. Then, second, I subdivide and ticket different kinds of quandary-freedom, antagonism-freedom and permission-unobstructedness.

There has not been much literature on the subject of these distinctions. Von Wright, (*An Essay in Deontic Logic and the General Theory of Action*) noticed what he called *predicaments* (resembling what I here call *quandaries*), such as that of Jephthah, in the Bible, *Judges* 11, who promised God to sacrifice the first living being he met on his return home victorious from battle, only to be greeted, when he did return, by his own daughter; and shows that, by the ordinary principles of deontic logic, if anyone finds himself committed to an inconsistent combination of actions, the situation is one he is obligated not to be in. (This is 'Jephthah's theorem', p. 79; see discussion by Prior in a review of von Wright's essay.) Nussbaum, (*Aristotle's De Notu Animalium*, p. 172-3) points out that considerations of practical conflict were important to the moral and logical theories of Plato and Aristotle. Thus Plato, particularly in *Republic*, Book 10, 604-06, criticises Sophocles' and other tragic dramatists' regular portrayal of the emotional trauma engendered by moral dilemmas, as appealing to the less rational part of the mind; and Aristotle, though his *Poetics* answers Plato by laying emphasis on tragedy's cathartic effects, also had to construct, in the *Nichomachean Ethics* and elsewhere, a logical theory – that of the so-called 'practical syllogism' – whose palpable object was to underpin rationality in moral matters and make it possible to argue dilemmas away. Nussbaum discusses the example, from Tacitus, (*Histories*, III, 51) of a soldier who encounters his brother on the opposing side in a battle. Lemmon, ('Moral Dilemmas') aims at characterizing the different varieties of moral dilemma, discussing mainly Sartre's discussion of 'bad faith' (in *Being and Nothingness*, p. 55-6) and the example (in *Existentialism and Humanism*, p. 35-6) of a man torn, in the Second World War, between fighting for the Free

French and caring for his sick mother, and reaches the heterodox conclusion (p. 150) that:

There seems no reason, therefore, why we should regard 'ought' and 'ought not' even as contraries, still less as contradictories. It seems to me that 'ought' and 'ought not' may well both be true, and that this description in fact characterizes a certain class of moral dilemma.

Van Fraassen, ('Values and the Heart's Command' and 'The Logic of Conditional Obligation') discussed a number of other examples and showed that Lemmon's suggestion could, in fact, be embodied in an otherwise consistent deontic logic. There has, of course, been much discussion of moral dilemmas, without much probing of their logic; (but see Walzer, 'Political Action: the Problem of Dirty Hands'; Marcus, 'Moral Dilemmas and Consistency'; and, for a modern rejection, Conee). I have myself written on this subject before, (in an article entitled 'Quandaries and the Logic of Rules') and the present chapter reproduces and develops some of the earlier material.

The first thing to be said about consistency, in the case of imperatives, is that it is not always so practically necessary as logicians are inclined to expect. In the case of indicatives – given, say, a set of propositions of a mathematical theory, or of a science, or of a scholarly book, or the testimony of a witness in a court case – the question of consistency looms large. Inconsistency discredits the theory, or the author or witness, or even wrecks his enterprise. But imperatives? Look at the following commonplaces:

1. $X$ tells $Z$ to do $D$;
   $Y$ tells him not to.
2. $X$ tells $Y$ I am obliged to order you to do $D$, and I hereby do so. But my private advice to you is not to.
3. $X$ tells each of $Y$ and $Z$, who are about to play singles tennis, *Go out and win!*

In (1), since $Z$ cannot obey both $X$ and $Y$ and may incur a penalty, he may find his situation vexing. But there is no question that the two orders can be simultaneously 'valid' ones, in the sense of being in force: and recognition of this fact does not wreck our logic, as would an attempt to regard each of two contrary indicatives as true. It is true that $Z$'s dilemma has some resemblance to the dilemma of which of two contrary indicative communications *to believe*; but disobedience to an order, unlike disbelief of a statement, does not reflect discredit on it or on its issuer. Does it follow, then, that $X$'s and $Y$'s imperatives are not really inconsistent, because not issued by the same person? It would be confusing to have to say this; it is surely not a *logical* matter who issues them.

Example (2) has been used by Warnock, 'Imperatives and Meaning', to argue, in effect, that imperatives have no logic, being too variable in force. (He says, p. 292, 'it is not possible to say what imperative sentences mean.') Unfortunately, an intermediate conclusion in this *reductio* seems to be that the imperatives X issues to Y *are* inconsistent in an uncomplicated sense, though what X says is saved from nonsense by the fact that one is an order and the other not. The correct lesson is not that imperative cannot contradict one another, but only that certain kinds of contradiction can be tolerated without disaster.

In the case of (3), I shall be told that the wording is misleading and that

> Go out and win!

means only

> Go out and try very hard.

But let us take it literally; is there any contradiction in telling Y to bring about a state S and Z to bring about the complementary state *non-S*? The question is verbal; the situation has some contradiction-like elements and some that are not, and the application of the word is unclear in it. But if we use it (and it is not unreasonable, though it would not be my choice) we are forced again to admit that imperative contradictions can have legitimate, undamaging uses.

### QUANDARIES

So let us suppose we are about to park in a parking lot, and that we observe two signs,

> Remove your ignition key

and

> Keys to be left in dash.

The imperatives in the signs may have different forces, and I may consider that I am not bound by either of them; but this question, as has been said, should at present be set aside. Let us speak as if I am so bound. I cannot obey both signs at once; I am in a *quandary*, and cannot act without infringing one or other of them. Doing nothing, of course, counts as doing something; and I can temporize only up to a certain moment of decision. There are, perhaps, drastic remedies such as driving out of the lot, blowing up the car or (if that counts) defacing the signs, but these can be regarded as out of court or as offending against yet other imperatives.

The simplest quandary is that generated by a pair of imperatives one of which is the type 1 or type 2 negation of the other. But there may, of course, be quandaries involving a set of three or more imperatives, or in which some imperatives are general rather than singular. A good way of defining a quandary, for a person subject to a set of imperatives, is as a circumstance in which there is *nothing he can do* that will not infringe at least one of the imperatives of the set; or, more accurately (to exclude the case of mere impossibility of a single imperative), a circumstance in which there is a deed $D$ such that either to do $D$ or not to do $D$ would infringe some imperative not otherwise infringed. *Quandary*, note, means *immediate quandary*; for although, in the ordinary use of the word, I am sometimes in a quandary over, say, a compulsory action whose non-performance will *later* get me into an immediate quandary, it is logically better to keep derived quandaries of this kind distinct from immediate ones. I may be unable to be a member of two rival religious or political organizations at once without quandaries over, say, when to pray or what to say; but this does not constitute a prohibition against *joining* them (however unwise that might be) and, if I were under imperative pressure to join them, my quandary would be a prospective, not actual, one – and consequently not, in the present sense, a quandary.

Generally, then, quandaries reflect an inconsistency in a set of imperatives or para-imperatives. But not every inconsistency generates a quandary. I am issued with a piece of paper that says at the top,

> The holder is entitled to proceed without hindrance in all parts of the precincts

and at the bottom,

> Admission is not permitted to security areas.

Security areas, let us assume, are within the precincts and part of them; what the issuer intended to say was that the holder might proceed in all parts of the precincts *except* security areas. What he has in fact said is inconsistent, since, in the case of security areas, he both permits and forbids access. On the other hand, there is no quandary. If I enter security areas I infringe the prohibition; but if I do not do so I infringe nothing at all. The inconsistency is not of such a kind that I cannot act without infringing an imperative.

In introducing negation type 4 in chapter 2 we drew a 'square of opposition' which, generalized, was of the form

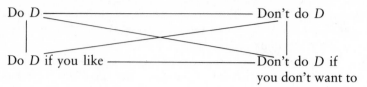

The four forms are interdefinable using one or another negation; but they do not enter equally into the generation of quandaries. The conjunction of the two top-row forms,

Do *D*

and,

Don't do *D*,

is quandarian, and these are the forms, to a sufficient approximation, of the respective signs in the parking lot; but forms at the extremes of diagonals – as are those on the admission pass – though inconsistent, generate no quandaries. They contradict one another not by making conforming action impossible, but only by both banning an action and permitting it.

It needs only a moment's further thought to see that imperatives of bottom-row forms cannot take part in the generation of quandaries at all. To say that I may do something-or-other if I like, or that I may refrain from doing it if I want to, gives me no instructions capable of being incompatible with other instructions. In setting out to determine the capacity of a given set of imperatives to generate quandaries, we may as well start by crossing out all the bottom-row, permissive ones and consider only those that are prescriptive or prohibitional. At least, this is an approximation to the truth; though we shall find later that we need to discuss whether permissives may sometimes play a subsidiary role by partly cancelling prescriptions or prohibitions.

The fact that we sometimes feel placed in a quandary when faced by a diagonal inconsistency such as that of the admission pass may be due to other factors. If I have a need or strong wish to go to security areas – because my business lies there, or because I have been told there is an especially fine view from the roof – I may be in a quandary as to whether to proceed. My plan to go there may be fortified by the apparent permission, only to be dashed by the restriction. But in this case the quandary is generated primarily not by the two imperatives on the card, but by the clash between the second, restrictive one of them and my needs or desires, namely, as it must be, by two imperatives of top-row forms.

Again, I might be in a quandary of sorts if I were uncertain which parts of the precincts were security areas and which were not, so that I feared crossing an unknown line; but, in this case, it would be lack of knowledge that generated the quandary, not the circumstances as such. The basic distinction between a quandarian (or, as we shall see, antagonistic) and a diagonal inconsistency can be maintained just so long as we can maintain the distinction between a top-row form and a permission.

Certain further kinds of quandaries, antagonisms and so on are dependent on the concept of agent-dependent possibility which we shall discuss in the next chapter. For example, Raz, (*Practical Reason and Norms*), speaking of 'exclusionary reasons' for a given course of action, discusses the case of someone who refuses to make a rational decision on some urgent issue because he or she is too tired, or feels too confused, to make it properly. We sometimes deliberately let opportunities slip, take an easy or conservative course, for no other reason; but may, of course, also face dilemmas over whether this is itself 'reasonable'.

## IMPERATIVE-GENERATING EVENTS

Before we get down to making a division of quandaries, let us look at an example that illustrates the importance of saying just *what* set of imperatives is regarded as operative or applicable on a given occasion. The difficulty arises from the fact that events affect the applicability or validity of the imperatives and, on some counts, can even be construed as bringing them into existence or cancelling them.

Let $P_0$, $P_1$, . . . be people (players, participants) and let $D_0$, $D_1$, . . . be deeds they may do. An *event* consists of the doing of a deed by a person, and is thus an ordered pair $\langle P_i, D_j \rangle$. I suspend, for the moment, any question about whether what a person does can be subdivided into elementary, personal deeds in this way, or whether there are not also such things as joint deeds, deeds with essential intensional elements, and so forth. Operative imperatives determine which events are 'legal' and which not. But they cannot always be applied to events in isolation from one another; they can prescribe or prohibit $E_2$, say, conditionally on $E_1$'s having occurred previously. This is particularly the case because the issuing of orders or advice, or the making of promises (and so forth), are themselves events, and have consequences for subsequent ones.

But if what happens at $E_1$ is that an imperative is issued that prescribes $E_2$ – if $E_1$ for example consists of John's asking Mary to hand him the screwdriver and $E_2$ is Mary's doing it – we have two choices what imperative or para-imperative to describe as being operative in respect of $E_2$. We can either say that the imperative,

Hand me the screwdriver,

issued by John, is operative in its own right; or we can say that some *rule* is in operation, such as,

Reasonable requests should always be granted,

which has as an instance the *conditional*,

If $E_1$ occurs, there is an obligation in respect of $E_2$.

Which we say does not matter where $E_2$ is concerned. (There would be a regress if we held that every event of imperative-issuing required an imperative or para-imperative backing to give it force, but that is not here in question.) On the other hand, it may alter what we say about which imperatives generate or are responsible for quandaries, and why.

So let us consider an example in which a quandary is involved. Suppose that two events take place in order,

$$E_0 = \langle P_0, D_0 \rangle$$

and

$$E_1 = \langle P_1, D_1 \rangle,$$

and that the question now arises of whether $P_0$ shall or shall not do deed $D_2$,

$$E_2 = \langle P_0, D_2 \rangle \ ?$$

And suppose that the occurrence of $E_0$, with or without some back-up rule, is enough to render operative an imperative to the effect that $P_0$ must or should do $D_2$, and, second, that the occurrence of $E_1$ brings it about in the same way that he *must not or should not*. For example, let $E_0$ be $P_0$'s promise to his girlfriend to meet her at six, and $E_1$ the recall of $P_0$ to his unit by his commanding officer, $P_1$, by five. $P_0$'s promise, perhaps together with the rule that we should keep our promises (especially to girlfriends), entails that he must meet her as planned; the occurrence of $E_1$, perhaps together with a rule about obeying lawful commands, entails that he must not. Let us suppose he does $D_2$, meets her.

In doing $D_2$, $P_0$ could seek to *excuse* himself on the grounds that he was in a quandary created by his promise $E_0$ and the subsequent recall order $E_1$. But the question of possible excuse leads us to look at the matter more synoptically and ask about the respective backings of the promise and the order, namely, about whether the quandary can be traced back to the operation of general rules such as the rule that we should keep promises, or obey orders. And as soon as we do this, the question of quandary-freedom or quandary-incurrence is less simple. There is at least one argument to the effect that $P_0$ has not broken either of these rules or, at least, cannot be held responsible for so doing. In effect, we can argue that the illegality is not in $E_2$ but in $E_1$, as follows.

For the sake of simplicity let us make the assumption that events before, after and in between the three we are considering have no effect on the considerations regarding these three. The overall effect of the imperatives is to divide possible sequences of events into *legal sequences* and *illegal sequences*. Any sequence of the form,

$$(S) \ldots, E_0, \ldots, E_1, \ldots, E_2, \ldots$$

– that is, any sequence of events in which $E_0$, $E_1$ and $E_2$ occur, in that order, independently of what is before, after or between – is illegal, because $E_2$ must not occur following $E_1$. But any sequence of the form,

$$(S') \ldots, E_0, \ldots, E_1, \ldots, E_2', \ldots$$

where $E_2'$ is any event ‹$P_0$, $D_2'$› of $P_0$'s not doing $D_2$ but doing in place of it, at the relevant time, some other deed $D_2'$, is illegal also, since, by the rules, $E_2$ ought to occur once $E_0$ has.

But if all sequences of forms $(S)$ or $(S')$ are illegal, then all sequences of the form,

$$(S'') \ldots, E_0, \ldots, E_1, \ldots$$

are illegal. In fact the set of sequences $(S'')$ is the join of the sets $(S)$ and $(S')$.

It follows that we must look for the source of the illegality not in $E_2$ or $E_2'$ – the doing of $D_2$ or $D_2'$ by $P_0$ – but in $E_0$ and $E_1$. In doing $D_2$, $P_0$ did not break the rules; they were already broken when he was put *by the occurrence* of $E_1$ in the position of having no legal continuation.

In the case of our example this does not seem a very plausible conclusion, since $P_0$'s orders of recall would normally be regarded as overruling his promise. But that is because we allocate the rules unequal weights. If we were to balance them by treating the claims of true love as equal to those of military duty, we could find ourselves reasoning that the Commanding Officer had no right to issue an order with the consequences that $P_0$ should have to break his promise at short notice.

But this is not all. Before we draw any morals, we should consider a further argument, to the effect that the illegality is not in $E_2$ or $E_1$, but $E_0$.

$P_0$ is court-martialled and pleads that the order of recall was invalid on the grounds just indicated. The court·dismisses the plea and reasons: 'Knowing that you might be recalled to your unit $(E_1)$, you had no right to make the promise $(E_0)$, and thereby put yourself *at risk* of a conflict of responsibilities'. How do we assess this reasoning?

Sometimes, perhaps, we are placed in quandaries through no fault of our own. By hypothesis, this is not the case here; not only is $P_0$ able to do something other than $D_0$, he is also in a position to predict the possibility that $P_1$ will do $D_1$ and that he, $P_0$, will then be in a quandary in respect of $E_2$. On the other hand (we suppose), if he does not do $D_0$, no such situation can arise. It can reasonably be argued that he should not do $D_0$. At least, if he does so, and if $P_1$ subsequently does $D_1$, he must take the consequences.

We can also very well imagine that $P_1$ subscribes to this reasoning and rejects any argument that affects the propriety of his doing $D_1$. '$PO_0$'s quandary', $P_1$ can say, 'is no concern of mine. It is not my business to save him from it'.

In effect, it is now argued that any sequence

$$\ldots, E_0, \ldots,$$

however continued, is illegal. Even if $E_0$ is not followed (separably) by $E_1$, the possibility that it *could* be so followed – with a consequent quandary for $P_0$ in respect of $D_2$ – is sufficient to demonstrate illegality in the sequence in respect of $E_0$.

So what do we say about the quandary-generating propensities of the imperatives that are applicable to the events? In the first place, if we consider just $P_0$'s promise and $P_1$'s recall order, it is clear that between them they generate a quandary for $P_0$ in the simplest sense possible; that is, they make it inevitable that there will be a situation in which there is nothing legal he can do. But we sometimes regard a set of imperatives as quandarian even when it does not do this. For example, we can reasonably regard the unqualified rule that we should keep promises and the unqualified rule that we should obey lawful commands, taken together, as themselves in conflict, just because occasions *may* arise in which a promise conflicts with an order and a quandary is generated. At the very least, we want to know what someone who finds himself placed in a quandary by a promise and an order should be expected to do about it; and that means supplementing or qualifying the rules. Just to say that people do not *have* to make promises or issue orders, or could, in principle, avoid making conflicting ones – and that consequently there is no logical inevitability of a clash between a promise and an order – is hardly enough. Rules should be designed to cover cases in which people get into, or are put in, quandaries unforeseen. At least there is something wrong with a set under which someone may get into a quandary by sheer force of circumstance, or be put in it by someone else through no fault of his own.

To pursue discussion of the concepts of illegality, fault and blame could lead us deep into morals. Is there anything *wrong* with quandaries? Is someone *to blame* for creating a situation in which he, or someone else, gets into one? We shall actually return to this question a little later. But it should be remarked, now, that it is possible for the logician to insulate himself from it – while still, perhaps using these moral words in a logical, not fully moral, sense – so long as his concern is simply to make clear which sets of rules or principles are potentially or actually quandary-generating. The quasi-moral concepts enter the logician's discussion when he tries to locate a failure to carry out an imperative; or, in reverse, when, given a quandary, he works backwards to locate the rules or imperative acts that generated it. What he says may, of course, be relevant to the making of moral judgements, but he need not take up moral attitudes himself.

Note further in passing that, although some of the difficulties in the example are connected with the fact that 'second-order' imperatives are involved – namely, imperatives in respect of acts that themselves enjoin, forbid or permit other acts – we cannot avoid these difficulties by confining ourselves to first-order ones. If $P_0$ orders $P_1$ to do $D$, $P_1$'s obligation can be specified without mention of the content of what $P_0$ says, in the alternative form of a conditional. Represent $P_0$'s issuing of the order as an event $E$; then we can regard $P_1$, if we wish – for all purposes except the abovementioned allocation of responsibility – as operating not under $P_0$'s order but under a *rule* of the form,

If $E$ occurs, do $D$.

If we refused to admit conditional imperatives of this simple kind our discussion would be elementary indeed.


FOUR KINDS OF QUANDARY-FREEDOM

But, given that sets of imperatives – rules, principles, para-imperatives or imperatives proper – may be open to objection as quandary-incurring in spite of the fact that they do not make quandaries inevitable, are there different senses of this quandary-incurrence or quandary-freedom? I proceed to describe four generic kinds. It should be remarked that this division – since quandary-freedom is discussed as a contribution to the explication, ultimately, of the concept of logical consistency – is made without invoking the distinction between top-row and diagonal inconsistencies. We have deferred diagonal inconsistency for later discussion, and confine ourselves at present to top-row forms.

The four kinds of quandary-freedom here listed are not exhaustive. But they are useful anchor-buoys.

### Absolute Quandary-Freedom

It is possible for a set of imperatives to be such that it could under no circumstances produce any quandaries at all. The most obvious example is the empty set; but we need not be so extreme. The set consisting of the single rule,

> We should keep our promises

is, to be sure, not absolutely quandary-free, since it is possible to get into a quandary by making incompatible promises; but if we were to replace it with rule,

> We would keep any promise that is not incompatible with previous promises

no quandary would be possible except on the supposition that it is possible to make two incompatible promises at the same time. In fact quite complicated sets of rules may be absolutely quandary-free, that is, such that none of their top-corner rules can possibly conflict. Absolute quandary-freedom can be achieved by declaring relevant rules to take precedence over others, as in,

> Do *A*.
> Do *B* unless it conflicts with doing *A*.
> Do *C* unless it conflicts with doing *A* or *B*.

Statutes and regulations often contain clauses aimed at resolving envisaged clashes in this way; for example (from the By-Laws of the University of New South Wales),

> None of the provisions of this chapter shall affect the authority of the Professional Board under which authority . . .

This does not in itself secure absolute quandary-freedom, since the Professional Board might enact quandaries; but it prevents, by fiat, a clash between Board decisions and the provisions of the chapter.

### Legislative Quandary-Freedom

An absolutely quandary-free set of imperatives has the property that it puts no one in a quandary, even if imperatives of the set are disobeyed many times over by one or another addressee. But there are many practical cases in which we settle for much less than this. We often reason that it is sufficient that quandaries should be avoided *provided all the actions of all addressees are legal.* Then if a quandary does occur it will be possible to put the blame on one or more previous infractions. I shall call this *legislative quandary-freedom*; unlike absolute quandary-freedom it can be achieved by *adding* imperatives to the quandary-infected set, namely, imperatives which will prevent the quandary from legally arising. The rule,

> We should keep our promises

does not lead to quandaries if there is added to it the rule,

> Promises should never be made that can produce inconsistencies with previous ones,

and the set consisting of just these two rules is legislatively quandary-free.

Most board and card games are quandary-free in at most this weakened sense. To take a rather artificial example, suppose that in Bridge, I play two cards on one trick; then I both must and cannot play a card on the last trick of the hand, since, first, the rules say I must play a card on each trick and, second, I cannot do so without somehow illegally getting an extra card. It follows that the system of rules of Bridge is not absolutely quandary-free; but it may be (and presumably is) legislatively so, since this situation could not have arisen unless a rule had been broken in the first place.

### Strategic Quandary-Freedom

Even legisative quandary-freedom may not be demanded in practical sets of imperatives, provided potential quandaries are predictable so that steps can be taken to avoid them. But in fairness to individuals subject to them it would often be reasonable to stipulate that no one should be put in a quandary by the actions of others, without a chance to avoid it by actions of his own.

What is demanded in this case is that, for each person, there should be a possible, legal *strategy* which, if he follows it, will keep him out of quandaries independently of what is done by others. If there is such a strategy for everyone, no one can be forced into a quandary, and, of course, it is possible that no one will be put in a quandary at all. The criterion is clearly weaker, in general, than that of legislative quandary-freedom, under which people stay out of quandaries just so long as they obey the rules. I shall call a set of imperatives such that there is a legal,

quandary-avoiding strategy for each person *strategically quandary-free.*
It is also possible that a set of imperatives should discriminate
between those subject to it in such a way that there exist quandary-
avoiding strategies for some people but not others; or that there exist
quandary-avoiding strategies for *groups*, of such a kind that their
members, jointly or severally, are kept free of quandaries provided the
appropriate co-operative action is taken by all group-members. We can
even imagine a case in which a set of rules is quandary-free for *P* if and
only if he takes certain actions which have as a consequence the
creation of a quandary for someone else. Since there can also be strategies
that facilitate, without guaranteeing, later absolute, or legislative, or
strategic, quandary-freedom the number of cases we might go on to
multiply is very great. But I shall not try to survey them in detail.

Strategic quandary-freedom easily becomes legislative quandary-
freedom if the set of imperatives by which it is generated is augmented
by one to the effect that everyone *ought* to take legal quandary-avoiding
action. In one natural interpretation, 'Jephthah's theorem' seems to say
that this is a principle of general application. But it is not one to which,
in fact, we would always subscribe, as can be demonstrated. Let us
suppose that a remote community in which bigamy of both sexes is
permitted achieves an overlay of Christianity. *X*'s wife *Y* contracts a
second marriage with their neighbour *Z*. *X* is bound to love, honour
and cherish his wife and not to covet his neighbour's wife; but they
happen to be the same wife, *Y*. And we shall assume that there is no
top-row rule, in the set made up of the older social mores and the newly
adopted Christian ones, that prohibits any of the actions leading to this
state of affairs. If the community, in adopting Christianity, had adopted
a prohibition of bigamy, the mores might have remained legislatively
quandary-free; but, let us suppose, no such explicit prohibition is in
force.

Now since no one *has* to marry anyone, the mores are strategically
quandary-free; but they are not legislatively so, since the decision
whether or not to contract a bigamous marriage is not itself the subject
of a quandary of the same kind as the one that ensues. In fact, *Y*, in
marrying *Z*, could indignantly claim that she is breaking no law and has
a right to do so, independently of any quandarian consequences for
anyone else. (After all, *X*, or *Z*, might conveniently drop dead before
any difficulty ensues.) This kind of claim is one that we continually
accept in cases into which probabilities enter. Let us suppose that *X*, in
marrying *Y*, knows that he is at some risk of quandary should *Y*
subsequently marry *Z*, but thinks the risk small. If *Y* does remarry, *X*
may reason, he will take the awful consequences; but this is no reason
for not marrying *Y* in the first place.

## Minimal Quandary-Freedom

Finally, a set of imperatives is quandary-free in a minimal sense if it is possible for everyone, subject to the set or not, to act legally, if necessarily co-operatively, in such a way that possibly no quandaries will arise for anyone. This seems a weak requirement, but it is the one that most naturally occurs to *You will . . .* theorists and, for that matter, most logicians who have not thought about the problem. In effect, it says just that there is a *possibility* that everyone's actions will be always legal; or, equivalently, that there is a possible universe in which no imperatives of the set are contravened. Another way of looking at it is as the limiting, weakest case of group strategic quandary-freedom, in which the 'group' is everyone, subject or not to the imperatives, and the task of keeping everyone out of quandaries may demand co-opertive action by the members of this maximal group.

Paradoxically, it does not follow from the fact that a set of imperatives is not even minimally quandary-free that the set makes a quandary inevitable. Let us suppose that $P_0$ tells $P_1$ to tell $P_2$ to do deed $D$, and also that $P_0$ directly tells $P_2$ not to; or, leaving $P_0$ out of it and reformulating the second-order imperative as a conditional – denoting the issuing of $P_1$'s order to $P_2$ as $E$ – let us suppose the following imperatives are in force:

$P_1$ must do $E$.
If $P_1$ does $E$, $P_2$ must do $D$.
$P_2$ must not do $D$.

Do the second two imply, by *modus tollens*, that $P_1$ must not do $E$? My logical intuitions are unclear. But, in any case, there is a quandary for $P_2$ unless $P_1$ infringes the first imperative of the three; there is no way in which everyone's actions can be always legal. On the other hand, if $P_1$ *does* infringe the injunction to do $E$, no quandary arises. At least one infraction must occur, but it is possible for it to occur wantonly, not as the result of a quandary.

### LOGICAL MODEL OF QUANDARIES

If we seek to sharpen up these definitions by stating them in the precise context of the semantic model of the preceeding chapter, we first run into the question of whether *possible*, as it occurs explicitly or implicitly in them, means *logically possible*, or *physically possible*, or *actively possible*, or *choosable*. For example, when we speak of a quandary as being *avoidable* in this or that circumstance (such as that in which a given strategy is adopted), it is not clear whether we should mean merely *logically avoidable*, or whether one of the stronger senses is more to the point.

To start with, we need to reconsider even the definition of *quandary* itself. In the case of a quandary generated by two imperatives that are mutual type 1 or type 2 negations – as are those of the parking-lot- – there is no doubt that the impossibility of conformity is logical. But it is easy to find cases in which one of the other senses is more appropriate. Let us suppose I am advised,

> In hot places like the Gulf you should keep your fluid intake up

and,

> But don't drink the water;

and that I have business in the Gulf that involves abstinence from alcohol for fear of offending teetotal clients. My succession of consequent quandaries is generated partly (but essentially) by physical limitations rather than mere logical ones, since there is no purely logical bar to my spiriting adequate quantities of some unoffending fluid out of the air by rubbing a lamp. A minor alternation to the example converts it into one in which action in conformity with the imperatives is not even physically impossible, but merely unchoosable; we can suppose that there is fluid available, but only in the shape of endless small cups of very sweet tea.

I shall avoid complications in the definition of *quandary* by generally treating the properties of imperatives as describable in terms of the strategies that are effective in carrying them out. This effectively limits us to *active* possibilities and means that physical restrictions, and restrictions of choosability in so far as they affect persons other than the doer, are automatically allowed as relevant. There may also sometimes be a 'quandary' when an imperative enjoins a deed unchoosable to the doer; but we can ignore this sense of the word as faulty or incompletely analysed, since cases of interest can as easily be treated by incorporating a para-imperative specification of the doer's 'desires' in the set. It follows that all quandaries, or at least all that will here be taken seriously, are active ones, and that purely logical or physical ones are a mere subset to be considered by those who will. This ties them also to given worlds and to temporal reference points; a quandary may exist in one world at one time but not in another or at others, and the existence of a quandary in world $w$ at time $t$ must be analysed in terms of strategies, or at least deeds, available to the subject in $w$ at $t$.

In reducing the logic of imperatives to that of *active* possibilities I do not want to pre-empt the occasional need to consider 'counterpossible' conditionals, in which we suppose not merely facts but also laws to be different from what they are, so that our logic is done against a background of a set of worlds that are *not* actively possible in the present sense. But inevitably – I think – this would have to be regarded as a second-order exercise, in which we suppose not merely that there are actively possible worlds other than the actual one, but also that there are, in some sense, other *possible* sets of actively possible worlds than the set we currently assume. There is no difficulty of logical principle in this assumption, or in a further extension to possible possible possibles, and so on. (But life is short.)

To achieve wholehearted satisfaction of an imperative $i$ – we said – starting at time $t$, the addressee $p$ (assuming, for the moment, there is just one) must have and follow a partial $i$-strategy at each $t'$ from $t$ on. As we defined *partial strategy* there always exists such a strategy; for, so long as the deeds available to him do not divide in such a way as to present him with a choice between at least two of (a) furthering an $i$-strategy, (b) ensuring that $i$ is dissatisfied, and (c) neither, he may follow a *null-strategy*, that is, do anything at all.

But to achieve wholehearted satisfaction of each or all of a set $I = (i_1, i_2, \ldots, i_n)$ of imperatives, starting at $t$, $p$ must similarly have and follow at each $t' \geq t$ a partial strategy that is simultaneously a partial $i_1$-strategy, a partial $i_2$-strategy, $\ldots$, and a partial $i_n$-strategy. And there may, of course, be no such strategy – namely, if $I$ creates a quandary. In fact, we seem to be able to define *quandary* formally as follows: There is a quandary for $p$ in $w$ at $t$ in respect of a set of imperatives $I$ if there is no deed of $p$ at $t$ that is a component of all the partial $i$-strategies, $i$ a member of $I$. But there is also something incoherent about this definition, unless we are prepared to make an apparently arbitrary distinction between the task of satisfying two or more imperatives singly and the task of satisfying them together. If I am given the two orders

Surrender the form to the accountant in the fees office

and,

Don't surrender the form to the accountant in the fees office,

it seems I am in a quandary and have nothing I can do, whereas if I had been given the conjunctive order,

Surrender, the form to the accountant in the fees office, but don't,

I would be entitled to shrug it off as impossible to satisfy, and do what I liked. And the problem is not, of course, just one of how we may best define *quandary*, or *impossible*. There is a difference in kind between an order which can be regarded as void through impossibility and a set of two or more orders, separately but not jointly obeyable, that create a problem of choice for the addressee.

The solution to the puzzle – if it is a puzzle – involves remembering the distinction we made in chapter 2 between separable and inseparable conjunctions. The inconsistency of an inseparable conjunction – namely, one in which imperative force attaches to the conjunction but not necessarily to the conjunctions – is fully specified by the statement that a null-strategy is a partial strategy for it. Presented with such an imperative, an addressee is in no greater quandary than he ever is in, in being given an impossible task, such as that of jumping over a 10-metre wall or expressing the square root of 17 as a whole number. But a separable conjunction of $i_1$ and $i_2$ is one such that if $i_1$ is not carried out then $i_2$ still must be, or if not $i_2$, $i_1$; and if it is impossible to do both, there is a problem which to choose. The availability of a null-strategy to satisfy the joint imperative $i_1$ & $i_2$ does not end the matter, because it is neither a partial $i_1$-strategy nor a partial $i_2$-strategy.

Quandaries are raised, then, by conjunctions of separately non-quandarian imperatives only when the conjunctions are separable ones. But in previous pages we have also seen that they may be raised by *rules*, such as,

> We should keep our promises,

that have separable instances. Two promises together constiute a separably, not inseparably, conjunctive promise; and the generality implicit in any rule of this kind descends separably to its instances. (Otherwise I could always evade a promise by making a contrary one and then doing what I liked.) The only kind of separability that does not create a quandary is that that applies to several addressees. Our two tennis players – both told to win – are not, in my individualist book, in a quandary until they have constituted themselves into a group with the resolve that a task of either is a task of both.

But the way in which a *rule* is decomposed into instances may change with time or, at least, may be different in different worlds. The rule about keeping promises, that is to say, enjoins the keeping of just such promises as have been made in a particular world. Consequently our definition of quandary was a little premature; we need to replace the concept of an arbitrary set $I$ of imperatives with that of an analysed set $I(p, w, t)$, whose members are the imperatives separably operative, as conjuncts or instances of members of $I$, on $p$ in $w$ at $t$. We need to be able to assume about the members of $I(p, w, t)$, first, that they do not resolve themselves further into separable conjuncts or instances, and second, that they do not combine *in*separably. (In theory, they may be infinite in number, though the supposition has a ring of implausibility about it.) And what we say about quandaries generated by $I$ for $p$ in $w$ at $t$ will now have to be said about this derived set. Specifically:

A set of imperatives $I$ creates a quandary for $p$ in $w$ at $t$ if the various partial $i$-strategies for $p$ in $w$, at $t$, for $i \in I(p, w, t)$, have no deed of $p$ in common at $t$.

I proceed to model the four quandary-freedoms.

*Absolute quandary-freedom* can be defined rather easily. A set $I$ of imperatives is absolutely quandary-free if there are no $p$, $w$ and $t$ such that there is a quandary in respect of $I$ for $p$ in $w$ at $t$. But perhaps it is necessary to emphasize what this definition leaves out. Since it does not refer to any particular world or state of the world, or to any particular person or time, it is independent of how separably general members of $I$ may be instantiated by events, that is, on there being any particular decomposition of $I(p, w, t)$. The deeds available to any particular $p$ may, of course, depend on circumstances, but the availability of 'legal' deeds, given any circumstance, is guaranteed.

Absolute quandary-freedom, in a variant sense, could alternatively be defined for a particular person $p$, or in a particular $w$; and we could replace applicability to all *logically* possible circumstances with applicability to some lesser class, such as all physically, temporally or actively possible ones or some other.

For *legislative quandary-freedom* we need the concept of a *legal history*, or set of worlds in which, up to some time $t$, all addressees of the given set of imperatives have done deeds which, whatever strategies they may have had, were deeds consistent with partial strategies for the satisfaction of all imperatives operative on them. That is, partial $i$-strategies (for $p'$ in $w'$ at $t'$) have been followed in $w$ by all $p'$ for all $t' <  t$, for all $i \in I(p', w', t')$. Let $J_t(I)$ be the set of such legal histories at time $t$. The set of imperatives $I$ is legislatively quandary-free if there is no person $p$ and time $t$ and world $w \in J_t(I)$ such that there is a quandary for $p$ in $w$ at $t$.

A strategy for satisfying $I$ – at least if we set aside certain degenerate cases such as that in which satisfaction of $I$ is impossible anyway and a null-strategy is acceptable – is naturally also a strategy for avoiding quandaries in respect of it. But the reverse is not necessarily the case, since it might be possible to ensure the avoidance of quandaries without doing anything to ensure satisfaction of $I$ – and even by wantonly infringing $I$ each time a quandary looked like coming up, before infringement was actually forced by the quandary itself. In effect, strategic quandary-freedom demands that there should exist a (complete) strategy for the satisfaction of the imperative

Avoid quandaries in respect of $I$;

and, in defining it above, we stipulated further that this strategy be everywhere legal, that is, be consistent with partial strategies for the satisfaction, in the usual sense, of $I$.

Let $W_{qfree}(p, I)$ be the set of worlds $w$ in which there are no quandaries for $p$ in respect of $I$, namely, such that at all times $t$ there exist partial $i$-strategies for all $i \varepsilon I(p, w, t)$. Now the set of imperatives $I$ is *strategically quandary-free* for $p$ in $w$ starting at $t$ if there is at least one strategy $q_t$ such that

$$\{W_{strat}(p, q_t) \cap W_{active}(w, p, t)\} \underline{C} W_{qfree}(p, I)$$

and which is such that the deed allocated to $p$ in any $w'$ at any $t' \geq t$ is a deed corresponding with a partial $i$-strategy for each $i \varepsilon I(p, w', t')$.

Note that

$$W_I \underline{C} W_{qfree}(p, I)$$

but not conversely.

Finally, *minimal quandary-freedom* consists in the existence of at least one infinite legal history, or possible quandary-free world; that is, a world such that there is no quandary for any $p$ at any $t$.

Generalizations of all these definitions to include or apply to groups of addressees are immediate.

## ANTAGONISMS

To speak of a *quandary* is to take the viewpoint of a recipient. But sometimes we want to regard top-row imperatives as inconsistent as they issue from the mouth of the issuer, although they create no quandary. When the tennis-coach says

Go out and win!

to each of the two players, neither is in a quandary; but it is certain that the exhortations cannot both be obeyed. The *antagonism* – a good jargon name for it – becomes a quandary (and ceases to be an antagonism) only if we imagine the players pooling their instructions and trying to meet them co-operatively. For a more ambiguous example, compare the dinner-hostess who, whether through confusion or malice, says separately to both Tom Smith and Stephen Brown,

Would you sit over there on the right of Janie Robertson.

Antagonistic imperatives do not have to have the same issuer; we can imagine that the players are given their instructions by separate coaches, or the dinner guests by competing hostesses. It follows that there is not necessarily anyone to blame, or to hold responsible, for an antagonism.

Antagonisms fall into the same categories as quandaries; antagonism-freedom can be absolute, legislative, strategic, minimal, or of other kinds. In fact their analysis is similar to that of group quandaries, and need not be duplicated here.

Lemmon briefly discusses the logic of antagonisms ('Deontic Logic and the Logic of Imperatives', p. 66).

### THE EFFECT OF PREMISSIVES

To import permissives into the model is to invite yet further multiple distinctions of kinds of inconsistency, namely, multiple varieties of diagonal inconsistency due to oppositions of permissives to top-row rules. We shall go on to look at these in a moment. But first let us look at what the presence of permissives leads us to say even about some of the cases in which our primary concern is with quandaries, and in which permissives seem at first to have nothing to contribute.

The case against $P_0$ who argued that his Commanding Officer had no right to issue the recall order would be very much strengthened if, besides the top-row imperatives that generated the quandary, there were also a bottom-row one of the form (say),

$P_1$ may do $D_1$,

that is,

The CO is entitled to issue the recall order

– or some more general permissive with this as an instance. If the CO is entitled to issue the recall order, there are grounds for reasoning that $P_0$ is *not* entitled to make his promise. The permissive, though it cannot contribute to the logical generation of a quandary, is relevant to deciding the legal status of deeds that generate it causally. This is because it is capable of contributing to a disjunctive syllogism such as,

Either $P_1$ must not do $D_1$ or $P_0$ must not do $D_0$.
But $P_1$ may do $D_1$.
Therefore, $P_0$ must not do $D_0$.

Once we have decided that there ought not to be a quandary and that the first premiss is therefore true, the permissive second premiss combines with it to produce the top-row conclusion.

We have already seen in the example of the bigamous Christians that a general principle to the effect that we have a duty to avoid quandaries would be a dubious one; sometimes (we think) we have a *right* to take actions which result in, or may result in, quandaries. And it is certain that people are sometimes regarded as having conflicting rights, and that exercise of these rights sometimes produces quandaries. In the case under consideration it is possible that there should also exist a permissive, or instance of a permissive, having the form

$P_0$ may do $D_0$;

that is, $P_0$ is entitled to make his promise to his girlfriend. (He might so plead at his court-martial.) But this is in contradiction with the conclusion of the disjunctive syllogism, and something is wrong. Either:

1. there is something wrong with the first premiss, and quandaries are sometimes just an unfortunate fact of life, for which no-one can be blamed; or
2. *having* a right is one thing but *exercising* it may bring untoward, possibly even punishable, consequences, from which the right does not provide immunity; or
3. (perhaps) *may* and *must not* are not always, when fully analysed, contradictories, but may be such that a *may* may invalidate a *must not* or a *must not* overrule a *may*.

Or something. Unless we can accept (1), (2) or (3), or some equally effective saving principle, we seem to be landed with a kind of inconsistency that is neither simply quandarian (nor antagonistic), nor simply diagonal, but an interactive mixture.

Possibility (3) needs to be looked at briefly, if only because it is clear that permissives and top-row imperatives may each vary considerably in force. When we gloss a permissive as an *entitlement* or a *right*, we give it a force that seems to make it capable, in suitable circumstances, of overriding and invalidating contrary top-corner imperatives. If I have a right to build a fence along my boundary, or to wear jeans in church, no one, at least who does not enjoy a status above that of the authority that established the right, has a right to stop me. But it is also sometimes said that conflicts of rights, or of rights with duties or obligations, far from being impossible, actually occur, and that their occurrence is no ground for denying any of the rights themselves. Professor $X$ and Dr $Y$ both have a right to sit in the common-room chair nearest the window – unless someone else is already in it, or has recently vacated it very temporarily intending to return, or . . . . Since we cannot complete the list of exceptions, we recognize the respective rights without them, and accept that conflicts may have to be dealt with by means not precisely laid down.

So (3) has difficulties. (2), on the other hand, is double-talk; the force of a right is to provide justification, and to say that a right does not always provide a justification is to take this force away.

Once again – as when we first discussed quandaries – we risk letting logic be invaded by concepts more at home in discussions of morality. The way out is to remind ourselves that the identification of *prima facie* inconsistencies is a necessary preliminary even to any moral dispute. Consider the set of four (para-)imperatives

If $P_0$ does $D_0$ he must do $D_2$.
If $P_1$ does $D_1$, $P_0$ must not do $D_2$.
$P_0$ may do $D_0$.
$P_1$ may do $D_1$.

namely,

If $P_0$ promises to meet his girlfriend he should meet her.
If the CO recalls $P_0$, he should not meet her.
$P_0$ has a right to plan (promise) to meet her.
The CO is entitled to recall him.

The question whether what they generate is an inconsistency, a paradox or a moral impasse is one it might be better not to attempt to answer. But it is certain that the kind of opposition in which they stand is worthy of note by the logician, or there would be no worry about them for anybody. And we need a descriptive framework in which to discuss it.

OBSTRUCTED PERMISSIONS

The permission to go anywhere within the precincts is, let us say, *obstructed* by the prohibition against entering security areas. More accurately, it would be possible to analyse it into two, as a conjunction of,

The holder may go anywhere *in security areas* within the precincts

and,

The holder may go anywhere *in non-security* areas within the precincts.

The second of these is not obstructed at all, but the first is obstructed by the added prohibition, as a simple consequence of the fact that it is in diagonal contradiction with it.

I shall speak of a permission as *obstructed* – lawyers might prefer the term *encumbered* – whenever its exercise is (totally) forbidden in this way by another imperative or imperatives. Alternatively we can see the permission together with the other imperative or imperatives as members of a set, and speak of obstruction within the set as a whole. In some ways this is a better way of speaking since it does not prejudge the question, if there is a clash between a permission or a prohibition, of which ought to give away. There might even be cases in which we prefer to speak of a top-row form as obstructed by a permission. This is particularly the case when the permission has the force of a *right* or *entitlement*. Rights are even sometimes called 'inalienable', with the implication that prohibitions cannot overrule them. On the other hand, top-row forms, if they have a moral force, are sometimes themselves regarded as expressing injunctions that are stronger than mere obligations, and we refer to them as *duties* and regard them as overriding mere permissions. This seems to raise, in turn, the question of whether there are even more vexatious kinds of diagonal contradiction, in which a *duty* obstructs a *right*, or vice versa; and there would be a wide range of similar questions if we were to consider, and take seriously, all the various other categorisations of top and bottom-row forms that sometimes enter morals – venial and mortal sin; the appellation *prima facie*; the distinctions between moral, prudential and aesthetic considerations, and those of, say, etiquette; those actions we regard as laudable but not forbidden; excusability; supererogation; and many others. (See, for example, Chisholm, 'Supererogation and Offence', and 'The Ethics of Requirement'; on the concept of a right, see Tranøy, 'An Important Aspect of Humanism', who notices that rights generate obligations or duties *in other people*, namely, obligations or duties to uphold them.)

But I shall not, here, pursue any of the distinctions these concepts generate, and I shall not be concerned to decide whether, when there is an 'obstruction', it is the top-row form that should override the permission or vice versa. Let us concentrate, instead, on the prior question of how and in what forms 'obstructions' occur. The terms *obstructed* and *unobstructed* are not intended to reflect the relative forces of the imperatives in connection with which they occur, any more than the word *quandary* prejudges the issue of whether one of two top-row forms may be invalidated by its conflict with another.

This said, we now need – particularly in view of the discussion of the preceding section – to face the fact that it is not always possible to describe individual permissions as *obstructed* and *unobstructed* in isolation from others. Permissions may be individually unobstructed but jointly obstructed; that is to say, they may also react with one another. If you prefer, a permission may be obstructed by a set of imperatives that essentially contains other permissions. If we did not recognize interaction between permissions we could not find anything wrong with the four imperatives in the preceding section. They do not make any quandary unavoidable; $P_0$ does not infringe any of them if he does not make his promise, nor the CO if he does not issue the recall order. And there is also no diagonal inconsistency; there is no need that is both permitted and forbidden, or both obligatory and omissible. Only if we make an inference involving all four imperatives do we encounter any kind of inconsistency at all.

But this is a relatively complicated case in which the objection to joint exercise of the permissions is that it leads to quandary. A simpler one would be: actions $A$ and $B$ are both permitted, but to do *both* is prohibited. (In the narrow lane behind my house we are permitted to park cars on the left, and we are permitted to park cars on the right; but we are not permitted to park on both left and right since this would block the lane.) And there are even cases in which it seems reasonable to speak of a permission as obstructed by another permission, without the intervention of any top-row form at all. Professor $X$'s and Dr $Y$'s rights to the same armchair are like this, since physical laws alone prevent simultaneous exercise. (But we shall make a special point about this in a moment.)

In speaking of obstruction of one permission by another a special exception needs to be made of alternative permissions such as the pair,

Go if you like.
Stay if you like.

We earlier called such sets of alternatives *hereses*. It is certain that the addressee cannot exercise *both* his permission to stay *and* his permission to go; but it would be silly to see this as a restriction on his choice. The conclusion ought rather to be that it is misleading to express the alternatives of a heresis as if they constituted separate permissions. Hereses can also, as we noted, be of general form, such as

Do anything you like;

but here, too, the instances cannot be regarded as mutually obstructing. Consequently, though nothing else about the analysis of obstruction is affected by the decision, I shall treat hereses differently from permissions of other kinds. For simplicity, let us assume that the sets of imperatives we are dealing with for the moment are absolutely quandary-free and antagonism-free, and construct a definition of what it is for there to be an *obstruction* for a given addressee at a given time in respect of a given set of imperatives. In the case of a set not containing hereses, there is an *obstruction* for such an addressee and time if there is no deed the addressee can do at that time that does not either infringe at least one top-corner imperative or forgo – that is, guarantee the non-exercise of – at least one permission. And in the case of a set containing hereses there is an obstruction if there is an obstruction in the case of some subset of it that has not more than one instance or member of each heresis.

VARIETIES OF UNOBSTRUCTEDNESS

If we continue, first, to confine ourselves to the case of sets that are absolutely quandary-free and antagonism-free, the analysis of obstruction is very similar to that of quandaries and antagonisms. Let us again consider our four special cases.

*Absolute unobstructedness*, such that no obstruction of permission can occur in any circumstance, so that every permission can be exercised without infringing any top-corner imperative, is commoner (if absolute quandary-freedom is common) than might be supposed – but only because it is achieved by fiat. It is common, that is to say, for a set of rules to contain no permissives except one, perhaps implicit, to the effect that everything is permitted that the rules do not forbid; or to contain no rules that are not permissive except one that forbids everything else. The rules of a board game, for example, often set out just the legal moves. Even when this is not so, rules often contain comparatively few top-corner imperatives, or comparatively few permissions, and are so formulated as to guard against obstructions, in recognition of the fact that those who read them may resent having to make cross-connections.

*Legislative unobstructedness* is also important in practice, namely, when legislation indirectly guarantees the exercisability of a right by prohibiting actions that would or might lead to a situation in which the right would be obstructed. Let us suppose that there is a right of employees to continued employment, but that tax laws or import-export quota restrictions are capable in some circumstances of driving an employing firm out of business and so making this employment impossible. In effect, the laws are capable of obstructing the employees' right. But we can also imagine that an unusually far-seeing government might insist on regulating the policies of a firm so threatened, to the extent needed to keep it able to meet its tax and quota obligations and stay in business. The employees' rights would then (in this respect) be legislatively, though not absolutely, unobstructed.

I do not think that people who demand legislation to guarantee our rights and freedoms always want legislation of this kind, or that they are always clear what will satisfy them. Sometimes absolute unobstructedness is demanded, achievable only by annulling all restrictions. Legislative unobstructedness, which, though it does not annul all restrictions, declares illegal at least one step in any chain of circumstances that might result in some restriction's becoming operative, does not guarantee exercise of rights at all, since whoever is responsible for the illegal step might still take it; but it would sometimes be regarded as satisfactory to the extent that, at law, the wrongdoer being identified, redress may be demanded. (And in, say, a board game the rules can be enforced retrospectively.) Even legislative unobstructedness, however, can be a high demand, and we may be satisfied to settle for less.

*Strategic unobstructedness* is achieved when, although obstruction can arise and even be legal, those that stand to be inconvenienced by it have a chance, if they wish, to take steps to ensure that it will not. Even this can be a strong demand in practical cases, since it implies that those who wish to exercise permissions need never depend on the not-choosably-inevitable help of others in order to do so. To have a strategically unobstructed freedom to get married, or play backgammon, or give or take employment, I must be in a position of being certain of persuading an appropriate partner or adversary to join me. And, especially when a permission is dignified with the title 'right' or 'freedom', something more than this seems to be demanded, namely, that relevant others *ought* or *have a duty* to co-operate in securing its exercise. Writing this *ought* into the rules as a top-corner imperative makes the unobstructedness legislative again. Strategic unobstructedness, however, when achievable, might be regarded as a satisfactory guarantee even of rights and freedoms.

*Minimal unobstructedness*, without which a permission would be totally pointless, is achieved whenever it is even remotely possible that a situation will arise in which it can be legally exercised.

As stated, these definitions are intended to apply only to sets of imperatives that are absolutely quandary-free and antagonism-free. Even in this case there is one small complication that can arise when exercise of a permission may have the consequence of generating an addition to the set of imperatives. This can happen either because the permission may be a permission to issue an order or other imperative, or (as we have seen, equivalently) because the set already contains a conditional imperative with the content of the permission as its antecedent. Suppose, for example, that the park-keeper has authority to order picnickers to keep off the grass, to be exercised at his discretion. Although his right is unobstructed, it may have consequences in quandaries for other people. In short, quandaries (or antagonisms) may be *produced* by the exercise of permissions.

They may also be removed. Legislative quandary-freedom or antagonism-freedom, that is to say, may be achieved if someone authorised to enact the appropriate additional imperatives chooses to do so; and, similarly, strategies may be enabled that create strategic freedom, or minimal. But the complication is not a very severe one, since permissions or conditional imperatives that are capable of having this effect are limited in kind, and easily identifiable. Exercise of a permission can have this effect, in short, only when the set being investigated contains a pair of imperatives of the form (where $P_0$ and $P_1$ do not need to be different),

$P_0$ may do $E$.
If $P_0$ does $E$, $P_1$ must do $D$.

– or a variant of it with state-defined instead of action-defined imperatives, or some elaboration of these. No permission-exercise can produce absolute quandary-freedom.

In reading all the above definitions, due account needs to be taken of the fact that individual permissions of a heresis, though not more than one of them can be exercised at a time, do not count as mutually obstructing.

## LOGICAL MODEL OF UNOBSTRUCTEDNESS

Provided certain complications do not arise, a precise formulation of the definitions of varieties of unobstructedness can be achieved within our model by reducing obstructions to quandaries. To say that a permission is obstructed by a top-corner imperative is to say that if the permission itself had top-corner force instead of bottom-corner there would be a top-row opposition between them. If the bottom-row forms in the square of opposition were, as it were, elevated to the top-row, the diagonal lines would conflate with the top-row side.

If a set is absolutely quandary-free, then, ignoring complications to be dealt with in a moment, we can test permissions for absolute/legislative/strategic/minimal unobstructedness by rewriting them all as top-corner imperatives – by deleting *if you wish*, or by turning *may* into *must*, or however else is grammatically appropriate – and testing the resulting set for the corresponding variety of quandary-freedom or antagonism-freedom. Note that mutually obstructing permissions, like Professor $X$'s and Dr $Y$'s rights to the armchair, become antagonisms. If we wish, we can sort out various sources of obstruction by rewriting the permissions one at a time instead of all together.

The complications concern (1) hereses, and (2) second-order

imperatives or their conditional counterparts of the kind we discussed a page ago. And hereses, in fact, create no problem, except tht we need to break them down as usual and consider their members separately. (Otherwise rewriting any two members of a heresis would create a quandary.) As before, given a set of imperatives containing hereses, if we form sets without hereses by deleting, in each case, all but one member of each heresis, and do this in all possible ways, each derived set can be tested for unobstructedness (of whatever variety) by rewriting its permissives, and the obstruction-properties of the parent set can be deduced.

In the case of second-order or conditional imperatives it will be sufficient to consider two cases, whose extensions will then be sufficiently obvious. They are those in which pairs of imperatives of the following forms occur:

1. $P_0$ do $E$,
   If $P_0$ does $E$, $P_1$ must do $D$;
2. $P_0$ may do $E$
   If $P_0$ does $E$, $P_1$ may do $D$.

(Again, $P_0$ and $P_1$ need not be different.) Case (1) is the case we considered a moment ago, where we noted that exercise by $P_0$ of his permission to do $E$ has the same consequence as adding an unconditional imperative:

$P_1$ must do $D$

to the set, and can therefore produce quandaries or antagonisms, or produce legislative quandary-freedom or antagonism-freedom where none was, or enable or illegalise strategies that produce strategic quandary-freedom or antagonism-freedom, or minimal. But rewriting $P_0$'s permission to do $E$ as a top-corner *injunction* to do it has the secondary effect of enjoining these consequences. Consequently, the alteration to the quandarian or antagonistic properties of the set produced by so rewriting it do not necessarily reflect obstruction of the permission itself.

But, fortunately, it is easy to separate the immediate and consequential effects of the rewriting. That being so, we can test for obstruction of the permission by rewriting it but omitting the imperative that is conditional on it.

In case (2), what is conditional on exercise of $P_0$'s permission is another permission. In this case, rewriting the first permission alone, deleting the conditional, tests adequately, as just mentioned, for obstruction of *this* permission; and then, rewriting of the second permission tests for obstruction of this in turn. So there is no difficulty.

It is necessary to remark that, since the second permission is conditional, so is its obstruction; but this does not complicate the definitions.

Chains of more than two imperatives, later ones conditional on the exercise of earlier, need to be treated similarly in a step-by-step fashion.

#### SUMMARY OF CONSISTENCY-TEST

It is now clear how any set of imperatives can be tested for what we must presumably continue to call, despite its disintegration into less logical-seeming sub-concepts, *consistency*. We do so in steps.

One, separate off and temporarily ignore all the permissives, leaving only top-corner forms. Analyse these, for each relevantly different *p*, *w* and *t*, into those separably operative, and test for quandary-incurrence, or for minimal/strategic/legislative/absolute quandary-freedom, or such other varieties as you care to invent.

Two, test the same sets for antagonisms, by 'grouping' participants in all possible ways *additional to* those in which the imperatives already group them, performing in each case the same test as for quandaries.

Three, if the permissions contain hereses, form in all possible ways heresis-free sets by deleting, in each case, all but one member of each heresis. For each of these:

Four, add the permissions to the top-corner imperatives; but ignore, at first, any conditional whose antecedent is the content of a separate permissive, or which comes later in a chain of such conditionals. Test for obstruction by rewriting permissives as top-corner imperatives and testing for quandaries or antagonisms *directly* produced by them (that is, other than as a consequence of enabling strategies).

Five, if necessary, add the deleted conditionals one by one and repeat.

The results yield the quandary, antagonism and obstruction properties of the original set of imperatives. If the set does not turn out to be absolutely free of quandaries, antagonisms and obstructions the tester then has the job of deciding how much he minds, and whether these explications of the concept of consistency embody what he wanted. But logic, at least of the kind we have been doing, cannot help him there. In essence, its own task is finished.

We have, however, one further piece of business. We should see what there is of relevance to say about differences of force.

FORCE

Earlier we considered, and rejected, the contention that there is 'no contradiction' in saying,

I am obliged to order you to do D, and I hereby do so.
But my private advice to you is not to.

The point is not that this is necessarily an unreasonable thing to say; rather, it is preferable to describe what is said as a piece of advice that *does* contradict an order. Having identified this clear logical fact we can go on, if we wish, to discuss whether the contradiction matters and in what sense one of the two imperatives might be said to override the other. But you cannot override something that is not, in the first place, an obstacle.

On the other hand, now that we know what 'simple' consistency and inconsistency are, it seems important to go on to ask in general how differences of force among the component imperatives might ultimately nullify, or modify, the conclusions reached, or might tender them trivial or irrelevant. If a conflicting command and piece of advice can, so to speak, pass one another by without meeting, does the same apply to *any* two imperatives of different forces? Does this, perhaps, even give us a test for saying what it is for two forces to be different? Or is it only that accountable imperatives 'miss' non-accountable ones? Or what?

The last suggestion can be disposed of immediately, since we can easily match a command with a request. The floor-manager says,

Officially you can't bring your dog in here, madam, and I have to instruct you to take him out. But please don't take any notice of that, he's a nice little chap.

In this vein we can match virtually any pair of forces, either way round; for example, invitation against request, as in,

I'm inviting you to my wedding; but please don't come;

or suggestion against advice, as in,

Think you could circle the rink backwards? Don't try, of course, you haven't learnt it yet.

But these examples fall into a pattern which, on inspection, is not quite what we claim it to be; the components differ not merely in force but also in seriousness or wholeheartedness of purpose. In several cases one imperative of the pair is a formal or vicarious one which the issuer frankly acknowledges to be issued in virtue of some obligation to which he incompletely subscribes. (And in the last case the suggestion was 'not wholly serious'.) Differences of force are consequently not the determining factor; the speaker makes clear which imperative he wants acted on, and, in the case of the conflicting one, pulls his punch. We can see this by constructing examples in which command is matched against command, as when one double agent who has infiltrated Smersh says to another, in the presence of Smersh colleagues,

Lock this list in the safe, comrade,

but adds in an undertone,

Leave it under the samovar for me to copy.

Or advice against advice; you are a maverick physician and I have an illness which would benefit from a certain illegal drug. You 'formally' advise the standard treatment, which you know to be less effective, but add,

Friend to friend, down in William Street you can get . . .

A speaker, in short, can issue imperatives in different capacities, wearing different hats, and withdraw his full support from one or another by making the limitation of that support clear. For a clincher – against those who think toleration of contradictions vitiates the logic of imperatives – let us match indicatives; the political PR men says to pressmen,

The Defence budget went through Cabinet unanimously

but adds

Actually, off the record, it squeaked through with the PM threatening everyone in sight.

This conclusion – that force is not the relevant feature in the examples – does not imply that force is irrelevant to deciding the practical effect of a contradiction. The recipient of contradictory COMMANDS – if they are wholehearted ones, from an issuer or issuers whose authority he recognizes or whom he must respect – is in a prototype quandary. But contradictory REQUESTS might be a different matter, since a request can often be refused summarily and without consequence and the presence of a counter-request might provide an addressee with the best of reasons for so refusing with a clear conscience. Or the choice might be made by weighing need, or personal obligation, or in any of a number of other untroubling ways. Similarly INVITATIONS. Contradictory ADVICE, at least from different advisers, is a commonplace and may again be unworrying; advice, again, need not be taken, and the grounds of choice are ideally fully rational. Choices between advice can be difficult, but they can also be so immediate as hardly to be choices at all. Combinations of imperatives of different forces do not introduce considerations different from these with pure ones.

So much for the problems of the addressee as agent. When imperatives come from a single source, quandaries and other conflicts flaw the issuer's putative 'plan'; and the analysis extends to most para-imperatives – PLANS, UNDERTAKINGS, INTENSIONS – without variation. They can also, of course, be deliberate, and intended to confuse; but this, again, is a feature they share with contradictions of indicatives.

# 6

# Imperfect Ability

It is one thing to say of a proposed course of action, in the terminology of chapter 4, that it is *actively possible*, and quite another to say that its agent *can* or *is capable of* putting it into effect.

Consider even prerequisite knowledge.

Call Joan about tomorrow, would you?

asks my wife, leaving the house. There is, let us suppose, no logical or physical bar to my calling Joan, and no question regarding choosability. (These were the elements of *active possibility*.) But where is that piece of paper with the number? I search the house, call inquiries, call a mutual friend, and so on. At best, the task is enlarged; at worst, my leads peter out and I fail at it.

But knowledge is only one element in the abilities an agent may have or lack. The others, as we find when we begin to explore, are almost bewilderingly diverse.

Knowledge of Joan's telephone number is 'propositional; the number *is* NNN or whatever. But it is also para-imperative; the family cat, whose ability to handle propositions is limited, would 'know' it in a suitable sense if he could be trained to push the right buttons on the dialler. Are there two different kinds of *knowledge how* and *knowledge that*? (It was Ryle who made the distinction for us ('knowing', also *Concept*, ch. 2.) Ryle's distinction is properly two overlapping ones. First, the para-imperative correlate of *knowledge that* is *knowledge to*, as when someone says,

He knows to go by the dockland route.

This specifies a task or action rather than a fact. But *knowledge how* or, better, *knowledge how to*, as in,

He knows how to get there,

specifies a task only to the extent of specifying, in indirect speech, an imperative QUESTION,

How do you get there?,

to which the particular imperative,

Go by the dockland route,

which *does* specify the task, is at most the correct, or a good, answer. In reverse, the most direct indicative correlate of *knowledge how to* is *knowledge whether*, as in,

He knows whether fish have ears,

which specifies the content of the knowledge only by specifying that it is whatever is the correct answer to the indicative question,

Do fish have ears?

Moreover, there are other relative-interrogative words besides *how* and *whether* – the 'six honest serving men' of the rhyme (but excluding *why*, which has special problems) – and they are all available in both indicative and para-imperative cases. Even *knowledge how* can be pure, indicative, as in,

He knows how fish spawn,

which says not that there is something he knows how to do, but that he knows the answer to the indicative question,

How do fish spawn?

The double distinction gives as a four-way table of parallels:

| | PROPOSITIONAL | PARA-IMPERATIVE |
|---|---|---|
| EXPLICIT | Knowledge that | knowledge (not) to |
| QUESTION- | Knowledge whether | Knowledge whether (not) to |
| SPECIFIED | (where . . . how) | (where (not) to . . . how (not) to) |

Ryle's cases are the *knowledge that* on the top left and the *knowledge how (not) to* at the bottom right. Note that imperatives can also have (inelegant, twenty-first century) subjects, as in *knowledge for X (not) to;* and that, even less elegantly, we can attach senses to formulations with other verbs than *know* and nouns that *knowledge – understand, appreciate,* even *believe, think.*

### CAN, POSSIBLE, KNOWLEDGE, ABILITY

*Knowledge how to*, whatever its relation to *knowledge that*, is certainly an ingredient in *ability*. But the connections and idiosyncrasies of the two terms have parallels also in near-synonymous ones. What we have the *ability* to do is what we *can* do, and what we *can* do it is *possible for us to* do. So *can, possible, knowledge* and *ability* all intertranslate; but a little uncertainly, so that as we move from one to another we risk shifting what we think we are saying. Let us take another look at *possible*.

Possibility, as in

It is possible to (climb the north face),

can be para-imperative too, and a distinction has often been recognized between *possible that* and what has usually been called *possible for*. Question-specified *possibles* seem to make no sense but, with this exception, *possibility* parallels *knowledge*. So-called epistemic modal logic is the attempted codification of a sense of *possible that* that can be glossed directly in terms of *knowledge that*; and writers on *possible for* sometimes tried to construct a parallel to it. It was noted, for example (by Kenny, ref.), that the fact that someone *will* do something does not imply that it is *possible for* him to do it. This is because there is an intensionality element. It could be the case that the Vicar will win the Church raffle, but

It is possible for the Vicar to win the Church raffle

and, particularly,

The Vicar has the ability to win the Church raffle

are capable of carrying the gloss that, if he wished, he could put the matter beyond doubt. (See Gert and Martin, 'Outcomes and Abilities' and 'What a Man does He Can Do' and Geach 'Reply', another of Kenny's examples divides choice-offering (heretical) disjunctions from plain ones; I can have the ability to *do A or B* without necessarily having the ability to choose which. But in the case of para-imperatives the conceptual connections between knowledge and ability are deeper and more ancient; there are links and crossovers among expressions for *know* and *can* in many or most languages, and they are often even etymological. (Old English *cennan* and *cunnan* – compare German *kennen* and *können*.) Knowledge, the makers of our languages seem to have believed, does not merely *give* ability: it is the same thing. (But facile identification is criticized by Carr, 'The Logic of Knowing How and Ability'.

Our related words divide in another important way. On the one hand we have the relatively abstract and ponderous *ability, knowledge* and *possibility* and, on the other, the workaday *can, know* and so on, whose study is, as much as anything, an exercise in grammar. *Can*, as it happens, is too grass-roots a word for our purposes. Aune, ('Can') distinguishes the *cans* of ability, right, inclination or probability, opportunity, and possibility. But other studies of *can* arrange its uses round different foci; Honoré, ('Can and Can't',) sums up:

In fact 'can' combines in a subtle way assessments of conduct in which achievement on the particular occasion is decisive with those in which the agent's normal achievements set the standard. (See also, Ehrman, 'Meanings of the Modals'.)

*Ability is para-imperative* Of the four linked concepts, *ability* is perhaps central. *But ability is para-imperative too*, and, unlike the others, exclusively so. Ability is *ability to* (do such-and-such or effect this or that state-of-affairs. True, we sometimes speak, using what has been called the 'mass-noun' sense (K. Baier, 'Ability, Power and Authority') of someone as 'having ability', without saying at what; but a gloss can always be demanded.

It follows that we can explore the logic of ability using the tools already developed for use on imperatives. In fact, much of what we said in chapter 2 about the grammar and logic of imperatives applies to abilities unchanged, or with at most minor changes.

1. Abilities are overwhelmingly 'plain predicate', with subject the 'owner' of the ability. I can't have an ability *for someone else* to do something, however able I may be to get him to do it. At best, a group of people might have an ability *for one of them* to do something – say, escape from gaol.

.2 In parallel with imperatives, verb forms other than the plain one (with *to*) are rare, modal auxiliaries are impossible, reflexives must refer to the ability-owner, and adverbs such as *probably* have specific limitations.

3. Stative verbs behave much as with imperatives; some are unacceptable, and all seem to call for paraphrase as agentives. An ability to *be tall* or *to have blond eyebrows* can only be an ability to do something about it. The ability *to recognize John* or *to appreciate Scarlatti* seem to be exercised non-deliberately, so that we could hesitate to list them as 'abilities' *tout court*.

4. Owner-action-reduction, whenever explication or gloss is needed, is called for and as methodologically fruitful as agent-action-reduction in the case of imperatives. There is one special point. Since 'the same' ability may be exercised by different people; or by the same person at different times, or, in principle, by the same person at the same time in different possible (possibly counterfactual) situations, action-reductions of abilities need to be indifferent as to time, situation ('world') and owner. In effect, they must be time-, world- and owner-*indexical.* (Those of imperatives, of course, may have to be also, but only to the extent that the imperatives themselves are so interpreted.) But the gloss is, as a rule, ready and natural, so that we have no need to remark on it.

Some abilities, too, are (what we shall call) *agglomerations* of action-reducible abilities, not action-reducible as whole (more on this later).

5. Abilities, like imperatives, are in respect of an immediate or remote future; I can *have had* an ability to do *D*, but I cannot have an ability *to have done D.*

6. Action-reductions of group abilities are closely parallel with those of imperatives with group addressees.

7. The analysis of imperative negation carries over to the negation of abilities, except that there is no obvious analogue of the distinction between top-row imperatives and permissives. Beside the ability to bring about *S* we can define (1) the ability to bring about non-*S*, (2) the ability to refrain from taking steps to bring about *S*, (3) the ability to refrain from taking *positive* steps; and we can have (4) *non-abilities.*

8. There is both a distinction between separable and inseparable conjunctive abilities and (as we noted) between choice-offering and non-choice-offering disjunctive ones.

The reason abilities do not have 'permissive' analogues is perhaps that they already resemble permissives. This is clear even in some of their associated terminology; an ability can be *exercised* as a permission can. The analogy extends to interrelations.

Perhaps perversely, *non*-abilities are easier to handle in logical applications than affirmative ones. Let us suppose we are in the position of issuing an imperative or imperatives to Richard Roe. And let us suppose we have a list of Richard's *non*-abilities; that is, a complete list of all the things he is quite unable to do. The items in the list may as well be expressed as negative plain predicates. If Richard cannot do arithmetic and cannot, say, keep his head in a crisis, these two facts can be put in the list, respectively, as,

Not do arithmetic,
Not keep head in crisis.

(or, for all it matters, with *Don't* instead of *Not.*) To check Richard's ability to do what we are about to enjoin him is now logically very simple; we make a combined list of the injunctions and his *non*-abilities, and check it for consistency.

## THE PARADOX OF APPLIED RESEARCH

Adding a set of non-abilities to a list of imperatives may, of course, generate not mere inconsistencies but quandaries, clashes between pairs or sets of top-corner imperatives. It is important to my firm to beat competitors to the market with a computerised waffle-iron, but we have not yet perfected a design that is sludge-free. To let the research department work on it longer would be to miss the market opportunity; to go into production now might be to market a failure.

Planning of any kind has costs, and takes time. Planning is, moreover – practically by definition – open-ended; results are incompletely predictable, or there would be no need for it in the first place. Truistically, good planning is the secret of *effective action*; but so is timeliness. When to stop planning and act? (see Wellman, 'The Justification of Practical Reason'.)

There is no way out of this quandary by meta-planning, pre-investigating what planning will be effective. There is also no way out by the use of 'intuition', 'expertise' or 'experience'. There are, perhaps, better or worse planners; but that is all.

## THE INGREDIENTS OF ABILITY

Besides knowledge, an agent facing a task (of any difficulty) needs the wit to organize it, self-control for its execution, and perhaps much more. How much more does he need, and what? The many-sidedness of the concept of ability is not revealed by our discussions, so far, of its grammar. What must we do to explicate it?

As it happens, we have a mentor; our position is very similar to that of Aristotle when he sought to explicate Practical Wisdom (or Prudence, *phronesis*), the faculty supposedly possessed by practical men who are good at decision-making. It is true that Aristotle seems to think he is dealing with a general ability that enables its possessor to do well at tasks of all kinds – a sort of practical IQ – whereas our more modest aim is to understand the range of factors that affect ability to cope with tasks or situations that are individual. Aristotle, too, is at time distressingly abstract and theory-laden; he spends his discussion-space juggling with twenty or so nouns denoting agglomerate mental faculties or abilities whose overlaps, interconnections and shades of meaning must have been obscure even to his Greek readers. But, regrettably or otherwise, it is not clear that matters have advanced much in the 2300 years since he wrote; and what he says is still capable of putting us on our modern road (see, mainly, *Nicomachean Ethics*, 1140a24-1145a12).

The ingredients of Practical Wisdom, as Aristotle expounds them, fall roughly into four groups:

1. A 'knowledge' group, comprising knowledge gained by Sensory Perception, *aisthēsis*; Scientific Knowledge, *epistēmē; and knowledge by intuitive Reason, noûs*. The last two together make up Philosophical Wisdom, *sophia*.
2. Art or Skill, *technē*, and Cleverness, *deinotēs*.
3. a group concerned with the weighing of ends, namely Deliberative Excellence, *euboulia*; Understanding, *sunesis* or *eusunesia*; and Judgement, *gnōmē*.
4. Moral Virtue, *aretē*.

Knowledge of the first kind, by Sensory Perception, *aisthēsis*, is necessary not merely to the planning of a task but to its execution. We can see this by imagining its lack. Can the blind man cross the park? He needs a substitute sense to find a route that avoids contingent obstacles. Perhaps he taps ahead with a stick; the knowledge is sensory, but he substitutes his sense of touch. In fact much of our knowledge of particular fact does not fit this rubric; if I find that piece of paper I shall use my eyes to read the number; but questions of the meaning and reliability of the marks on the paper make the knowledge I glean 'sensory' only in a derived sense. However, noting Aristotle's conflation of cases at this point, let us pass on.

Much of our knowledge is not knowledge of particular fact, but Scientific Knowledge, *epistēmē*, knowledge of laws governing what happens. To obey the imperative,

Cook the port for 6.30 dinner

I need to know not just wht time it is and how much the leg weighs but the law relating the cooking-time of pork to its weight. If this law is not already in my possession I get it from available sources or, in the last resort, by some process of research. At all events, the contrast with knowledge gained immediately by Sensory Perception is sharp, since the general knowledge needed in the execution of a task will *not* be obtainable in this way, but at best beforehand or by some side-process such as taking time off to look it up.

But Aristotle thinks there is a third, more elevated, variety of knowledge, namely, knowledge by intuitive Reason, *noûs*. The word *noûs*, besides being the ordinary word for Mind or Intellect, can also refer to the meaning of a word or expression, so that knowledge of this third kind is some kind of amalgam of the innate, the Kantian synthetic *a priori*, and the analytic. It is possible to imagine tasks whose performance depends on appreciation that $7 + 5 = 12$, that every effect has a cause, or that all brothers are male; and Aristotle himself would have put a good deal of what we regard as 'scientific' knowledge in this category also. For present purposes we do not need to labour any distinction there might be between knowledge of this type and of the preceding one; Aristotle himself puts them together under the title of Philosophic Wisdom, *sophia*. For that matter we shall not need to distinguish either of these kinds of knowledge from any sort of knowledge that is long-lasting relative to the task in hand and can be regarded as 'background' – for example, in the case of most ordinary tasks, geographical facts, the law of the land, facts of manners and customs, and other non-particular kinds of 'common knowledge'.

Aristotle, himself a practical man at heart, is quick to point out that Philosophic Wisdom does not guarantee the Practical Wisdom that it is our task to explicate. The philosophers Thales and Anaxagoras, he thinks, had a lot of the first and not much of the second. (Thales? What little we know of him gives us a different picture; but no matter.) Aristotle accordingly continues his list of the ingredients of Practical Wisdom with *technē*, Art, Craft or Skill, and *deinotēs*, Natural Ability or Cleverness; the difference seems to be that the former is a learnt or practised ability and the latter inborn. The second is an unanalysed grab-bag, and the extent to which *any* abilities are inborn rather than learnt is, perhaps, debatable. But to ignore it would be to deny that agents ever differ in natural ability and, in consequence, in the strategies open to them. Where learnt skills are concerned we are on safer ground, but their relevance implies a complication of action-reduction theory, since the learning of a skill may itself be a part of the task. An actor who is told,

I want you to understudy Phillip at the Bicentenary Pageant

must mentally action-reduce the mask into, among other things, an unspecified period of script-learning, character-study and attendance at rehearsals. There is also an ambiguity; it is often not clear whether possession of the ability to develop an ability should be regarded as itself that ability. In the case of the actor, there are equity precedents for how much preparation is 'reasonable'. But Napoleon said that there is no such word as *can't*, from which it seems to follow that it would be wrong or misleading to say that I do not have the pianistic ability to play Chopin's *Fantaisie Impromptu* – despite the fact that my current level of competence is *Chopsticks* (see Kenny, 'Human Abilities and Dynamic Modalities', p. 213.) What it is appropriate to say sometimes turns also on the amount of help understood to be available from others; apes *can* converse with humans (in sign-language), but not without being taught. Medieval philosophers regularly noted and debated an Aristotelian distinction between *potential* and *actual* senses of *can*, in debating the fallacy of 'different modality' (see my *Fallacies*, p. 106-7).

Aristotle's third group breaks quite different ground. Adding Cleverness and Skill to Sensory Perception and the philosophical and scientific varieties of knowledge is still not enough to make up Practical Wisdom, since however knowledgeable and skilful people may be they may lack Judgement and may consequently direct their activities to the wrong goals. Aristotle says slightingly of people of this kind that they are concerned only with means, not with ends, and turns his attention to faculties more concerned with the weighing of ends, namely *euboulia*, Deliberative Excellence or Good Counsel; *sunesis* or *eusunesia*, Understanding; and *gnōmē*, Judgement. Does it need argument that the addition of faculties of this kind to our list of ability-ingredients is necessary and does not take us beyond our original brief? The fact is that even quite ordinary imperatives,

> Drive a good bargain.
> Cook it well, but don't overdo it.
> At this point add some discussion of consilience

– which specify tasks at which success or failure is a matter of shades of grey rather than white or black – *presuppose* the possession of judgemental abilities by the addressee. Driving a good bargain is partly a matter of appreciating whether a price of *X* thousand dollars, when circumstances are weighed up, is a good one or not; whther a particular piece of cooked pork is well-done can, truistically, only be judged by applying standards of taste; and the right amount of discussion of consilience cannot be calculated by any formula. It follows that of two agents who have the same factual and theoretical knowledge and are equal in technique one may succeed, one fail, at the same task, if only the first is capable of making the appropriate judgements.

Aristotle himself goes close to admitting that he cannot clearly analyse and separate the members of the grab-bag of concepts introduced so far, when he says (1143a25):

Now all the states we have considered converge, as might be expected, to the same point; for when we speak of Judgement and Understanding and Practical Wisdom and Intuitive Reason we credit the same people with possessing Judgement and having reached the years of Reason and with having Practical Reason and Understanding.

But we have not yet finished, because even all the faculties of the three groups together – that is (roughly), of knowledge, technique and judgement – do not get us to the essence of Practical Wisdom. This is because they do not necessarily lead to action. He says about Understanding (1143a8),

Practical Wisdom issues commands, since its end is what ought to be done or not to be done; but Understanding only judges.

And he would presumably have been prepared to say the same about the others. So Practical Wisdom is, by definition, not merely the faculty that makes the right actions possible but the faculty that ensures that they are performed. Although we need not follow Aristotle in detail through his attempt to find the extra ingredient, two points must be made. The first is that yet a further faculty, *aretē*, Goodness or Excellence or Virtue or Character or Merit, seems both to presuppose Practical Wisdom and to be presupposed by it. (see 1144b1-1145a11 and Ackrill pp. 28-9). The word *aretē*, in Greek, does have a less 'moral' flavour than its usual English translations suggest; but the fact that Aristotle links it at all to Practical Wisdom means that he uses the latter term, at least to some extent, as an honorific, moral one, in a way it would be inappropriate for us to copy if all we have in mind is the explication of an agent's ability to act on a given imperative. Yet we also cannot entirely dismiss the claims of *aretē* to consideration, if only because an imperative cannot always be considered in isolation from the content of other imperatives and para-imperatives relevant to the action-reduction of the governing one. What does the agent do when the governing one is blocked or when literal conformity is undesirable. I can't find Joan's number, but how much does it matter? Isn't there some other way of securing the end to which calling Joan was to be the means? Or is there something else I ought to be doing that is more important than this hunt for that slip of paper? The question is not just how to ring Joan, but *what I should be doing now*, in this situation in which the task if ringing Joan is one competing element. (Mr Punch issued a famous piece of advice to those about to marry.)

We cannot, in short, define Practical Wisdom narrowly in terms of ability to carry out literally and without criticism injunctions already issued. But the critical ability the agent can be expected to make use of to assess his injunctions in their overall situation resembles *aretē* more than it does any of the earlier ingredients.

Finally, let us turn to Aristotle's worry about what it is that guarantees that the appropriate action – granted the knowledge, skill, judgement and moral sense to select it – will actually be put into effect. No one counts as having Practical Wisdom who does not eventually put into practice what his faculties dictate. Aristotle never quite solved the problem of what the extra faculty is, but his attempts to grapple with it – particularly on the negative side, in analysing what it is that sometimes leads people to act in ways they know *not* to be sensible or rational – can at least show us that there is a gap in our list. This negative faculty, or anti-ability, is *akrasia*, Incontinence, or Weakness of Will, and Aristotle devotes a long, deep and analytical discussion to it (1145a15-1152a35).

I have found that piece of paper and taken it to the telephone; but Joan will be in full flight at this time of the morning, and the prospect of half an hour of her is daunting. There are, of course, ways of making myself make the call, but because of my anti-ability, the process is harder and takes longer.

Neither 'incontinence' nor 'weakness of will' is quite the right name for what I suffer *vis-à-vis* Joan; and they are similarly misdescriptions of a different kind of case. You are the President of a Corporation whose Pillworth plant must be closed, causing widespread hardship in the town. The decision is inevitable, yet you pause, try to fault the logic. Some will say 'He doesn't have the courage', but is that quite right? Others will call your decision hasty and ruthless even when you make it. True, you hesitate irrationally long; but you would hardly respect someone in the same position who did not. Can we meet the problem of *akrasia* by postulating the necessity of an extra ingredient such as Will? The move achieves very little, though it has been made by various writers throughout philosophical history. For present purposes it is sufficient that we note the relevant senses of *ability* and the other words. There are recognized, if controversial, senses in which the agoraphobe *does not have the ability* to go out the door; I *can't* stop myself from blinking when the light flashes; and it *is not possible* for you as Pillworth President to sign those documents till you have searched your soul. Note also that *belief* can be akratic (see Rorty 'Akratic Believers'; Heil 'Doxastic Incontinence').

'WOULD ... IF ...'

How are we to put together an analytical, unitary account of ability in modern dress?

The *would ... if ...* theory of ability was put up – and knocked down again – by J.L. Austin ('Ifs and Cans') in comment on Moore ('Ethics' pp.28-31). It is virtually the only analytical theory of ability, though much has been built on it (see Tichý and Oddie 'Ability and Freedom' etc.). Statements of it vary; in some ways it is not so much a theory as a box to put one in. Austin's version glossed

X can do A

as (with qualifications)

X would do A if he/she/ ... chose

And something may need to be added about opportunity. But even then this fits only some kinds of ability; it fails our last ingredient. Will, since akratic agents are precisely those who cannot, or have difficulty in, choosing. Tichý and Oddie (note 6) point out that *skill* is not always necessary to ability under Austin's gloss, since, although I might be unable to spell *committee* I can carry around a card with the correct spelling on it. On the other hand the 'Church raffle' example, which has something been held to expose a weakness, can perhaps be accommodated if the same amount of intensionality is read into the example as into the definition: thus The Vicar can ... is simply ambiguous as between 'at will' and 'by chance' senses, and would weaken the analysis only if it had to assume the latter.

Yet once we have accepted that the way to specify an ability with precision is by means of an action-reduction, we have already adopted something very close to a *would ... if ...* theory. For since an ability is something someone *has*, it has to be regarded as a built-in (whether practised or natural) repertoire, routine, procedure, ploy or program, that can be *activated, mobilized* or *called up* (or, as the computer people say, *booted*) as occasion demands, to become a part of its owner's behaviour. To avoid the question of who or what initiates the process, let us use an impersonal formulation and say that the ability *is exercised* when it *is activated*. Under this rubric we can fit machines as easily as humans, animals and the rest; thus

This machine has the ability to dig post-holes at the rate of one every two minutes

is glossed without problem. But so, in at least the simplest cases, is self-activation by humans – as when the juggler slips into his three-ball act.

It follows that we do not need to involve ourselves, any more than anywhere else in this book, in questions of mechanism or determinism. As we said, there is a sense in which the issuing of an imperative *implies* the possibility of influencing a free agent – though it also presumes the possibility of a causal influence on that agent. These are neither arguments for determinism nor arguments against; they are neutral comments on how we speak and behave. The issue has been so widely debated that it is no longer necessary to apologize for a 'mechanistic' model of mental events. The word implies little more than that the model is precise and well-formulated, and it could even be argued that a model that is *not* mechanistic in this sense is defective. Determinism is, for some people, more of a bogey, but the issue is a different one and can be debated independently – and elsewhere.

Can a computer, then, or its program, exhibit skill, judgement and understanding, display practical wisdom, suffer from weakness of will? Ready yes-answers to these questions would be naive; but philosophical luddism is not called for either. No one doubts that a sufficient (and sufficiently intelligent) research-effort into the development of a detailed descriptive analysis of these concepts, capable of commanding agreement among users of them – rather than into actual realization of a machine or program, which is a relatively small problem – could make possible very close *imitation* of the behaviour they describe; and whether this is enough – whether this behaviour would be 'the real' thing – is a question whose own nature is unclear. (Human beings have been semi-seriously, somewhat more than fancifully, personifying machines for centuries.) However, none of these issues touch what we have been saying; we are insulated from them. (For some modern discussions of the 'intentionality of action' see Dennett *Brainstorms*, ch. 1; Boden *Minds and Mechanisms*, ch. 2.)

Only the simplest abilities fit the *exercised when activated* analysis directly. The exercise of some abilities demands successive activation of separate parts; other display yet other structures. A terminology for several kinds of ability-structure might be helpful. (The list-cannot be regarded as exhaustive.)

Let us call an ability *atomic* if it cannot be broken into abilities requiring (or susceptible to) separate activation. A 'basic action' ability would have to be atomic; but the juggler's three-ball act can also be considered so since it proceeds without separate activations of separate parts. An ability exercised in sections separately activable is *molecular....* The ability to make a wooden box or hang a door has as parts various sub-abilities such as the ability to nail, the ability to saw, and abilities to chisel, drive screws, and so on, but although we describe it as a single ability these parts are activated in irregular sequence as parts of a whole the owner has – it seems clearest to say – the knowledge to organize. Our formulation catches the sub-abilities, less certainly the whole.

*Agglomerate* abilities – such as the ability to speak Tamil – are families (in Wittgenstein's sense *Philosophical Investigations*, I, 67) of atomic or molecular abilities, separately activable, but not necessarily in special sequence. Someone who has the ability to speak Tamil does not necessarily have a routine of Tamil-speaking he turns on; he has a range of sub-abilities such as knowledge of the meaning of this or that word, ability to construct this or that form of sentence. The sub-abilities again fit some version of the *exercised when activated* analysis; the agglomeration of them does not.

It seems worth saying that most of the faculties Aristotle nominates as ingredients of Practical Wisdom are agglomerate.

But the ability to speak Tamil is not even very accurately described when it is called *agglomerate*; for bilingual speakers have a tendency to 'switch' whole behaviour-patterns. Let us speak of *behaviour-mode abilities*, that are not so much 'activated' as 'enabled'. Once you enable your Tamil-speaking mode you become in possession of the agglomerate ability to speak Tamil, with its separately activable parts. But your behaviour-mode can be *dis*abled again, and your usual, or another, mode enabled in its place.

Atomic abilities are their own action-reductions; molecular abilities action-reduce to atomic. The components of agglomerate abilities have separate action-reductions, but the abilities themselves have none. Behaviour-mode abilities, on the other hand, have action-reductions in the sense that there can be an action-reduction of a period of behaviour within the mode.

Richard Roe's list of *non*-abilities may as well, for easiest theoretical handling, be a list of negated atoms.

KNOWLEDGE AGAIN

Little more need be said about most of the Aristotelian ingredients of ability. We have no theory of them; but *if* there were agreement in the words' application, and *if* we were prepared to do the work of finely codifying them, it would not be any lack of conceptual framework that would hold us up. Knowledge is a different matter; and, particularly, knowledge of the first kind, by Sensory Perception. This is because it complicates the picture of action-reductions.

In chapter 4 we defined a *strategy* as an allocation of a deed to each time for each (past) history at that time; and an *i-strategy* (of $p$ in $w$ at $t$) as a strategy all of whose actively possible outcomes achieve extensional satisfaction of imperative $i$. If the set of (past) histories at $t$ is $Q_t$ and $p$ is subject to some $i$, $P$ is subject at any $t$ to a strategy-component of the general form

> If the history is $q_t^1$, do $d^1$,
> If the history is $q_t^2$, do $d^2$,
> . . .
> If the history is $q_t^n$, do $d^n$.

At first sight, the formulation appears to give us unlimited scope to allow that $P$ may take into account knowledge of empirical fact; but, realistically, it denies him any such scope, since, he has *no* way of saying which of $q_t^1$, $q_t^2$, . . . , $q_t^n$ is the true world history and cannot make his choice of deed at all. We have made no provision for distinguishing between knowledge available to the agent and knowledge not.

Let us return to the problem of the blind man crossing the park. Making simplifying assumptions about the park and its paths, we can imagine designing for him an action-reduction consisting of a fixed, finite sequence of moves each of one of the forms 'Take one step forward', 'Turn right', 'Turn left'. If he memorised this sequence and followed it with precision, he *could* 'cross the park'; and this is the 'alethic' solution to his problem. But it would be misleading to say that he did it himself if he had to rely on our predesigned plan. For an 'epistemic' solution which he might be capable of putting into effect unaided, we assume he can detect obstacles with his stick, and detect also when he is finally across. He now follows a 'computer program', such as

> START: If no obstacle ahead, go to GO; otherwise –
> Turn left
> Take one step forward
> Turn right
> Repeat from START
> GO: Take one step forward
> If not at far boundary, repeat from START; otherwise –
> FINISH

This particular, simple program guides him round the left-hand end of any rectangular obstacle. Pseudo-instructions such as 'Repeat from START', internal to the program, could in principle be eliminated, since the elements of the (bounded) task could be arranged in tree-form, without looping. But to be able to execute *pari passu* a conditional instruction such as 'if no obstacle ahead, . . . ,' the agent needs current knowledge by Sense Perception.

The programming technique is wellworn, and there is no conceptual strain in supposing that strategies or action-reductions be laid out using it. Since, here, every conditional is followed by an *otherwise*, the forks are all two-way (though this is not essential); alternatively, each *if* could be rewritten *iff*. One important assumption about these forks is, however, made; the agent's situation at the moment the conditional is encountered in the program is always such that he knows whether the antecedent is true or false. If it is possible he does not, the program is faulty or, at least, incomplete; it should have had earlier instructions (such as 'Tap with stick' and 'If resistance encountered, . . .') ensuring that the needed knowledge was 'collected'.

Several new elements in turn need to enter our chapter 4 model. Any particular piece of empirical knowledge available to an agent will be equivalent to a *partial past world-history (ppwh)*, that is, disjunction of complete (past) world-histories. But *ppwhs*, for any agent, time and world, divide in two – those the agent can, and those he cannot, come to know by instant, *pari passu* observation. Those he *can* so come to know – though not only those – can serve as the antecedents of conditional instructions operative on that $o$, in that $w$, at that $t$.

But sometimes, knowledge is available only some longer or shorter time before it is needed; and, if this is so, it must be 'remembered', that is, stored in coded form for later reference by the program, or allowed to modify the program itself in a way that achieves the same effect. (The choice between these alternatives is a detail for the programmer.) Either way, the program must contain *alterable* elements. Again, this is a commonplace of computer practice; but it is unusual, to say the least, as a feature of a logical theory. In effect, we are required to model an agent's strategy as a mechanism in two-way contact with his postulated environment; it not only represents what he *does* in carrying out his imperative (or exercising his ability), but it is itself regularly and systematically altered by that environment – namely, when he makes (as it specifies he must) empirical observations.

Knowledge of more general kinds – of relevant laws, or of non-permanent facts of a background character – clearly also needs to be stored earlier for use later. But since (at least if non-future-referent) it can also be expressed by *ppwhs*, it raises no theoretical demands different from that by Sensory Perception.

A different demand is raised by the fact that agents sometimes come to know things by drawing conclusions (or otherwise extrapolating from things known); it becomes necessary to admit the possibility of knowledge-items generated 'internally' by the operation of a set of laws – psychological, logical or whatever – supplementing the 'external' physical ones. We made this assumption earlier in a limited way in defining choosability; we are now forced into making it more generally, and into building into the concept of a strategy or an action-reduction a model – special, perhaps to each agent – of available reasoning processes and tendencies in their use.

The complete description of the state of the world at any instant must also now include specification of the contents of all knowers' knowledge-stores or other alterable contents of the action-reductions of their abilities, and of other action-reductions in train; and world-histories must incorporate such specifications for all (non-future) instants. Hence knowledge of a state or a history might in principle have to include knowledge of this knowledge, . . . The regress does not necessarily create logical difficulties, though it does set some theoretical limits to the possible contents of knowledge (see Radford, 'Knowing and Telling'). I shall not attempt to construct any part of this burgeoning model, which is clearly beginning to resemble a design for a robot, in detail.

UNCERTAIN OUTCOME

The word *knowledge* has been the wrong one for us to use, virtually throughout this chapter – begging, as it does, all questions of reliability. In fact, a proportion of what we observe we misobserve, and part of what we learn or infer we mislearn or misinfer – or misremember. Although there are techniques of checking and hedging that can be used to minimize the damage 'misknowledge' causes, action based on it must sometimes be defective, and unpredictably so.

Can we define an ability in terms of a *stochastic* outcome? Yes, the word itself refers to marksmanship, and there can be good and bad marksmen. But a good marksman achieves, at best, a 'usual' or 'average' success; and we cannot say that his ability is an ability *to do* anything less shadowy than this. (*Would . . . if . . .* fails, except with stochastic words after the *would*.)

A further, theoretically distinct, source of uncertain outcome is our inability to predict the deeds of other agents. These deeds may be, in intention or in fact, cooperative with, competitive with, or indifferent to, our own. They may also be done on the basis of their doers' uncertain predictions about ourselves.

None of this calls, here, for more than a comment. But is there some special kind of ability that is needed by those who must act on unreliable information? The answer, of course, is that there are several well-studied branches of theory that are relevant – probability theory, so-called 'decision'-theory, 'bargaining'-theory, and the 'theory of games'. These other large areas of study consequently overlap the considerations of this book.

# 7
## Imperatives in Dialogue

At the beginning of this book I set aside for later treatment the question what sort of *entities* the imperatives are that the logician could or should take an interest in and talk about. Are they utterances, locutions, speech-acts, acts of linguistic communication, . . . ? We gave a tentative nod to the last-mentioned. A main difficulty is that these entity-terms are all imperfectly defined; and the question even of what *logic* is, when it operates in this enlarged field, is not so definitely settled that it could not break out anew.

Now, we have a lot of case-law. And from one point of view, the problem is rather easy; it is a matter of what kinds of *indexicality* imperatives are to be allowed to have if we are to be able to say the logically interesting things about them. If we had been determined to be guided by the analogy of 'propositions', we would have looked for entities that were independent of time, place and circumstances of utterance (including utterer and utteree), so that 'the same' entity could drop up on arbitrarily different occasions or be the logical content of speech-acts otherwise unlimitedly diverse. But it is now clear that, although it would be counterproductive to deny ourselves the facility of talking loosely about 'the same' imperative's 'different' materialisations, many of the properties we regard as logical depend on details of occasion. A given imperative form of words uttered to different people, though it may contain no terms commonly regarded as indexical, calls for action now by one of them, now by another; at different times, even if it refers to the same end-state of the same person, it may call for more urgent action, or less; and so on. And if *effectiveness* is a logical property – and it did seem worth while so to regard it – it even makes a difference who the utterer is, what his social relation is to the utteree, and perhaps what the likelihood is of his helping of hindering the execution and what parallel inducements or distractions he offers. Not all of our distinctions call for all of these specifications, but the need to invoke one or another kind of indexicality is much greater in the case of imperatives – if the *interesting* things are to be said – than it is in the case of indicatives.

The reader who has lived with this situation through half a dozen chapters may now be ready to go a little further with me and accept the fact that too nice a distinction between 'sentences, utterances, locutions, speech-acts and acts of linguistic communication' is for the pedants. And in any case, if we turn, as I now propose, to that neglected area of logical or linguistic study, pragmatics – or, as I prefer to call my own version of it, dialectic – we are likely to find that many of our logical categorizations need to be suspended or rethought. This is the area in which we discuss not the grammatical structure of sentences, or their logical forms or meanings, or the logical relations between them, but the way they fit together as parts of linguistic discourse and interchange. In fact, I think, this study is last where it ought to be first; we are familiar with its raw material as a part of our everyday experience, whereas that of the other logical and linguistic studies has to be extracted by a process of isolation and analysis. In spite of this, dialectic is still treated by most logicians and many linguists as an arcane study calling for conjecture, sensitivity to nuance, and a Wittgensteinian contentment with the 'making of philosophical remarks'.

Yet it is here, if anywhere – following the commonplace that to discover the meaning of a word, or phrase, or discourse, we must look at how it is *used* – that we find out what an imperative *is*, and for that matter an indicative also. And it is here we should look for a basis for the distinction between commands, requests, advice and the other imperative varieties; and for clear explications, if we pursue the study far enough, of the multiple concepts of negation, conjunction, generality and the other logical concepts; and for all other definitions or explications of this kind, perhaps even including those of *truth*, *meaning* and ethical or para-ethical terms such as *good* and *right*. These seem extravagant claims until we reflect that most of what is being said is that the terms in question are to be seen as linguistic tools and as definable, if at all, by explaining their role in the widest field of the study of language.

There are those who would immediately look to find these distinctions behind language and language-use, supposedly more fundamental than it. The account of meaning given by Grice, for example (also Leonard, Schiffer), makes undefined use of mentalistic terms such as *belief* and *intention*, and differentiates imperatives from indicatives by giving separate accounts of their correlates in the minds of utterer and addressee. Thus Grice's definition of 'utterer's meaning', paraphrased and with the omission of details not presently relevant, is, for indicatives,

For utterer *u* to mean, by saying *x* to *A*, that *S*, is for *U* to intend to produce in *A* (by means of *A*'s recognition of *U*'s intention) the belief that *S*

– and, for imperatives,

For *U* to mean, by saying *x* to *A*, that *A* is to do *D*, is for *U* to intend to produce in *A* (by means of *A*'s recognition of *U*'s intention) the intention to do *D*.

(Earlier, for imperatives, the account ran more nearly 'for *U* to intend . . . to bring it about that *A* does *D*'.)

Indicatives are calculated to produce *beliefs*; imperatives, to produce *intentions* or perhaps, directly, *actions*. So far, so good; indicatives and imperatives are differentiated; and from some points of view *beliefs* and *intentions* are well enough understood to need no further glossing. But they lead us quite outside the description of language-use; and whatever is ultimately decided, it is surely clear that patterns of language-use can be studied, at first, 'straight', with less metaphysical commitment or controversy. There would be accounts of the concepts of belief and intention that lead back into considerations of language-use, such that Grice's account must be seen as back-to-front or circular. Under some interpretations, it is even plainly inaccurate; the thoughts, either of utterer or addressee, that accompany an utterance need not have any connection with its meaning (for other criticism, see Carr, 'Speaker Meaning').

The commonest account of the difference between indicatives and imperatives is one that puts them into a context of use in an environment. Wittgenstein's builder (*Philosophical Investigations*) uses the words,

Five slabs!

as an order to his assistant, as part of a 'game' in which the assistant subsequently brings five slabs; and it is explained that the same words could, in another 'game', be used to report the number of slabs in a pile. Wittgenstein does not elaborate on the 'games', but it seems clear that what distinguishes the imperative is the addressee's immediate, subsequent *action*. We could object: a report that there were five slabs in a pile could also lead to immediate action, and more specification is required. But to find it we must look elsewhere. For Wittgenstein, the lack of detail was not a matter for excuse, since he thought language-games were in principle infinitely variable. David Lewis (*Convention*) has added a suggestion: Paul Revere (in Longfellow's poem) arranged with the sexton of the Old North Church to report the arrival of the British redcoats by displaying lanterns in the tower,

One if by land, or two if by sea,

so that Paul Revere might ride off to warn the defence – to Lexington, let us assume, in the first case, or to Concord in the second. But what is the grammatical status of the sexton's lantern-signals? Are they indicatives,

The British are coming by land (sea),

or imperatives,

Ride to Lexington (Concord)?

It depends, it seems on the authority relationship between the sexton and Paul Revere. If Paul Revere is in charge, he expects *information* from his subordinate to which to base his decision how to act. But if the sexton were a senior officer of the resistance his signals would be imperatives, specifying *action* which he would regard himself as entitled to demand independently of whether the British were coming by land, sea or at all. It is a matter of which of the two, Paul Revere or the sexton, has discretionary powers of choice – Paul Revere to decide what to do when he gets the signal, or the section to decide which signal to send. These are, of course, two clear-cut cases among others less so.

Note that it is not here plausible to say, without qualification, that signals specify *action* to be performed. It has been said to be a mark of imperatives that they 'lead from linguistic behaviour to nonlinguistic behavior' (Belnap, *An Analysis of Questions*); but indicatives, as much as imperatives, are as often as not uttered so that their addresses will act on them, or language as a whole would be singularly pointless. And in this case, whether the signals in the tower are taken as indicative or imperative, Paul Revere will ride, and ride immediately. The indicative/-imperative distinction is, rather, reduced to a social one; imperatives are locutions spoken by those in, or exercising, some kind of authority. Subject to many qualifications, this might be made to work as a definition. On the other hand, it is not clear that the delineation of authority-relationships is anyone's best starting-point. Are we sure we can explain social distinctions without circular recourse to those between indicatives and imperatives?

The picture of imperatives that is promoted by these accounts of their differentiation – consistent even with that of Grice – is as of *immediate* COMMANDS. A form of sentence is uttered, or a light hung in a tower, and *action* follows. The linguistic communication, note, is one-way; the addressee's *action* is his only relevant response. It is true that, if there is a sequence of such commands, what happens can be presented as a sort of dialogue of which the actions are part:

Instructor: Left-hand lane.
    Pupil: (Crosses to left-hand lane.)
Instructor: Pull up close and brake gently.
    Pupil: (Pulls up close and brakes gently.)
Instructor: Hand brake.
    Pupil: (Applies hand brake.)

– and so on. The imperatives we issue to animals fit this pattern – it is a sort of 'Giddap' – 'Whoa' theory. But it is, at best, a parody of a true dialogue; and, even as a picture of what happens, it is incomplete. The driving-pupil's acceptance of the instructor's orders is implicit not just in the fact that he acts on them, but on the fact that he knows that the instructor observes his actions, and that the instructor knows he knows . . . it is true that there can be other cases, such as that in which immediate commands are issued 'blind'; but they are atypical even of immediate commands, hence bad guidance to imperative differentiation. The link between language and action needs more sophisticated description than this; and it becomes necessary to re-emphasize that indicatives and imperatives, within an account of any sophistication, need to be seen as parts of a common language, and to be distinguished by their roles and relation within it.

Perhaps surprisingly, one of the best-known attempts to define and formalize such a joint language is subject to some of the same charges. Winograd ('Understanding Natural Language') designed a simulated 'robot' capable of receiving indicative, interrogative and imperative inputs, making rational replies to them, and taking appropriate action, in a model world in which variously coloured and shaped objects were manipulable with a grab-arm. It was a 'slave' machine in the sense that, subject to logical and physical constraints, it did what it was ordered to do and believed what it was told. The interest of the project is in the sophistication of the robot's ability to handle language. A possible dialogue (input and output by keyboard and screen):

    – Pick up a big red block
    – OK
What does the box contain?
    – The blue pyramid and a blue block.
How many blocks are not in the box?
    – Four of them.
Is at least one of them narrower than the one which I told you to
    pick up?
    – Yes, the red cube.
    – Put the littlest pyramid on top of it.
    – OK.

The program for the machine has to parse input sentences; to distill them for meaning; to keep a stock of facts in linguistic form, and relate them to the simulated physical world; make deductions, answer questions and interpret such things as descriptive phrases; and evolve strategies for, say, circumventing obstacles when carrying out orders. Faced with impossible tasks or questions, or undefined words or nonsense-grammar, it formulates appropriate objections.

Unfortunately, despite the prodigious array of features, the imperatives that figure in the dialogues between operator and robot – as Winograd himself might be among the first to admit – are of an extremely limited kind. The master-slave relationship between operator and robot, and the fact that only the operator issues imperatives, virtually ensures that only COMMANDS are represented, never requests, and never any non-wilful, accountable imperatives at all. There is therefore no representation of how an imperative may be justified or argued for, or of the logic this would require. There are no permissives, and there are no questions of the kind that require imperative answers. Even commands are all, again, of the *immediate* type, virtually mere names of ACTIONS, and are carried out, if at all, before conversation proceeds. Undertakings, unless we count the accompanying *OK*, are therefore unnecessary. It is not explained how the program will deal with a conjunctive command when it can obey only one of the conjuncts, but this would presumably be either by treating it as inseparable and objecting to the whole or by taking the conjuncts ordinally. Quantifiers can occur inside the scope of an imperative operator, but there is no provision for general imperatives such as RULES, and consequently no need for deductions involving them.

The fact that all the imperatives handled are immediate ones, and that none of them are of ongoing application, means that the robot never needs to store up undertakings for future occasions. This fact even greatly reduces the amount of strategic planning it needs to do, since although it could be necessary to plan for simultaneous satisfaction of all conjuncts of a conjunctive command, each whole new command can always be considered on its merits without reference to *other* imperatives held in store as undertakings. Strategies, in short, can always be total ones, for the uninterrupted carrying out of tasks of limited duration.

## TOWARDS A NOTATION

To a dialectical system, we need not so much a formal notation as an analytic shorthand. Since the object is to explicate the workings of natural language, it is natural language that it should deal with. But a compendious notation for selected features is as useful as in any theoretical study, to sharpen distinctions.

To the case of an all-indicative dialectical system (such as those of my *Fallacies*, ch. 7, and 'Mathematical Models'; Mackenzie, 'Begging the Question': Barth and Krabbe, *From Axiom*; Hintikka and Saarinen, 'Information-Seeking'), 'propositions' are most naturally represented in one of the standard notations, say, as 'states-of-affairs', $S_0, S_1, S_2, \ldots$, representing partial descriptions of some notional universe. In the case of a system that incorporates imperatives, we shall need much more. First, it is important to an imperative who the *subject* is, and who the *addressee*; and the phenomenon of the differential addressing of locutions – to one rather than another of those present and participating – cannot be ignored. (It is not, of course, always irrelevant in the indicative case; but it is possible to go some way without it.) Thus if $P_0$ says, to $P_1$ and $P_2$ together, that $P_1$ is to do $D$ this is, to $P_1$, an instruction to do $D$, and to $P_2$ an instruction that $P_1$ do $D$, whence it is really neither of these things alone; and $P_1$ says it to $P_0$ and/or $P_2$ it is at least an undertaking, if not some kind of deviant 'vicarious' instruction, whence it is not these things either. Without differential addressing we cannot make sense of these distinctions. Incidentally, it should be noted that there is no reason for potential subjects of third-person imperatives to be restricted to actual participants.

It will often be convenient to notate the addressee of a locution $L$ as if in an explicit vocative, and, for generality, let us make provision for putting the speaker in too. The speech-act that consists of $P_0$'s uttering to $P_1$ the locution $L$ can be represented,

$$P_0: P_1, L.$$

Where $L$ is indicative, it may as well be represented summarily as a (partial) world-state-description $S$; thus,

$$P_0: P_1, S$$

represents $P_0$'s addressing to $P_1$ a statement whose content is $S$. Where the locution is imperative, we shall in general also need to notate a subject; and since (as we noted earlier) state-defined imperatives are somewhat more general than act-defined ones, and imperatives speech-act can best take the form,

$$P_0: P_1, P_2 \; achv \; S,$$

where '*achv*' means 'achieve', and what is being represented is $P_0$'s saying to $P_1$ that $P_2$ is to (act so as to) achieve world-state $S$. The 'states' $S_0, S_1 \ldots$ of our now joint indictive-imperative language must be construed rather more widely than is usual in all-indicative logic, namely, as 'partial world histories' after the manner of chapter 4.

The easiest way to notate a 'Second-person' or 'plain-predicate' imperative is as a degenerate case,

$P_0; P_1, P_1 \, achv \, S,$

where the subject is explicitly the same as the addressee. Note, incidentally, that our doctrine that every imperative has an *addressee-action-reduction* has the consequence that every imperative can be put into this form. In fact, in reference to imperative commitment, we shall have to stipulate that every third-person imperative,

$P_0: P_1, P_2 \, achv \, S$

has a reduction or related form notable in some such was as,

$P_0: P_1, P_1 \, achv \, (P_2 \, achv \, S).$

Here $P_1$ is being enjoined to achieve a world-state within which $P_2$ achieves S.

When $P_0$ makes a statement and $P_1$ agrees with it, as in,

$P_0: P_1, S$
$P_1: P_0, S,$

the content 'S' of the agreeing statement is the same as that of the original. This feature is reproduced in the case of at least the simplest imperatives, where an addressee's agreement to an imperative is interpretable as an undertaking. An undertaking, in short, is an imperative locution whose subject is the utterer. The interchange,

$P_0: P_1 \, P_1 \, achv \, S$
$P_1: P_0, P_1 \, achv \, S$

represents an injunction of $P_0$ to $P_1$, followed by $P_1$'s acceptance of it. Only in the case of a third-person subject will it be necessary to qualify this pattern; thus,

$P_0: P_1, P_2 \, achv \, S,$

which enjoins $P_1$ (as primary agent) that $P_2$ is to achieve S, must be addressee-action-reduced before being transformed, and the corresponding undertaking is consequently not,

$P_1: P_0, P_2 \, achv \, S$

(which would be an imperative addressed back to $P_0$), but

$P_1: P_0, P_1 \, achv \, S).$

The simplest kinds of group-directed imperatives are easily accommodated by allowing groups to replace individuals. In particular, a (two-person) 'Let's-imperative is one whose subject is the utterer and addressee jointly, as in,

$P_0$: $P_1$, $\{P_0, P_1\}$ *achv S.*

This must be analysed as some kind of combined imperative and undertakings, and 'agreement' simply interchanges the two. (This, at least, is a first account; the detailed action-reduction may well be more complex.)

As we represent matters, a vocative prefixed to an imperative singles out not merely an addressee as it does in the case of indicatives and other locutions, but also the agent who is to be responsible for taking action; and this may be an oversimplification in the case of a many-person dialogue, in one sense, all understood listeners are addressees, and the vocative attached to an imperative singles out an *enjoinee*. More complicated stipulations would be necessary to deal with cases of multiple utterers, enjoinees and subjects; and with a variety of possible cases of misreference or ambiguity. But I do not take these up.

REFUSING

An addressee can *reject* an imperative, in the extreme case, by making a contrary undertaking; or he can refuse to make an undertaking either way. There are various other possibilities connected with different ones of our five negations of chapter 2. Given propositional negation applying to states, with $\bar{S}$ as the complementary state to $S$, the type 1 rejection of,

$P_0$: $P_1$, $P_2$ *achv S*

is,

$P_1$: $P_0$ $P_2$ *achv* $\bar{S}$

in the third-person case, and correspondingly in the degenerate cases. $P_1$ confronts the imperative that $P_2$ achieve $S$ by issuing one of his own, that $P_2$ achieve $\bar{S}$ instead. This does not reject the original imperative at all, except by implication since the two cannot be jointly satisfied. For a locution that *explicitly* rejects an imperative we need an 'illocutionary' negation, type 5. Looking ahead to dialectical system-building, let us write '*nocom*' (for 'no commitment') for this negation, applicable to indicatives and imperatives alike, and with a range of dialectical effects to be described in due course. An interchange in which locution $L$ is rejected without replacement is of the form

$P_0$: $P_1$ L

$P_1$: $P_0$, *nocom* L,

and, in particular, that type 5 rejection of,

$P_0$: $P_1$, $P_2$ *achv* S

is

$P_1$: $P_0$, *nocom* $P_2$ *achv* S.

Note that '*nocom*' must stand over a *whole* locution; with this proviso, degenerate cases again fall into place.

For a type 2 negation an indicator can be placed before '*achv*'; to help avoid misreading it should be a special one, say '*nst*' (for 'no-steps', for 'Don't take steps to'). I shall not here attempt a formulation of negation type 3.


CONDITIONALS, PERMISSIVES

Conditional imperatives, though they raise difficult points of logic, seem to raise none of grammar; we can surely, given a state-description S, prefix '*If S*,' to any locution L – indicative or imperative – without fear of solecism. In the case of imperatives, however, the *if*-clause should be placed after the subject, to indicate the person on whom the condition operates; there is a subtle difference between, say,

$P_0$: $P_1$, ($P_2$, *if* $S_0$, *achv* $S_1$)

and

$P_0$: $P_1$, *if* $S_0$, $P_2$ *achv* $S_1$,

in which the condition defaults to the addressee, and an equivalent more explicit form is,

$P_0$: $P_1$, ($P_1$, *if* $S_0$, *achv* ($P_2$ *achv* $S_1$)).

*Permissives*, as we saw, are commonly expressed by attaching to what is apparently an imperative a pseudo-conditional clause *if you wish*. Although this is not a true conditional – *Smoke if you wish* is not a conditional *injunction* to smoke – so treating it is probably the simplest way of incorporating permissives into our scheme. Let us write '*ifw*' (for 'if-wish', that is, 'if he/she/they/you . . . wish') to represent the psuedo-conditional clause, and consequently, for example,

$P_0$: $P_1$, $P_2$ *ifw achv* S

for $P_0$'s locution to $P_1$ to the effect that $P_2$ be permitted to achieve $S$. The placing of the *ifw* resolves, if necessary, the ambiguity concerning who has discretion to make the choice. This is (one case of) our negation type 4 whereby an imperative may be (confrontationally) rejected as in the interchange,

$P_0$, $P_1$, $P_2$ *achv* $S$
$P_1$: $P_0$, $P_2$ *ifw achv* $\bar{S}$.

Again, the addressee of a plain-predicate imperative can claim privilege to make up his own mind, as in the interchange,

$P_0$: $P_1$, $P_1$ *achv* $S$
$P_1$: $P_0$, $P_1$ *ifw achv* $\bar{S}$.

### THE VARIETIES

The imperatives we are representing are – except for one or two special points – indifferent as between COMMANDS, REQUESTS, ADVICE and imperatives of parallel varieties. But it would be counterproductive, from the dialectical point of view, to try to build the distinctions between these varieties into our dialectical notation; because it has been clear, throughout our discussion of them, that distinctions of force *are* largely a dialectical matter – of how locutions are traded – and not a matter of logical form. So, by distinguishing notationally between, say,

$P_0$: $P_1$, command $(P_2$ *achv* $S)$

and,

$P_0$: $P_1$, advise $(P_2$ *achv* $S)$

we would prejudge just the kind of issue on which a dialectical system is capable of throwing light. Development of our notation, if any, should lie in other directions.

One 'logical' limitation, though it will not much concern us, should be noted. Generally states-of-affairs $S_0$, $S_1$, $S_2$, . . . can be regarded as incorporating any distinctions made in general statements, with 'all', 'some', 'always' and so on. But the fact that we have separately notated imperative *subjects* means that imperatives with separably general subjects – in particular, with 'everybody', 'nobody' and so on – have been dropped out. We shall remedy the situation *ad hoc* as needed.

## A BASIC QUESTION-ANSWER SYSTEM

The parallelism between imperatives and indicatives, though not exact, has been in some sense maximized by the notation we have been devising. It is appropriate to consider now a basic dialectical system within which the parallelism is as far as possible still preserved. It can accommodate indicative and imperative questions.

A *dialectical system* is, as elsewhere in my own and other writings cited above (also Mackenzie 'The Dialectics' and Walton, 'Logical Dialogue-Games') a system of rules for the conduct of dialogue. Although the aim is obviously to explicate real-life dialogues, a *formal* system – like other formal systems within logic – aims not at descriptive accuracy but at analysis of particular features found to be of interest.

The 'formal' rules of the systems described in this chapter are informally presented. I assume that there is a fixed set of *participants* $P_0$, $P_1$, $P_2$, . . . , who politely take turns in uttering *locutions* (of some language) in suitable sequence. The dialogue is public to all of them. An important aid in the formulation of rules (of what constitutes a proper dialogue) is the concept of *commitment*; broadly, utterance of a locution *commits* the utterer in respect of the subsequent dialogue – not wilfully to repeat the utterance, not to utter locutions that immediately contradict it, and so on. Commitments may sometimes be withdrawn or lapse; it is convenient to think of the *current* commitments of each participant as recorded – publicly, since the dialogue is public – on a board or slate, whose contents at any time partially govern what it may be proper for one or another participant to say next. A commitment slate is an edited summary of the dialogue's preceding history. Various questions can be raised about the commitment-concept itself, such as the extent to which logical consequences of commitments are themselves commitments. Particular stipulations can be made as we need them.

*Questions* are most simply regarded as the sets of their possible answers; thus the question with the three possible indicative answers $S_0$, $S_1$, and $S_2$ can be represented,

$$(S_0, S_1, S_2)?$$

(The number of possible answers need not be finite; but we shall contine ourselves to simple cases.) A more careful definition is needed when imperatives are included: a *question* is any set of (say) two or more indicatives, or imperatives, or a mixture; a complete answer to it consists of any one of the indicatives or imperatives, or any heresis, or choice-offering disjunction, of the imperatives. For example, possible answers to,

$P_0$, $P_1$, $(S_0 \; P_0 \; achv \; S_0$, $P_1 \; achv \; S_1)$?

are,

$P_1$: $P_0$, $S_0$
$P_1$: $P_0$, $P_0 \; achv \; S_0$
$P_1$: $P_0$, $P_0 \; achv \; S_1$
$P_1$: $P_0$, $(P_0 \; achv \; S_0$ or $P_1 \; achv \; S_1)$.

That the disjunction in the last case is choice-offering can be made explicit by adding permissives,

and $P_0$ *ifw achv* $S_0$ and $P_1$ *ifw achv* $S_0$.

The general form of a locution-act of one participant $P_1$ addressing another $P_2$ is

$P_1$: $P_2$, $L$

where $L$ is a *locution* of one of the following varieties:

1. a statement $S$ $(S_0, S_1, S_2, \dots)$ or negation $\bar{S}$;
2. an imperative $P \; achv \; S$ (or $P \; achv \; S$), where $P$ is a person (not necessarily an actual participant) or group;
3. a conditionalized statement or imperative as already described;
4. a permissive with the pseudo-conditional *ifw*;
5. any of these preceded by *nocom*;
6. a question;
7. in selected cases, conjunctions and disjunctions of other locutions.

A *contribution* is a locution-act or uninterrupted string of locution-acts uttered by one participant, not immediately preceded or followed by other locution-acts of the same participant. Except as specified, we shall assume that each contribution consists of a single locution-act; but in appropriate circumstances it is necessary to permit more than one – for example to permit a participant to reject all proffered answers to a question, with a string of '*nocom*' locutions.

Although the listed locution-varieties are limited in scope (and we shall augment them a little later), their use permits a great variety of kinds of dialogue. The participants can make statements or withdraw them, issue imperatives or withdraw them, accept or reject statements or imperatives made to them, ask and fully or partly answer yes-no questions or questions with any finite number of alternative answers and imperative questions of the same types – including questions concerning undertakings, permissions, group-action and so on – or reject questions by indicating non-commitment to any of their answers.

The following snatches of dialogue illustrate special points.

$P_0$, $P_1$, $(S_0, P_0 \; achv \; S_1)$?
$P_1$: $P_0$, $S_0$

('Did you ring the plumber or shall I?' 'I have.')

$P_0$: $\{P_1, P_2\}$, $(P_0, P_1, P_2 \; achv \; S_0, \{P_0, P_1, P_2\} \; achv \; \bar{S}_0)$?
$P_1$: $\{P_0, P_2\}$, $\{P_0, P_1, P_2\} \; achv \; S_0$
$P_2$: $\{P_0, P_1\}$, $(P_2 \; achv \; (\{P_0, P_1, P_2\} \; achv \; \bar{S}_0); \{P_0, P_1\} \; ifw \; achv \; S_1)$

('Shall we go to dinner now?' 'Yes, let's.' 'No, but you two go on if you like.') It can be convenient to notate a conjunction ';'.

$P_0$: $P_1$, $(P_0 \; achv \; S_0, P_0 \; achv \; S_1)$?
$P_1$: $P_0$, $(nocom; P_0 \; achv \; S_2)$

('Shall I look on the shelves? Or the sorting-trolley?' 'Neither; use the desk copy.') It is convenient to let '*nocom*', alone, stand for the rejection of a preceding statement or imperative or of all alternatives of a preceding question.

$P_0$: $P_1$, $(P_0 \; achv \; S_0, P_0 \; achv \; (P_2 \; achv \; S_0))$?
$P_1$: $P_0$, $(P_0, if \; S_1, ifw \; achv \; S_0; P_0, if \; \bar{S}_1, achv \; (P_2 \; achv \; S_0))$

('Shall I do it myself or get John to do it?' 'You can do it yourself if you're sure you know how; get John to otherwise.') Conditionalization of answers can make good sense, though it is subject to some restrictions not here stated.

The *commitment* of each participant is a set of indicatives and/or imperatives, null at the start of a dialogue and subsequently defined recursively, any indicative or imperative being added to it when uttered by or addressed to him/her, deleted if he/she utters a withdrawal in the shape of a *nocom*-locution. Questions (for the present) do not affect commitments. That the *addressee* of an utterance is committed by it is an expression of the principle 'Silence gives consent', and its function is to guarantee that participants do not 'talk past one another' An addressee may, of course, immediately reject any commitment with a '*nocom*'.

We cannot realistically stipulate that participants are alive to all the logical relations between the various locutions of any dialogue; but it would be equally unrealistic to suppose that they appreciate none of them. For the sake of making some distinction, let us stipulate (without detail) that there are relations of *immediate consequence* and *immediate inconsistency*, and derived relations as needed, between the locutions, that embody the participants' (assumed common) intuitive logical appreciations. Now, here is a simple set of rules for question-answer dialogues. Lacking qualifications, it is over-stipulative; but all the dialogue-fragments so far used as examples, at least, conform with it.

1. Except as in (3), or in immediate agreement or disagreement with a statement or imperative by another participant, no statement or imperative must be uttered by any participant when the commitments of all other participants either contain it or contain an immediate antecedent of it, or when that of the utterer contains anything immediately inconsistent with it.

2. No contribution must contain more than one question.

3. When a given contribution contains a question, the following contribution must be by one of its addressees and contain an answer, or a rejection of the question with one or more *nocom*-locutions.

4. No question must be asked by any participant whose commitment has any answer as an immediate consequence, or with whose commitment any answer is immediately inconsistent.

5. When the commitment of any participant is immediately inconsistent he must, as part of his next contribution (if any), utter one or more *nocom*-locutions that render it consistent.

6. Except as in (3), a *nocom*-locution must not occur unless the statement or imperative it contains is already a commitment of the speaker.

7. No locution containing '*achv S*' may be uttered by any participant whose commitment, together with the content of any conditionals standing over the '*achv S*', is immediately antecedent to or inconsistent with *S*.

Rule (1) bans repetitiveness or self-contradiction; the ban on immediate consequences is severe in that it prevents the step-by-step drawing out of an argument. Rule (3) is indifferent as between a 'Don't know' locution (for which we have no expression) and a rejection of the question's presupposition. A question should possibly also commit its asker to its presupposition, namely, to a statement representing the disjunction of its answers, but a rule to this effect requires that the language be able to express all such disjunctions or equivalents of them. Rules (1) and (4) are reasonable on the assumption that the object of statements is to inform and that of imperatives is to give instructions, and that the corresponding objects of indicative and imperative questions are to seek information or instructions respectively; these rules require alteration if the relevant locutions are to be allowed to have other functions, Rule (6) is dispensable and merely outlaws unnecessary 'negative' locutions. Rule (7) bans the use of imperatives already held to be inevitably satisfied or dissatisfied.

## THE 'WHY?' QUESTION

The word *Why?*, in English, is multiply ambiguous; it can be a request for a causal explanation, a motive, a rational explanation, or rational justification or support, of a statement, an imperative or an action. I use it here exclusively in the sense of a request for rational justification; the other senses obtrude just occasionally where they overlap this one. To meet a why?-challenge to a statement or imperative it is necessary to produce one or more others which represent or are key steps in a rational (not necessarily deductive) argument supporting it.

Since susceptibility to support by argument is characteristic particularly of imperatives of the ADVICE and related varieties, we called these (in chapter 1) *accountable*, by contrast with those of the COMMAND and REQUEST varieties, which are *wilful*. However, another factor governing availability of *why?*-challenges to an imperative should be considered first.

An imperative, as we noted, may become unusable with the passage of time; it may *lapse*, in the sense that its satisfaction, or its dissatisfaction, may become temporally inevitable. This may, moreover, happen within the course of a dialogue, and we seem to need, after all, to modify our linguocentric stance to the extent of recognizing that it is outside facts that determine whether an imperative has lapsed or remains 'open' to take part in dialectical transactions. *Immediate* imperatives, in particular, lapse almost as soon as uttered, namely, as soon as the time for action arrives or has passed. *Why?*-challenges are inappropriate to these not because they are of the COMMAND variety (which they may not clearly be) but because they are immediate; there is simply no time between the issuing of the imperative and the time at which it would be too late to carry it out or desist from doing so.

Hence the main variety-differentiation the question of the availability of *why?*-challenges accomplishes for us is not that between wilful and accountable imperatives but that between immediate ('Whoa' – 'Giddap') imperatives and others. Details, to be sure, remain in part vague or specific to individual cases; but to stop and question an immediate imperative is to change its nature. It changes, as it were, the nature of the Wittgensteinian 'game' (and is, of course, clearly recognizable as a change in a dialectical pattern). Any genuine attempt at justification must be post-mortem.

The question whether a given, or a typical, *immediate* imperative is COMMAND, ADVICE or whatever must be answered, if at all, by appeal to other considerations – those, perhaps, of authority-relationship or relative expertise. But, in general, because of the non-availability of the key test, it will not be possible to answer it.

So let us turn to clearly *non*-immediate imperatives. And the first case that should claim our attention is that of dialogues during which there is no question of any relevant imperative's lapsing. We suppose, in short, that there are *no* temporal constraints on the issuing and meeting of '*Why?*'-challenges, since the relevant action is all future to the dialogue itself. This means that the dialogue can be regarded as being, as medieval logicians would have put it (Hamblin, *Fallacies*), *in eodem tempore*, conducted 'at a single point of time'. During the dialogue, no changes can take place in any of the properties of locutions in respect of their temporal references; and the justification of imperatives '$P$ *achv* $S$' can be discussed without question of their lapsing as the dialogue proceeds.

Rational justification of imperatives is not well understood. The premisses of Aristotle's practical syllogism, its unavoidable prototype, give respectively an end and a means; the end is usually evaluative or deontic and more general than the conclusion. The means-premiss gives neither a necessary nor a sufficient condition nor any strict causal connection, and sometimes the only thing singling out one means from others is that it is itself evaluable as 'good' or 'the best'. I make no attempt, here, to codify any dialectic embodying these complications. Let us suppose simply that an imperative can be supported by citing another *imperative*, and that *why?*-challenges are demands for such support. Although a pale parody of what is needed, these simplistic assumptions will set us on our road. We write '*why $P$ achv $S$?*' for a challenge to the imperative locution '$P$ *achv* $S$', or, for short, '*why?*' in reference to an imperative in a preceding contribution. (We shall have no need to consider justifications of indicatives.) Rules are added:

8. A *why?* or *why $P$ achv $S$?* challenge must be a whole contribution addressed only to a participant whose commitment contains $P$ *achv* $S$ or to a group all of whose commitments do so.

9. When a given contribution contains a *why?* or *why $P$ achv $S$?* challenge, the following contribution must be by one of its addressees and either begin with '*nocom $P$ achv $S$*' or a plain '*nocom*' or must consist of a single unconditional imperative.

Example:

$P_0$: $P_1$, $P_1$ *achv* $S_0$
$P_1$: $P_0$, *why?*
$P_0$: $P_1$, $\{P_0, P_1\}$ *achv* $S_1$.

('Put the rubbish in the bin'. 'Why?'. 'Let's avoid littering the area.')

A plain *nocom* is a rejection of the challenge; a single imperative is a proferred justification. Note that rule (7) banning the use of imperatives held to be lapsed prevents the use of these imperatives as justifications. That an imperative is challenged and duly justified does not, of course, identify it as accountable and non-wilful; for issuers of commands may speak as if from an assumption of pooled interests of commander and commandee – perhaps, but not necessarily hypocritical. Similarly issuers of requests. The availability of *why?*-challenges does not divide accountable imperatives from wilful ones.

But this is by no means the last word. Note, first, that the imperative offered as backing of a genuinely accountable imperative ought itself to be fully accountable, and challengeable as such in turn. An accountable backing can be properly offered for a wilful imperative, but not *vice versa*. It follows that we can identify an imperative as wilful if we can identify its issuer's justification as wilful. The issuer, for example, may reply 'Because *I want to* (achieve so-and-so)'; we have no notation for this, but another case might be that in which the proffered backing is an undertaking,

$P_0$: $P_1$, $P_1$ *achv* $S$
$P_1$: $P_0$, *why?*
$P_0$: $P_1$, $P_0$ *achv* ($P_1$ *achv* $S$).

The pattern is again available for (hard-pressed) requests.

Can an issuer of advice *refuse* to back it? A dialogue such as,

$P_0$: $P_1$, $P_1$ *achv* $S$
$P_1$: $P_0$, *why?*
$P_0$: $P_1$, *nocom*

– though we have nominated it legal – could be held to type the imperative as non-accountable. No doubt, in some cases, the refusal might be otherwise explained away; but there is, least, a *prime facie* case.

When advice is *rejected* – in virtually any form – the rejection is as challengeable as the advice:

$P_0$: $P_1$, $P_1$ *achv* $S_0$
$P_1$: $P_0$, *nocom*; $P_1$ *achv* $\bar{S}_0$
$P_0$: $P_1$, *why?*
$P_1$: $P_0$, ($P_0$, $P_1$) *achv* $S_1$.

But must the backing then be accountable? Would, for example,

$P_1$: $P_0$, $P_1$ *achv* ({$P_0$, $P_1$} *achv* $S_1$)

be available as an alternative last line? ('Sit down and be comfortable'. 'No, I shall leave in a moment.') Yes; advice may be based on a perception of what the advisee *wants*. But an adviser can also press arguments that would override this. The subsequent course of the dialogue can determine the issue; the advisee who is prepared to debate his rejection helps to determine as accountable not merely the rejection but the original. Rejections of other kinds – such as with '*inst*' or '*ifw*' – seem not to raise different considerations.

The backing offered for accountables is not only usually more general – evaluative or deontic, what the traditional moral philosopher calls 'universalisable' – than the imperative being backed; it is quite inappropriate for it to be *less so. By comparison with typical imperatives, evaluative and deontic locutions are impersonal or interpersonal, and a 'Something ought to be done to achieve so-and-so' or 'Such-and-such shouldn't be the case' can hardly be justified by anything resembling our 'P achv S'.* The point cannot be pursued in detail without elaborating our notation; but if, temporarily, we let plain '*achv S*' represent an 'Impersonal imperative' we can express some sort of distinction by saying that '*achv $S_1$*' can justify '*P achv $S_0$*' but not vice versa. (The notation is inadequate to capture some subtleties – in particular concerning conditionalization.)

Even given an extended dialogue-sample, nothing we have said goes far enough to permit reliable division of accountable imperatives from wilful; and perhaps nothing could. At best, strong pointers are provided. If we go on now to consider subvarieties; COMMANDS and REQUESTS (in the wilful category) seem best distinguished by conceiving utterer and utteree to stand in an authority-relationship; and DEMANDS from these by conceiving them as 'socially irregular', in the sense that there is a relationship they step out of. And these distinctions, fashioned outside and often independently of dialogue, not only have dialectical manifestations but are regularly signalled and reinforced by them. An authority-relation of a sort, perhaps quite temporary, can develop or dissipate at short notice and consist of little more than a pattern of behaviour displaying a peck-order. DEMANDS *become* COMMANDS after, for a while, they have been regularly acceded to, or REQUESTS if they have not; and REQUESTS can similarly merge into COMMANDS, and vice versa. It is not so clear that this process is not dialectical; though I do not suggest that this is the place to start trying to model it.

In the accountable category, the main distinction we have not discussed – between ADVICE and SUGGESTIONS – can perhaps be disposed of with the remark that though the rejection of a piece of advice may need to be reasoned for, the rejection of a suggestion can always be wilful.

## THE 'HOW?' QUESTION

The question *How?* asked of imperatives, in English, is ambiguous as between manner and means; I use it here as a request for a specification of means. *How?* can be asked of a certain class of indicatives too, namely, those that describe deliberate actions or, somewhat less certainly, non-deliberate actions or the happenings of some personifiable natural agent. (In the latter case it may resemble the *Why?* that asks for a cause.) But *How?* can always be asked of imperatives.

In the case of a *how?*-challenge to an imperative it is hardly possible, in practice, to conceive of a 'complete' answer, since the breakdown of a task into more elementary ones can proceed to any degree of fineness. (Only 'basic actions' could end the process. A. Baier, 'Ways and Means' regards this as definitional of them.) In a sense, the reply to a *how?*-challenge is an inverse of that to a *why?* one; it specifies a means to an enjoined end, rather than an end for an enjoined means. ('Let's avoid littering the area.' 'How?' 'Put your rubbish in the bin') The specification of means is imperative, but indicative information may be needed as well, or may be the missing link in an action-reduction otherwise obvious. However, I shall again be content with a simplistic addition to our system. Let '*how?*' and '*how L?*' (for any imperative $L$) be added to our locutions, and the following to our rules:

10. A *how?* or *how P achv S?* challenge must be a whole contribution addressed only to a participant whose commitment contains *P achv S* or to a group all of whose commitments do so.
11. When a given contribution contains a *how?* or *how P achv S?* challenge, the following contribution must be by one of its addressees and either begin with *nocom P achv S* or a plain *nocom* or must consist of a conjunction of (one or more) possibly conditional imperatives and possibly conditional choice-offering disjunctions of imperatives.

In short, the rules are as for why?-challenges except that answers may consist of complexes of imperatives instead of just single ones.

Examples:

$P_0$: $P_1$, $P_1$ *achv* $S$
$P_1$: $P_0$, *how?*
$P_0$: $P_1$, $P_1$ *achv* ($P_2$ *achv* $S$)

('Fix the swivel-arm.' 'How?' 'Get Bloggs on to it.')

$P_1$: $P_0$, *how* $\{P_0, P_1\}$ *achv* $S_0$
$P_0$: $P_1$, ($P_1$ *achv* $S_1$; $P_0$ *achv* $S_2$)

('How shall we arrange for you to arrive first?' 'You take the high road and I'll take the low road.')

$P_1$: $P_0$, *how* $P_1$ *achv* $S_0$?
$P_0$: $P_1$, (*if* $S_1$, $P_1$ *achv* $S_2$; *if* $\bar{S}_1$, ($P_1$ *achv* $S_3$ *or* $P_1$ *achv* $S_4$))

('How should I go home?' 'If it rains, stick to the expressway; otherwise by the old road or the second turn-off.')

Just a few comments need to be made, in connection with *how?*-questions, concerning the differentiation of varieties.

First, the issuer of a *wilful* imperative, though he may choose to answer a *how?*-question, cannot be expected to do so or even to know the answer; the choice of means, or even the task of finding a means, can be delegated, and the issuing of the imperative could even be regarded as implying delegation. The case is a little different if the imperative is accountable; for advice is not very good if there is a question of how to put it into effect, and the advisor's expertise should normally extend to this. If he cannot so extend it at least to the extent of providing key features of an answer he has not, quite, given advice.

It seems to follow that the dialogue,

$P_0$: $P_1$, $P_1$ *achv* $S$
$P_1$: $P_0$, *how?*
$P_0$: $P_1$, *nocom*,

other things being equal, types the imperatives as wilful.

But SUGGESTIONS ('You could . . .', 'Why not . . .') come into their own in answers to *how?* to accountables. We have no notation to distinguish them clearly from fully-fledged advice-imperatives; but, oddly, even in natural language, they merge with permissives. We can have:

$P_0$: $P_1$, $P_1$ *achv* $S_0$
$P_1$: $P_0$, *how?*
$P_0$: $P_1$, ($P_1$ *ifw achv* $S_1$; $P_1$ *ifw achv* $S_2$)

('Find it in the work-area.' 'How do I do that?' 'Search the desks if you like. Or you can see if the sorters have spotted it.') Suggestions may often be a matter of denying imagined prohibitions.

Answers to *how?*-questions are, of course, RECIPE-like; questioned in turn with *why?*, they call for answers that are more impersonal and 'universalizable'. But this fact is incidental to the differentiation issue. Note that a *how?*-challenge to a permissive is answerable in *the same* terms as one to the corresponding imperative. The means to implementation are the same and do not divide the cases.

## THE ACTION LINK

How people really decide to act, or what action they take when they do so, is not a dialectical matter, if only because it is not linguistic. It is true that some parts of it can be verbalized, and that drives, intentions, wishes, resolutions, decisions, . . . are (in their relevant roles) what we have called *para-imperative*; this says that their contents are specified in the same way as those of imperatives (*to* instead of *that*) and that they share some part of imperatives' grammar and other features. (Vendler, and others have made parallel lists.) This means that there can at least sometimes be a logical process associated with the answering of a (usually, self-addressed) question 'What to do, now?'). The relevant influences are all regarded as equivalent to imperative ones, and so expressed, beside expressions of the relevant perceived or recieved facts; after which the determination of the consequences for action may be mechanical. The relevant logic is an adaptation of that of our chapter 5.

Life is not like that, and the process is not merely artificial but is, at best, a theoretical reconstruction of what really goes on. But there is a dialectical correlate. The set of imperatives *in the commitment* of any participant in a dialogue can have (logically) *immediate consequences* for action, immediate or at whatever time. Since these are, in principle, public to all participants, they are at least capable of being conceived as relevant to the dialgoue and of influencing it. The question what each participant is *committed* to do, now or at any time, is one to which all participants notionally keep track of the answer.

The sense in which imperatives 'lead from linguistic behavior to non-linguistic behavior' is this: Action in accordance with commitment has a conventional claim on participants, resembling the convention that what they say obeys dialectical rules. To flout commitments to action is to weaken the conventions that give meaning to the language. The 'committed-action convention' is like the 'truth-telling convention' of Searle, (' Classification) and Lewis (*Convention*; see Wunderlich, 'Assertions, Conditional Speech Acts').

'Points of order' of the kind with which participants regulate their own dialogue (see my *Fallacies*, pp. 283-4, and Mackenzie. 'How to') can as readily be raised to promote and maintain this kind of convention. The pressure they exert is not necessarily, of course, pressure to action; it can as easily be pressure to retract a commitment.

## BELIEF AND INTENTION

There are two parts of the soul, said Aristotle (1140b25), that can follow reasoning. Are there?

If the distinction between indicatives and imperatives had to be based (à la Grice) on that between beliefs and intentions, Aristotle's dichotomy would be central to all our considerations. But what, again, really goes on in our minds as we contemplate, utter and reason?

Indicative commitments are not beliefs, though critics of the *genre* often, confusedly, seem to think so. The utterer of a lie is as committed by it as if it were not one; he incurs a commitment that is not a belief. If commitments were the same as beliefs it would be impossible for anyone ever to tell a lie.

In fact, so far as commitments are concerned, the actual mental contents – beliefs or whatever – of utterers have no relevance. As I speak, I may be thinking something else entirely, or nothing. It makes no difference to the conversational functioning of what I *say*.

Hobbesian corporate persons such as the Electricity Supply Company (as pointed out to me by J.D. Mackenzie) incur commitments, and can perhaps even be regarded as constituted by the fact that they do so; but they do not have beliefs. The personal beliefs of the Secretary or Chief Accountant do not qualify.

Imperative commitments,now – for the same reasons – are not intentions, or wishes, or volitions, or anything of that kind. There can be 'lies' in which they are incurred without mental accompaniments, or with irrelevant or contrary ones.

In specifying that participants, commitments are null at the start of a dialogue we made an – admittedly partly arbitrary – determination which (of course?) was in no way meant to imply that participants start beliefless, or that this is likely to be the presumption of those they talk to (see Walton, Logical Dialogue Games). The only way the postulation of existing *commitments* should be justified would be by the production of evidence concerning previous relevant conversations between the same participants, or – though the supposition is a stretched one – by the language-community's being so tightly-knit that its members could be regarded as born or educated into certain generally recognized pre-agreements.

But the strongest argument for the recognition of the distinction is methodological. A concept of dialectical commitment, indicative or imperative, is natural and intuitive as soon as we theorise about how people talk to one another. The question of what a language-user is *committed* to by what he says involves practical, but no burning theoretical, obscurities. In essence, his commitment is an edited transcript of what he *says*.

A language-user's (or anyone else's) beliefs or other mental contents are, by comparison, often not well-defined at all – determined by induction from behaviour-analysis, even counterfactual what X *believes* is what he/she *would* tell you *if* you got him/her in an honest, clear-headed and frank mood. It is true that the terms *honest* and *frank* themselves raise questions (the *same* questions!); but the independent tests of their applicability – consistency, accompanying behaviour, conformity to a view of human nature (in general, or of the relevant speaker in particular) – cannot be ignored where any communication that is not superficially verbal is considered.

The concept of indicative commitment is not an abstraction from or idealization of that of belief; it is the other way round. Let us imagine conversations in which honesty, clear-headedness and frankness are complete – in which, as it were, the speakers commitments have become internalized – and we have reached the first stage of an analysis of what it is for people to have in their heads – as ultimately required by the use of the concept of belief – stores of (propositional) *beliefs*. In short, the concept of belief is an idealization of that of indicative commitment.

The parallel with imperatives is immediate enough not to need to be traced in detail. The concepts of intention, wish, will ... are idealizations at imperative commitment, for different imperative varieties.

# Bibliography

Achinstein, Peter. From Success to Truth. *Analysis* **21** (1960), 6-9.

Ackrill, John Lloyd (ed.) *Aristotle's Ethics*. London, Faber, 1973.

Acton, H.B. 'The Expletive Theory of Morals', *Analysis* **4** (1936), 42-5.

Alchourrón, Carlos E., 'Logic of Norms and Logic of Normative Propositions', *Logique et Analyse* **12** (1969), 242-68.

Aldrich, V.C. ('Do Commands Express Propositions?', *Journal of Philosophy* **40** (1943), 654-7.

Anderson, Alan Ross. 'Some Nasty Problems in the Logic of Ethics', *Noûs* **1** (1967), 345-60.

*The Formal Analysis of Normative Systems*. Federal Report no. 2, Contract no. SAR/Nonr-609(16), Office of Naval Research, Group Psychology Branch, New Haven, 1956. Also in Rescher, N. (ed.) *The Logic of Decision and Action*, Pittsburgh, University of Pittsburgh Press, 1966; p. 147-213. With new preface and supplementary bibliography.

Angstl, Helmut. On the Logic of Norms: A Natural Deontics', in *Ratio* **19** (1977), 58-67.

Anscombe, Gertrude Elizabeth Margaret. *Intention*. Oxford, Blackwell, 1957.

Anselm of Canterbury, Saint. Lambeth Manuscript 59, in Schmitt, F.S. and R.W. Southern (eds.), *Memorials of St Anselm*, London, Oxford U.P., 1969, 333-54.

Apostel, Leo 'Practical Modalities, Practical Inference and Practical Knowledge'. *Communication and Cognition* 6(1976), 173-218.

Åqvist, Lennart. 'Choice-Offering and Alternative-Presenting Disjunctive Commands'. *Analysis* **25** (1965), 185-7.

'A Binary Primitive in Deontic Logic'. *Logique et Analyse* **5** (1962), 90-7.

'Deontic Logic Based on a Logic of "Better"'. *Acta Philosophica Fennica* **16** (1963), 285-90.

'Good Samaritans, Contrary-to-Duty Imperatives and Epistemic Obligations'. *Nous* **1** (1967), 361-79.

*Performatives and Verifiability by the Use of Language. A Study in Applied Logic of Indexicals and Conditionals*. Uppsala, Filosofiska Föreningen och Filosofiska Institutionen vid Uppsala Universitetet, 1972 (*Filosofiska Studier*, 14).

*A New Approach to the Logical Theory of Interrogatives*. Tübingen, TBL Verlag Gunter Barr, 1975. (New Edition.)

'On the "Tell Me Truly"' Approach to the Analysis of Interrogatives').
University of Uppsala, unpublished paper, 1980.

Arbini, Ronald, 'Tag-Questions and Tag-Imperatives in English', *Journal of Linguistics* 5 (1969), 205-14.

Árdal, Páll S. 'Threats and Promises: a reply to Vera Peetz'. *Mind* 88 (1979), 586-7. 'And That's a Promise'. *Philosophical Quarterly* 18 (1968), 225-37.

Aristotle *Nichomachean Ethics*.
*The Movement of Animals.*
*Poetics.*

Armstrong, David M. *'Meaning and Communication'*. *Philosophical Review* 80 (1971), 427-47.

Atiyah, P.S. 'Promises and the Law of Contract'. *Mind* 88 (1979), 410-18.

Aune, Bruce 'Can', in Edwards, P. (ed) *The Encyclopaedia of Philosophy* vol. 2., New York, Macmillan, 1967 18-20.

Austin, John. *The Province of Jurisprudence Determined* (1832). London, Weidenfeld & Nicolson, 1954. (Library of Ideas)

Austin, John Langshaw. 'Other Minds'. *Proceedings of the Aristotelian Society*, supplementary volume 20 (1946), 148-87. Also in Flew, A. (ed.) *Logic and Language* Oxford, Blackwell, 1961, 123-58.

'Ifs and Cans'. *Proceedings of the British Academy* vol. XLII, (1956), 109-32, reprinted in Austin, J.L. *Philosophical Papers* (ed.) Urmson and Warnock. Oxford, Clarendon, 1961.

*How to do Things with Words* (ed.) J.O. Urmson Oxford, Clarendon, 1962.

'Three Ways of Spilling Ink'. *Philosophical Review* 75 (1966), 427-40.

Ayer, Sir Alfred Jules. *Language Truth and Logic*. London, Gollancz, 1936.

Baier, Annette C. 'Ways and Means. *Canadian Journal of Philosophy* 1 (1971), 275-93.

'The Search for Basic Actions'. *American Philosophical Quarterly* 8 (1971), 161-70.

'Intention, Practical Knowledge and Representation' in Brand, Myles and Walton, Douglas *Action Theory*. Dordrecht, Reidel, 1976 27-43.

Baier Kurt. 'Ability Power and Authority'. Paper to AAP Conference, Canberra, August 1974.

Barnes, Winston H.F. 'Ethics without Propositions'. *Proceedings of the Aristotelian Society, supplementary volume* 22 (1948), 1-30.

Barth, E.M. and Krabbe, E.C.W. *From Axiom to Dialogue: A Philosophical Study of Logics and Argumentation*. Berlin and New York, Walter de Gruyter, 1982.

Beardsley, Elizabeth Lane. 'Imperative Sentences in Relation to Indicatives'. *Philosophical Review* 53 (1944), 175-85.

Belnap, Nuel D., Jr. *An Analysis of Questions: Preliminary Report*. Santa Monica, California, System Development Corporation, 1963. (Technical Memorandum TM1287/000/00.)

Bennett, Jonathan. 'Whatever the Consequences' *Analysis* 26 (1966), 83-102. 'Acting and Refraining'. *Analysis* 28 (1967), 30-1).

Bentham, Jeremy. *An Introduction to the Principles of Morals and Legislation*. London, Athlone Press, 1970.

Bible Book of Judges 11.

Bird, G.H. 'Confusing the Audience'. *Analysis* 35 (1975), 135-9.

Boden, Margaret A. *Minds and Mechanisms; Philosophical Psychology and Computational Models*. Sussex, Harvester, 1981.

Bohnert, H.G. 'The Semiotic Status of Commands'. *Philosophy of Science* 12 (1945), 302-05.

Bolinger, Dwight. 'The Imperative in English' in *To Honor Roman Jakobson: Essays on the Occasion of his Seventieth Birthday* The Hague, Mouton, 1967; vol. 1, 335-62. (Janua Linguarum, series maior, 31.)

Bosanquet, Bernard. *Logic, or the Morphology of Knowledge*. Oxford, Oxford University Press, 1888. 2nd ed. 1911.

Bosque, Ignacio. 'Retrospective Imperatives'. *Linguistic Inquiry* 11(1980), 415.

Boyd, Julian and Thorne, James Peter. 'The Semantics of Modal Verbs'. *Journal of Linguistics* 5 (1969), 57-74.

Brand, Myles. 'Danto on Basic Actions'. *Nous* 2 (1968), 187-90.
'The Language of Not Doing'. *American Philosophical Quarterly* 8 (1971, 45-53.

Brentano, Franz Clemens. *Vom Ursprung sittlicher Erkenntnis/The Origin of the Knowledge of Right and Wrong* translated by Cecil Hague. New York, Dutton, 1902.

Broad, C.D. 'Some Reflections on Moral-Sense Theories in Ethics'. *Proceedings of the Aristotelian Society* 45 (1944-45), 131-66.

Broadie, Alexander. 'Imperatives'. *Mind* 81 (1972), 179-90.

Burch, Robert William. 'Cohen, Austin and Meaning'. *Ratio* 15 (1973), 117-24.


Carnap, Rudolf. '*Philosophy and Logical Syntax*'. London, Kegan Paul, 1935.
'Testability and Meaning'. *Philosophy of Science* 3 (1936), 419-71 and 4 (1937), 1-4.

Carr, D. 'The Logic of Knowing How and Ability', *Mind* 88 (1979), 394-409.
'Speaker Meaning and Illocutionary Acts'. *Philosophical Studies* 34 (1978), 281-91.

Castañeda, Hector-Neri. 'The Logic of Obligation'. *Philosophical Studies* 10 (1959), 17-23.
'Outline of a Theory on the General Logical Structure of the Language of Action'. *Theoria* 26 (1960), 151-82.
'Imperatives, Decisions and Ought's: A Logico-Metaphysical Investigation' in Nakhnikian, G and Castañeda, H.N. (eds) *Morality and the Language of Conduct* Detroit, Wayne State University Press, 1963, 219-99.
'A Problem for Utilitarianism'. *Analysis* 28 (1968), 141-2.
'There are Command Sh-Inferences'. *Analysis* 31 (1971), 13-19.

Chellas, Brian F. *The Logical Form of Imperatives* Stanford, Perry Lane Press, 1969. 'Imperatives' in *Theoria* 37 (1971), 114-29.

Chisholm, Roderick M. 'Supererogation and Offence: A Conceptual Scheme for Ethics'. *Ratio* 5 (1963), 1-14.
'The Ethics of Requirement'. *American Philosophical Quarterly* 1 (1964), 1-7.
'The Agent as Cause' in Brand Myles and Walton, Douglas (eds) *Action Theory* Dordrecht, Reidel, 1976, 199-212.

Chomsky, Noam. *The Logical Structure of Linguistic Theory* New York, Plenum Press, 1975.

Clark, Herbert H. 'Responding to Indirect Speech Acts'. *Cognitive Psychology* 11, (1979), 430-77.

Cohen, Laurence Jonathan. 'Do Illocutionary Forces Exist?' *Philosophical Quarterly* 14 (1964), 118-37.

Cohen, Ted. 'Illocutions and Perlocutions. *Foundations of Language* 9 (1973), 492-503.

Collingwood, Robin George. *An Essay in Metaphysics*. Oxford, Clarendon Press, 1940.

Conee, Earl. 'Against Moral Dilemmas'. *Philosophical Review* 91 (1982), 87-97.

Copp, David. 'Hobbes on Artificial Persons and Collective Actions'. *Philosophical Review* 89 (1980), 579-606.

Cornides, Thomas. 'Der Widerruf von Befehlen'. *Studium Generale* 22 (1969), 1215-63.

Cresswell, Maxwell J. 'Some Further Semantics for Deontic Logic'. *Logique et Analyse* 10 (1967), 179-91.

*Logics and Languages*. London, Methuen, 1973.


Danielson, Sven. 'Definitions of "Performative". *Theoria* 31 (1965), 20-31.

Danto, Arthur, C. 'What We Can Do. *Journal of Philosophy* 60 (1963), 435-45.

'Basic Actions'. *American Philosophical Quarterly* 2 (1965), 141-8.

'Freedom and Forbearance'. Lehrer, K. (ed.) *Freedom and Determinism* New York, Random House, 1966, 45-63.

*Analytical Philosophy of Action*. Cambridge, Cambridge University Press, 1973.

D'Arcy, Eric. *Human Acts: an Essay in Their Moral Evaluation* Oxford, Clarendon Press, 1963.

Davison, Alice. 'Indirect Speech Acts and What to do with Them', in Cole, Peter and Morgan, Jerry (eds) *Syntax and Semantics vol 3: Speech Acts*. New York and London, Academic Press, 1975, 143-85.

Dennett, Daniel C. *Brainstorms: Philosophical Essays on Mind and Psychology*. Sussex, Harvester, 1978.

Diggs, B.J. 'A Technical Ought', *Mind* 69 (1960), 301-17.

Dinello, Daniel. 'On Killing and Letting Die'. *Analysis* 31 (1971), 83-6.

Downing, Bruce T. 'Vocatives and Third-Person Imperatives in English'. *Papers in Linguistics* 1 (1969), 570-92.

'Subjunctive Conditionals, Time Order and Causation'. *Proceedings of the Aristotelian Society* 59 (1958), 125-40.

'Opposite Conditionals and Deontic Logic'. *Mind* 70 (1961), 491-502.

Dubislav, W. 'Zur Unbegrundbarkeit der Forderungssatze'. *Theoria* 3 (1937), 330-42.

Dummett, Michael. 'Truth' *Proceedings of the Aristotelian Society* 59 (1958), 141-62. Reprinted in Pitcher, G. (ed.) *Truth*. Englewood Cliffs, Prentice-Hall, 1964.

'Bringing About the Past'. *Philosophical Review* 73 (1964) 338-59. Reprinted in Gale, Richard M. (ed.) *The Philosophy of Time*. London, Macmillan, 1968; 252-74.

Duncan-Jones, A.E. 'Assertions and Commands'. *Proceedings of the Aristotelian Society* 52 (1952), 189-206.

Ehrman, Madeline Elizabeth. *The Meanings of the Modals in Present-Day American English*. The Hague, Mouton, 1966. (Janua Linguarum Series Practica no 45).

Falk, W.D. 'Goading and Guiding'. *Mind* 62 (1953), 145-71.
Field, G.C. 'Note on Imperatives', *Mind* 59 (1950), 230-2.
Fillmore, Charles. 'Subjects, Speakers and Roles'. *Synthese* 21 (1970), 251-74.
Fitzgerald, P.J. 'Acting and Refraining', *Analyse* 27 (1966), 133-9.
Fraassen, Bas C. Van. 'The Logic of Conditional Obligation'. *Journal of Philosophical Logic* 1 (1972), 417-38.
'Values and the Hearts Command'. *Journal of Philosophy* 70 (1973), 5-19.
Fries, Charles Carpenter. *The Structure of English*. New York, Harcourt Brace, 1952.

Gale, R.M. 'Do Performative Utterances Have any Constantive Function?' *Journal of Philosophy* 67 (1970), 117-21.
Garner, Richard T. 'Some Doubts About Illocutionary Negation. *Analysis* 31 (1971), 106-12.
Geach, Peter Thomas 'Imperative and Deontic Logic'. *Analysis* 18 (1958), 49-56. Reprinted in Geach, P.T., *Logic Matters*. Oxford, Blackwell, 1972.
'Ascriptivism'. *Philosophical Review* 69 (1960), 221-5. Reprinted in Thomson, J. and Dworkin, G. :eds.) *Ethics*. New York, Harper & Row, 1968, 22-6.
'Reply to Gert and Martin. *Analysis* 33 (1973), 173 and 191-2.
Gean, W.D. 'Reasons and Causes'. *Review of Metaphysics* 19 (1965-66), 667-88.
Gert, Bernard and Martin, James A. 'Outcomes and Abilities'. *Analysis* 33 (1973), 188-92.
'What a Man Does He Can Do?' *Analysis* 33 (1973), 168-73.
Geukens, Steven K.J. 'The Distinction between Direct and Indirect Speech Acts: Towards a Surface Approach'. *Journal of Pragamtics* 2 (1978), 261-76.
Gibbons, Peter C. 'Imperatives and Indicatives'. *Australasian Joural of Philosophy* 38 (1960), 107-19 and 207-19.
Gombay, Andre. 'What *is* Imperative Inference?' *Analysis* 27 (1967), 145-52.
Gordon, David and Lakoff, George. 'Conversational Postulates'. *Papers from the Regional Meetings, Chicao Linguistic Society* 7 (1971), 63-84.
Graham, Keith. *J.L. Austin: A Critique of Ordinary Language*. Hassocks, Harvester, 1977. (Harvester Studies in Philosophy)
Grant, Colin King. 'Promises'. *Mind* 58 (1949), 359-66.
'Imperatives and Meaning'. The Royal Institute of Philosophy *Lectures vol. 1: The Human Agent, 1966-1967*, London, Macmillan, 1968.
Green, Georgia M. 'How to Get People To Do Things With Words: The Whimperative Question' in Cole, Peter and Morgan Jerry (eds.) *Syntax and Semantics, vol. 3: Speech Acts*. London, Academic Press, 1975; 107-41.
Greenspan, Patrica S. 'Conditional Oughts and Hypothetical Imperatives'. *Journal of Philosophy* 72 (1975), 259-76.
Grice, H.P. 'Meaning'. *Philosophical Review* 66 (1957), 377-88.
'Logic and Conversation' in Cole, Peter and Morgan, Jerry (eds.) *Syntax and Semantics, vol 3: Speech Acts* London Academic Press, 1975; 41-58.

Gruner, Rolf. On the Action of Social Groups' *Inquiry* 19 (1976), 443-54.

Gustafson, Donald. 'Expression of Intention'. *Mind* 83 (1974), 321-40.

'The Range of Intention'. *Inquiry* 18 (1975), 83-95.

Hall, Everett Wesley. *What is Value? An Essay in Philosophical Analysis.* New York, Humanities Press, 1952.

Halldén, Sören. *On The Logic of 'Better'.* Lund, Gleerup, and Copenhagen, Munksgaard, 1957. (Library of Theoria).

Hamblin, Charles Leonard. *Fallacies.* London, Methuen, 1970.

'Mathematical Models of Dialogue' *Theoria* 27(1971) 130-55.

'Quandaries and the Logic of Rules'. *Journal of Philosophical Logic* 1 (1972) 74-85.

Hanson, William H. 'Semantics for Deontic Logic'. *Logique et Analyse* 8 (1965), 177-90.

'A Logic of Commands' in *Logique et Analyse* 9 (1966), 329-348.

Hare, Richard Mervyn. 'Imperative Sentences'. *Mind* 58 (1949), 21-39. Also in R.M. Hare. *Practical Inference.* London, Macmillan, 1971.

*The Language of Morals.* Oxford, Oxford University Press, 1952. 'Some Alleged Differences between Imperatives and Indicatives'. *Mind* 76(1967), 309-26. Also in R.M. Hare. *Practical Inference* London, Macmillan, 1971.

'Meaning and Speech Acts'. *Philosophical Review* 79 (1970), 3-24. Also in R.M. Hare. *Practical Inference.* London, Macmillan, 1971.

'Wanting: Some Pitfalls' in Binkley, R., Bronaugh, R. and Marras, A. (eds) *Agent Action and Reason.* Toronto, University of Toronto Press, 1971. Also in R.M. Hare. *Practical Inference.* London, Macmillan, 1971.

Harrison, Jonathan. 'Knowing and Promising'. Mind 71 (1962), 443-57.

Hart, H.L.A. 'The Ascription of Responsibility and Rights'. *Proceedings of the Aristotelian Society* 49-50 (1948-50), 171-94.

Hartnack, Justus. 'The Performatory Use of Sentences'. *Theoria* 29 (1963), 137-46.

Hedenius Ingemar. 'Performatives' *Theoria* 29 (1963), 115-36.

Heil, John. 'Doxastic Incontinence. *Mind* 93 (1984), 56-70.

Heringer, James Tromp JR. 'Some Grammatical Correlates of Felicity Conditions and Presuppositions'. *Ohio State University Working Papers in Linguistics* 11 (1972), 4-110.

Hintikka, Kaarlo Jaakko Juhani. 'Questions About Questions', in Munitz, Milton K. and Unger, Peter K. (eds) *Semantic and Philosophy.* New York, New York University Press, 1974.

Hintikka, Kaarlo Jaako Juhani and Saarinen, Esa, 'Information-seeking Dialogues; some of their logical properties', *Studia Logica* 32 (1979), 355-63.

Hobart, R.E. (Pseudonym for Miller, Dickinson S.) 'Free Will as Involving Determinism and Inconceivable Without It'. *Mind* 43 (1934), 1-27.

Hobbes, Thomas. *Leviathan* (1651). London, Dent, 1914. (Everyman's Library 691).

Hofmann, T.R. 'Past Tense Replacement and the Modal System'. Harvard University Computation Laboratory, Mathematical Linguistics and Automatic Translation, *Report no NSF-17 to the National Science Foundation,* 1966 VII-2 – VII-21.

Hostadter, Albert and Mckinsey, J.C.C. 'On the Logic of Imperatives'.

*Philosophy of Science* 6 (1939), 446-57.
Holdcroft, David. *Words and Deeds: Problems in the Theory of Speech Acts.* Oxford, Clarendon, 1978.
Honoré, A.M. 'Can and Can't' *Mind* 73 (1964), 463-79.
Houston, J. 'Truth Valuation of Explicit Performatives' *Philosophical Quarterly* 20 (1970), 139-49.
Hume, David. *An Essay Concerning Human Understanding and other Essays.* New York, Washington Square Press, 1963.
Husserl, Edmund. *Loqische Untersuchungen.* Leipzig, 1913.

Ibanez, Roberto. 'Uber die Beziehungen zwischen Grammatik und Pragmatik: Konversationspostulate auf dem Gebiet der Konditionalität und Imperativität'. *Folia Linquistica* 10 (1977), 223-48.
Inwagen, Peter Van *see* McKay, Thomas and Inwagwen, Peter, Van

Jackson, Frank. 'Weakness of Will'. *Mind* 93 (1984) 1-18.
Jespersen, Otto. *The Philosophy of Grammar* (1924). New York, Norton & Co, 1965. (The Norton Library)
Johnson, Marion R. 'Questions and Requests', *Ohio State University Working Papers in Linguistics* 21 (1976), 145-52.
Joos, Martin. *The English Verb; Form and Meaning.* Madison and Milwaukee, University of Wisconsin Press, 1964.
Jørgensen, J. 'Imperatives and Logic'. *Erkenntnis* 7 (1937) 288-98.
Kading, Daniel. 'How Promising Obligates'. *Philosophical Studies* 22 (1971), 57-60.
Kamp, Hans. 'Free Choice Permission *Proceedings of the Aristotelian Society* 74 (1973-74), 57-74.
Kanger, S. *New Foundations for Ethical Theory*, Pt I, Stockholm 1957. (Mimeographed) Later version under same title in Hilpinen, Risto (ed) *Deontic Logic: Introductory and Systematic Readings.* Dordrecht, Reidel, 1971, 36-58.
Kant, Immanuel. *Fundamental Principles of the Metaphysics of Ethics.* Translated by Thomas Kingsmill Abbott. London, Longmans, 1959.
Katz, Jerrold Jacob and Postal Paul M. *An Integrated Theory of Linguistic Descriptions.* Cambridge, Mass., M.I.T. Press, 1964.
Kenny, Anthony. *Action, Emotion and Will.* London, Routledge & Kegan Paul, 1963.
'Human Abilities and Dynamic Modalities' in Manninen, Juha and Tuomela, Raimo (eds.) *Essays on Explanation and Understanding*, Dordrecht, Reidel, 1976, 210-32.
Kiparsky, Paul and Kiparsky, Carl. 'Fact' in Bierwisch, Manfred and Heidolph, K.E. (eds) *Progress in Linguistics*. The Hague, Mouton, 1970.
Krabbe, E.C.W. *see* Barth, E.M. and Krabbe, E.C.W.
Kraemer, Eric Russert. 'Intentional Action, Chance and Control'. *Analysis* 38 (1978), 116-17.
Kripke, Saul A. 'Semantic Analysis of Modal Logic I, Normal Propositional Logics. *Zeitschrift fur Matematische Logik und Grundlagen der Mathematik* 9 (1963), 67-96.

Lakoff, George *see also* Gordon, David and Lakoff, George

Lakoff, George. 'On the Nature of Syntactic Irregularities'. Harvard University Computation Laboratory. Mathematical Linguistics and Automatic Translation. *Report no 16 to the National Science Foundation.* 1965.

'Static Adjectives and Verbs in English'. Harvard Computation Laboratory. Mathematical linguistics and Automatic Translation. *Report No 17 to the National Science Foundation.* 1966, 1-16.

'A Note on Negation'. Harvard University Computation Laboratory. Mathematical Linguistics and Automatic Translation. *Report no 17 to the National Science Foundation.* 1966, III, 1-8.

'Linguistics and Natural Logic'. *Synthese* **22** (1970), 151-271.

Lakoff, Robin T. 'The Logic of Politeness. *Papers from the Regional Meetings, Chicago Linguistic Society* **9** 1973), 292-405.

Langford, C.H. 'The Notion of Analysis in Moore's Philosophy', in Schilpp, P.A. (ed.) *The Philosophy of G.E. Moore.* New York, Tudor, 1942. (Library of Living Philosophers).

Laplace, Pierre Simon De. *Essai Philosophique sur les Probabilites.* Paris, 1812.

Lee, Chungmin 'The Performative Analysis of 'Why not U?'. *Language Sciences* **25** (1973), 39-41.

Lemmon, E.J. 'Moral Dilemmas'. *Philosophical Review* **71** (1962), 139-58.

'On Sentences Verifiable by their Use'. *Analysis* **22** (1962), 86-9.

'Deontic Logic and the Logic of Imperatives. *Logique et Analyse* **8** (1965), 39-71.

Leonard, Henry S. 'Interrogatives, Imperatives, Truth, Falsity and Lies'. *Philosophy of Science* **26** (1959), 172-86.

Levenston, E.A. 'Imperative Structures in English'. *Linguistics* **50** (1969), 38-43.

Lewis, David K. *Convention: A Philosophical Study.* Cambridge, Mass., Harvard University Press, 1969.

'General Semantics'. *Synthese* **22** (1970), 18-67.

'Completeness and Decidability of Three Logics of Counterfactual Conditionals' *Theoria* **37** (1971), 74-85.

*Counterfactuals.* Oxford, Blackwell, 1973.

'A Problem About Permission' in Saarinen, E., Hilpinen, R., Niiniluoto, I. and Hintikka, M.P. (eds) *Essays in Honour of Jaakko Hintikka.* Dordrecht, Reidel, 1979, 163-75.

Lewis, David K. and Stephanie R. review of: Olson, R. and Paul, A. *Contemporary Philosophy in Scandinavia.* London, Johns Hopkins Press, 1972. In *Theoria* **41** (1975), 39-60.

Llewelyn, John Edward. 'What is a Question?' *Australasian Journal of Philosophy* **42** (1964), 67-85.

Loewer, Barry. 'Counterfactuals with Disjunctive Antecedents'. *Journal of Philosophy* **73** (1976), 531-7.

Londey, David. 'On the Action of Teams'. *Inquiry* **21** (1978), 213-18.

Lowe, E.J. 'Neither Intentional nor Unintentional' *Analysis* **38** (1978), 117-18.

Lyons, Daniel. 'Welcome Threats and Coercive Offers'. *Philosophy* **50** (1975), 425-36.

McGinn, Colin. 'Semantics for Non-indicative Sentences'. *Philosophical Studies* **32** (1977), 301-11.

McKay, Thomas and Inwagen, Peter Van. 'Counterfactuals with Disjunctive Antecedents'. *Philosophical Studies* **31** (1977), 353-6.

Mackenzie, James D. 'How to Stop Talking to Tortoises'. *Notre Dame Journal of Formal Logic* **20** (1979), 705-17.

'The Dialectics of Logic'. *Logique et Analyse* **24** (1981), 159-77.

'Begging the Question in Dialogue'. *Australasian Journal of Philosophy* **62** (1984), 174-81.

McKinsey, J.C.C. *see* Hofstadter, Albert and McKinsey, J.C.C.

Macklin, Ruth. 'Reason vs. Causes in Explanation of Action'. *Philosophy and Phenomenological Research* **33** (1972-73), 78-89.

McLaughlin, R.N. 'Further Problems of Derived Obligation'. *Mind* **64** (1955), 400-02.

Mally, E. *Grundgesetze des Sollens: Elemente der Logic des Willens.* Graz, 1926.

Mannison, Donald S. 'Doing Something on Purpose but not Intentionally'. *Analysis* **30** (1969), 49-52.

Marcus, Ruth Barcan. 'Moral Dilemmas and Consistency'. *Journal of Philosophy* **77** (1981), 121-36.

Margolis, Joseph. 'Actions and Ways of Failing'. *Inquiry* **3** (1960), 89-101.

Margolis, Joseph. 'Danto on Basic Action'. *Inquiry* **13** (1970), 104-8.

Martin, James A. *see* Gert, Bernard and Martin, James A.

Martin, Jane R. 'Basic Actions and Simple Actions'. *American Philosophical Quarterly* **9** (1972), 59-68.

Mayo, Bernard. 'Deliberative Questions: A Criticism'. *Analysis* **16** (1955), 64-6.

Mayo, Bernard and Mitchell, Basil George. 'Varieties of Imperatives'. *Proceedings of the Aristotelian Society: supplementary Volume* **31** (1957), 161-90.

Menger, Karl. 'A Logic of the Doubtful. On Optative and Imperative Logic'. *Reports of a Mathematical Colloquium* **2** Notre Dame University, Indiana, Notre Dame University Press, 1939 53-64.

Mitchell, Basil George *see* Mayo, Bernard and Mitchell, Basil George

Mohan, Bernard A. 'Principles, Postulates, Politeness'. *Papers from the Regional Meetings, Chicago Linguistic Society* **10** (1974), 446-59.

Moore, George Edward. *Principia Ethica.* Cambridge, Cambridge University Press, 1903. *Ethics.* London, Oxford University Press, 1912.

Morillo, Carolyn R. 'Doing, Refraining, and the Strenuousness of Morality'. *American Philosophical Quarterly* **14** (1977), 29-39.

Moritz, Manfred. 'Imperative Implication and Conditional Imperatives'. *Modality, Morality and Other Problems of Sense and Nonsense. Essays dedicated to Sören Halldén.* Lund, Gleerup, 1973.

Morris, Herbert. 'Imperatives and Orders'. *Theoria* **26** (1960), 183-209.

Moser, S. 'Some Remarks about Imperatives'. *Philosophy and Phenomenological Research* **17** (1956), 186-206.

Nesbitt, Winston. 'Value-Judgements, Prescriptive Language and Imperatives' *Philosophical Quarterly* **23** (1973), 253-7.

Nowell-Smith, P.H. *Ethics.* London, Pelican, 1954.

Nussbaum, Martha Craven. *Aristotle's De Motu Anaimalium: text with translation, commentary and interpretive essays.* Princeton, New Jersey, University Press, 1978.
Nute, Donald. 'Counterfactuals'. *Notre Dame Journal of Formal Logic* **16** (1975), 476-82.

Oddie, Graham *see* Tichý, Pavel and Oddie, Graham
O'Hair, S.G. 'Performatives and Sentences Verifiable by their Use'. *Synthèse* **17** (1967), 299-303.
Olivecrona, Karl. *Law as Fact.* London, Stevens, 1971. 2nd. ed. (extensively rewritten from the 1st ed. 1939).
Opalek, Kazimierz. On the Logical-Semantic Structure of Directives'. *Logique et Analyse* **13** (1970), 169-96.

Partee, Barbara Hall *see* Stockwell, Robert Paul, Schachter, Paul and Partee, Barbara Hall.
Pears, D.F. 'Are Reasons for Actions Causes?' in Stroll, A. (ed) *Epistemology.* New York, Harper & Row, 1967, 204-28.
Peetz, Vera. 'Promises and Threats'. *Mind* **86** (1977), 578-81.
Plato. *The Republic* Translated by A.D. Lindsay. London, Dent, 1935.
Postal, Paul M. *see also* Katz, Jerrold Jacobs and Postal, Paul M.
Postal, Paul M. 'Underyling and Superficial Linguistic Structure'. *Harvard Educational Review* **34** (1964), 246-66.
Pratt, Vaughan R. 'Semantical Consideration on Floyd-Hoare Logic'. *17th IEEE Symposium on Foundation of Computer Science.* 1977, 109-121.
Price, A.W. 'Doing Things Explicitly with Words. *Philosophical Studies* **36** (1979), 345-357; 352.
Prichard, Harold, Arthur. *Moral Obligation.* Oxford, Oxford University Press, 1949.
Prior, Arthur, N. 'Review: G.H. von Wright *An Essay in deontic Logic and the General Theory of Action'. Ratio* **12** (1970), 175-8.
*Objects of Thought.* Ed. by P.T. Geach and A.J.P. Kenny Oxford, Clarendon, 1971.

Quirk, Randolph et al. *A Grammar of Contemporary English.* London, Longmans, 1972.

Radford, Colin. 'Knowing and Telling'. *Philosophical Review* **78** (1969), 326-36.
Rand, R. 'Logik der Forderungssätze'. *Revue internationale de la Théorie du droit* (also known as *Internationale Zeitung für Rechtsphilosophie*) **1** (1939), 308-22. English translation: 'The Logic of Demand-Sentences'. *Synthese* **14** (1962), 237-54.
Raz, Joseph. *Practical Reason and Norms.* London, Hutchinson, 1975. 'On the Nature of Rights, *Mind* **93** (1984), 194-214.
Reichenbach, Hans. *Elements of Symbolic Logic.* New York, Mcmillan, 1947.
Rescher, Nicholas. *The Logic of Commands.* London, Routledge & Kegan Paul, and New York, Dover, 1966.

Robins, Michael, H. 'The Primacy of Promising' *Mind* **85** (1976), 321-40.

Rorty, Amelie Oksenberg. 'Akrasia and Conflict'. *Inquiry* **23** (1980), 193-212. 'Akratic Believers', *American Philosophical Quarterly* **20** (1983), 175-83.

Ross, Alf. 'Imperatives and Logic'. *Theoria* **7** (1941), 53-71. Also in *Philosophy of Science* **11** (1944), 30-46.

Ross, John Robert. 'On Declarative Sentences, in Jacobs, Roderick A. (comp.) *Readings in English Transformational Grammar*. Waltham, Ginn & Co. 1970, 222-72.

Russell, Bertrand. *'An Inquiry into Meaning and Truth*. London, Allen & Unwin, 1940.

Ryding, Erik. 'The Sense of "Smoking Permitted", A Note on Erik Tranøy's "An Important Aspect of Humanism"'. *Theoria* **24** (1958), 188-90.

Ryle, Gilbert *The Concept of Mind*. London, Hutchinson, 1949.
'Knowing How and Knowing That'. *Proceedings of the Aristotelian Society* **46**, (1945-46), 161-84.
*Dilemmas*. Cambridge, Cambridge University Press, 1954. 'Comment on Mr Achinstein's Paper' *Analysis* **21** (1960), 9-12.

Sadock, Jerrold M. Saarincn, Esa, *see* Hintikka, Kaarlo Jaako Jahami and Saarinen, Esa. 'Hypersentences'. *Papers in Linguistics* **1** (1969), 283-370. 'Whimperatives'. *Papers in Linguistics Monograph Series 1* (1970), 223-238, 111, 116.

Sartre, Jean Paul. *Existentialism and Humanism*. London, Methuen, 1948.
*Being and Nothingness: an essay on phenomenological ontology*. London, Methuen, 1957.

Schachter, Paul. 'Imperatives' in *The Major Syntactic Structures of English* Stockwell, Robert Paul, Schachter, Paul and Partee, Barbara Hall (eds.) New York, Rinehart & Winston, 1973, 633-71.

Schiffer, Stephen R. *Meaning*, Oxford, Oxford University Press, 1972.

Schmerling, Susan F. 'Asymmetric Conjunction and Rules of Conversation', in Cole, Peter and Morgan, Jerry (eds) *Syntax and Semantics; vol. 3: Speech Acts*. London, Academic Pres, 1975, 211-31.

Schneewind, Jerome. 'A Note on Promising'. *Philosophical Studies* **17** (1966), 33-5.

Scruggs, Johnny V. (Thesis: *A Praxeological Theory for Action-Guiding Discourse*. University of New South Wales, 1976.

Searle, John R. *Speech Acts*. Cambridge, Cambridge University Press, 1969.
'Indirect Speech Acts' in Cole, Peter and Morgan, Jerry (ed.). *Syntax and Semantics; vol 3: Speech Acts*. London, Academic Press, 1975, 59-82.
'A Classification of Illocutionary Acts. *Language in Society* **5** 1976), 1-23.

Segerberg, Krister. 'Applying Modal Logic'. Paper read at New Zealand Philosophy Conference, Dunedin, 1980.

Segerstedt, Torgny T. 'Imperative Propositions and Judgements of Value'. *Theoria* **11** 1945), 1-19.

Sellars, Wilfrid. 'Imperatives, Intentions and the Logic of "Ought"', in Castañeda, Hector-Neri (ed.) *Morality and the Language of Conduct*. Detroit, Wayne State University Press, 1963.

Sextus Empiricus. *Against the Logicians*. London, Heineman, 1933-1949. (Loeb Classical Library no. 291).

Sigwart, Cristoph. *Loqik*, Tübingen, 1873. *Logic* English translation by Helen Dendy from the 2nd. ed. of 1888. London, 1890, 140.

Sloman, Aaron. 'Transformation of Illocutionary Arts'. *Analysis* 30 (1969), 56-9.

Sobel, J. Howard. ' "Everyone", Consequences and Generalization Arguments'. *Inquiry* 10 (1967), 373-404.

Sosa, Ernest. 'Actions and Their Results', *Logique et Analysee* 8 (1965), 111-25.

Stalley, Richard F. 'Intentions, Beliefs and Imperative Logic'. *Mind* 81 (1972), 18-28.

Stalnaker, Robert C. 'Possible Worlds'. *Nous* 10 (1976), 65-75.

Stevenson, C.L. *Ethics and Language*, New Haven, Yale University Press, 1944.

Stopes-Roe, Harry V. 'Recipes and Induction: Ryle v. Achinstein', *Analysis* 21 (1960), 115-20.


Tacitus. *Histories*, III, 51.

Thalberg, Irving *see also* Weil, Vivian M. and Thalberg Irving

Thalberg, Irving. 'Mental Activity and Passivity'. *Mind* 87 (1978), 376-95.

Thorne, James, Peter *see also* Boyd, Julian and Thorne, James Peter Thorne, James Peter. 'English Imperative Sentences'. *Journal of Linguistics* 2 (1966), 69-78.

Tichý, Pavel and Oddie, Graham. 'Ability and Freedom'. *American Philosophical Quarterly* 20 (1983), 135-47.

Toulmin, Stephen Edelston. *An Examination of the Place of Reason in Ethics*. Cambridge, Cambridge University Press, 1950.

Tranøy, Knut Erik. 'An Important Aspect of Humanism'. *Theoria* 23 (1957), 36-52.

Turnbull, R.G. 'Imperatives, Logic and Moral Obligation. *Philosophy of Science* 27 (1960), 374-90.


Ukaji, Masatomo. *Imperative Sentences in Early Modern English*. Tokyo, (Kaitakusha 1978.


Vendler, Zeno. 'Verbs and Times'. *Philosophical Review* 66, (1957), 143-60. *Res Cogitans: An Essay in Rational Psychology*. New York, Cornell University Press, 1972.

Vermazen, Bruce. 'The Logic of Practical "Ought"-Sentences'. *Philosophical Studies* 32 (1977), 1-71.


Wachtel, Tom. 'A Question of Imperatives'. *Papers and Studies in Contrastive Linguistics* 10 (1979), 5-31.

Walton, Douglas N. 'Omitting, Refraining and Letting Happen'. *American Philosophical Quarterly* 17 (1980), 319-26. *Logical Dialogue-Games and Fallacies*. Lanham, University Press of America, 1984.

Walzer, Michael. 'Political Action: The Problem of Dirty Hands'. *Philosophy and Public Affairs* 2 (1975), 160-80.

Warnock, Geoffrey. 'Imperatives and Meaning', in Lewis, H.D. (ed.) *Contemporary British Philosophy*, London, Allen & Unwin, 1976, 292-305.

Wedeking, Gary A. Dissertation: *A Critical Examination of Command Logic*. St. Louis, Washington University, 1969.

Weil, Vivian M. and Thalberg, Irving. 'The Elements of Basic Action'. *Philosophia* 4 (1974), 111-38.

Wellman, Carl. 'The Justification of Practical Reason. *Philosophical and Phenomenological Research* 361 (1975-76), 531-44.

Westphal, Fred. 'Utilitarianism and "Conjunctive Acts": a Reply to Professor Castaneda'. *Analysis* 32 (1972), 32-5.

Winograd, Terry. 'Understanding Natural Language'. *Cognitive Psychology* 3 (1972), 1-191.

Wisdom, John. 'Ludwig Wittgenstein, 1934-1937. *Mind* 61 (1952), 258-60.

Wittgenstein, Ludwig. *Philosophische Untersuchungen/Philosophical Investigations*. Translated by G.E.M. Anscombe, Oxford, Blackwell, 1953.

Wright, Georg Henrik Von. *Norm and Action*. London, Routledge & Kegan Paul, 1963.

'Deontic Logics'. *American Philosophical Quarterly* 4 (1967), 136-43.

*An Essay in Deontic Logic and the General Theory of Action*. Amsterdam, North-Holland, 1968.

Wunderlich, Dieter. 'Assertions, Conditional Speech Acts and Practical Inferences. *Journal of Pragmatics* 1, (1977), 13-46.

Zimmerman, David. 'Force and Sense'. *Mind* 89 (1980), 214-33.

# Author Index

Achinstein, Peter 12
Ackrill, John Lloyd 209
Acton, H.B. 115
Alchourron, Carlos E. 70
Aldrich, V.C. 102
Anderson, Alan Ross 154
Angstl, Helmut 154
Anscombe, Gertrude Elizabeth
  Margaret 40
Anselm of Canterbury, Saint 54, 66
Apostel, Leo 138
Åqvist, Lennart 27, 76, 154
Arbini, Ronald 48
Ardal, Pall S. 34
Aristotle 88, 168, 205-10, 240
Armstrong, David M. 39
Atiyah, P.S. 38
Aune, Bruce 203
Austin, John 19
Austin, John Langshaw 22, 23, 28,
  42, 104, 128, 131, 211
Ayer, Sir Alfred 21

Baier, Annette C. 140, 237
Baier, Kurt 10, 203
Barnes, Winston H.F. 115
Barth, E.M. 224
Beardsley, Elizabeth Lane 72
Belnap, Nuel D., Jr. ix, 27, 80, 221
Bennett, Jonathan 66
Bentham, Jeremy 19, 89
Boden, Margaret A. 212
Bohnert, H.G. 94, 102
Bolinger, Dwight 50, 72, 81, 106

Bosanquet, Bernard 27
Bosque, Ignacio 50
Boyd, Julian 9, 105
Brand, Myles 57, 66, 140
Brentano, Franz Clemens 18
Broad, C.D. 115
Broadie, Alexander 10, 46
Burch, Robert William 23

Carnap, Rudolf 21, 114
Carr, D. 203, 220
Castañeda, Hector Neri 35, 74, 91,
  102, 115, 135
Chellas, Brian F. 138
Chisholm, Roderick M. 31, 66, 147,
  190
Chomsky, Noam 104
Clark, Herbert H. 8
Cohen, Laurence Jonathan 23
Cohen, Ted 23
Collingwood, Robin George 93, 147
Conee, Earl 169
Copp, David
Cornides, Thomas 71
Cresswell, Maxwell J. 131, 133, 154

Danielson, Sven 131
Danto, Arthur C. 57, 140
D'Arcy, Eric 19
Davison, Alice 8
Dennett, Daniel C. 212
Diggs, B.J. 83
Dinello, Daniel 66
Downing, Bruce T. 52, 87

Dubislav, W. 101, 115
Dummett, Michael 50, 81, 82, 84, 87
Duncan-Jones, A.E. 102

Ehrman, Madeline Elizabeth 105

Falk, W.D. 116
Field, G.C. 12, 27
Fillmore, Charles 44
Fitzgerald, P.J. 66
Fraassen, Bas C. Van 169
Fries, Charles Carpenter 2

Gale, R.M. 131
Garner, Richard T. 70
Geach, Peter Thomas 70, 116, 202
Gean, W.D. 94
Gert, Bernard 202
Geukens, Steven K.J. 7
Gibbons, P.C. 103, 106, 107
Gombay, Andre 76
Gordon, David 7, 10
Graham, Keith 23
Grant, Colin King 34, 36, 37, 38, 39
Green, Georgia M. 8, 22
Greenspan, Patricia S. 83
Grice, H.P. 7, 23, 219, 240
Gruner, Rolf 60
Gustafson, Donald 42

Hall, Everett Wesley 73
Hallden, Soren 154
Hamblin, Charles Leonard 169, 208,
    224, 234, 239
Hanson, William H. 116, 154
Hare, Richard Mervyn 9, 18, 25, 27,
    30, 70, 73, 90, 91, 102, 114, 139
Harrison, Jonathan 131, 44
Hart, H.L.A. 131
Hartnack, Justus 131
Hedeneius, Ingemar 131
Heil, John 210
Heringer, James Tromp, Jr. 8, 83
Hintikka, Kaarlo Jaakko Juhani 27,
    224
Hobart, R.E. (*pseudonym for* Miller,
    Dickinson S.) 146

Hobbes, Thomas 10, 60
Hofmann, T.R. 8, 117
Hofstadter, Albert 101, 139
Holdcroft, David 10, 22
Honoré, A.M. 203
Houston, J. 131
Hume David 4
Husserl, Edmund 128

Ibanez, Roberto 72
Inwagen, Peter van 86

Jespersen, Otto 10
Johnson, Marion R. 72
Joos, Martin 2, 39, 47, 51, 105
Jørgensen, J. 71, 101

Kading, Daniel 37
Kamp, Hans 76
Kanger, S. 115
Kant, Immanuel 10, 12, 14, 15, 113
Katz, Jerrold Jacob 51, 104, 106, 107
Kenny, Anthony 36, 54, 202, 203
Kiparsky, Carl 130
Kiparsky, Paul 130
Krabbe, E.C.W. 224
Kraemer, Eric Russert 42
Kripke, Saul A. 154

Lakoff, George 7, 10, 130, 131
Lakoff, Robin T. 8, 54
Langford, C.H. 103, 107
Laplace, Pierre Simon de 145, 146
Lee, Chungmin 11
Lemmon, E.J. 115, 130, 168, 169,
    187
Leonard, Henry S. 102, 115, 219
Levenston, E.A. 47, 61
Lewis, David K. 27, 71, 86, 103, 112,
    131, 147, 220, 239
Lewis, Stephanie R. 27
Llewelyn, John Edward 27, 78
Loewer, Barry 76
Londey, David 60
Lowe, E.J. 42
Lyons, Daniel 34

McGinn, Colin 23
McKay, Thomas 86
MacKenzie, James D. 224, 239, 240
McKinsey J.C.C. 101, 139
Macklin, Ruth 94
McLaughlin, R.N. 75
Mally, E. 101
Mannison, Donald S. 42
Marcus, Ruth Barcan 169
Margolis, Joseph 57, 162
Martin, James A. 202
Martin, Jane R. 140
Mayo, Bernard 26, 78
Menger, Karl 74
Mitchell, Basil George 26
Moore, George Edward 136, 211
Morillo, Carolyn R. 66
Moritz, Manfred 89
Morris, Herbert 9
Moser, S. 94

Nesbitt, Winston 78
Nowell-Smith, P.H. 115
Nussbaum, Martha Craven 168
Nute, Donald 86

Oddie, Graham 138, 211
O'Hair, S.G. 131
Olivecrona, Karl 19
Opalek, Kazimierz 115

Pears, D.F. 94
Peetz, Vera 34, 38
Plato 168
Postal, Paul M. 51, 104, 106, 107
Pratt, Vaughan R. 139
Price, A.W. 131
Prichard, Harold Arthur 37
Prior, Arthur, N. 115, 168

Quirk, Randolph 46, 48

Radford, Colin 216
Rand, R. 115
Raz, Joseph 173
Reichenbach, Hans 23
Rescher, Nicholas 102

Robins, Michael H. 37
Rorty, Melie Oksenberg 210
Ross, Alf 71, 77, 115
Ross, John Robert 27, 48, 101, 128, 129, 130, 133
Russell, Bertrand 97, 99, 100
Ryding, Erik 76
Ryle, Gilbert 12, 55, 200, 201

Saarinen, Esa 224
Sadock, Jerrold M. 128, 129, 130, 133
Sartre, Jean Paul 168
Schachter, Paul 24, 29, 46
Schiffer, Stephen R. 23, 219
Schmerling, Susan F. 73
Schneewind, Jerome 39
Scruggs, Johnny V. 76
Searle, John R. 22, 23, 24, 28, 38, 39, 70, 99, 239
Segerberg, Krister 139
Segerstedt, Torgny T. 18, 116
Sellars, Wilfrid 116
Sextus Empiricus 97
Sigwart, Cristoph 27
Sloman, Aaron 70
Sobel, J. Howard 54
Sosa, Ernest 60
Stalley, Richard F. 89
Stalnaker, Robert C. 147
Stevenson, C.L. 114
Stopes-Roe, Harry V. 12

Tacitus 168
Thalberg, Irving 50, 140
Thorne, James Peter 9, 47, 105
Tichý, Pavel 138, 211
Toulmin, Stephen Edelston 116
Tranøy, Knut Erik 76, 190
Turnbull, R.G. 102

Ukaji, Masatomo 2

Vendler, Zeno 22, 23, 28, 32, 34, 43, 44, 54, 55
Vermazen, Bruce 41

Wachtel, Tom 49
Walton, Douglas N. 66, 229
Walzer, Michael 169
Warnock, Geoffrey 170
Wedeking, Gary A. 116
Weil, Vivian M. 140
Wellman, Carl 205
Westphal, Fred 74

Winograd, Terry 222
Wisdom, John 4
Wittgenstein, Ludwig 36, 220
Wright, Georg Henrik Von 60, 70,
    76, 115, 125, 138, 139, 168
Wunderlich, Dieter 239

Zimmerman, David 70

# Subject Index

Abilities 200–17
  agglomerate 204, 213
  atomic and molecular 212–13
  behaviour–mode 213
ability, ingredients of 205–13
action–reduction principle 58, 124
  and abilities 204
action, joint and group 35, 58–60,
    165–6
actions and states 54–55
  basic, 57–8, 140–1, 237
addressees, multiple 35, 59–60
addressee–action–reduction–principle
  see action–reduction principle
adjectives, Japanese 57
advice 10
  indicative 11, 26
  philosophical 4, 21
antagonisms 168, 186–7
antagonism–freedom 168
applied science 14
Arabic 99
art or skill (techne)
  as ingredient in ability 206–07
authorisations 30
authority
  and permissives 30
  social, rational, coercive 10–11

Beliefs 219–20
  akratic 210
  as idealised commitments 240–1
Bengali 25

Causation
  agent and event 147
Chinese 95
choice, principles of 145–6
cleverness (deinotés)
  as ingredient in ability 206–07
choosability 148
commands 5–6
commissions 5
commitment 229–32
concessives 30
conjunction 71
  separable and inseparable 73–5,
    165, 184
continuous tenses
  in imperatives 49
  and performatives 132
convention
  committed action 239
  truth-telling 239
corporate persons 60, 240
counsel see Advice
covenants 33

Decisions 42
declaratives see indicatives
decrees 29
deeds and happenings 140
demands 9–10, 26
designs 32, 39
desires 36, 42
determinism 212
  Laplacian 145

259

dialectic
  as logic of dialogue 45, 94
dilemmas, moral 168–9
directives 5
discretion 13, 221
  ambiguity of, in permissives 31, 67, 228
disjunction
  choice-offering and
    alternative-presenting 75–8, 202

Effectiveness 137, 162
English 46–51
enticings 44
ethics 14, 18, 19–20
  imperative theory of 18, 20, 40
exercitives 23, 28, 33
exclamations 24, 97, 115

Fiats 101–02, 129
force,
  illocutionary 22–3, 35
  and mood 23

Heresis *see* disjunction, choice-offering

Imperatives
  accountable 19
  categorical 4, 16
  conditional 83–7, 166, 177
  consistency of 167–99
  first-person 39
  first-plural 35, 58–9
  formal 25
  frequency of 2
  future-tense 25
  hearer-interested 22
  group 53, 60
  hypothetical 15–17
  immediate 25, 26, 41, 223
  in dialogue 218–41
  in indirect speech 62–3
  philosophical 4–5, 15
  plain-predicate 47–50
  polite 6–9
  sanctioned 22
  scientific 11

in semi-indirect speech 63
variable terminology of 26
varieties (distinguished) 5–26, 228–36
varieties, table of 44–5
wilful 11, 15, 20, 22, 23
imperative-generating events 173
inconsistency
  diagonal and top-corner 172
indicatives and imperatives 3
inference, imperative 87, 91
influencings 44
instructions 11–13
interjections *see* exclamations
intuitive reason (*noûs*)
  as ingredient in ability 206
intellect
  speculative and practical 14
intentions 33, 23, 41–3
  as idealised commitments 240–1
  statements of 33
invitations 24, 29

Japanese 7, 57
Jephthah's theorem 168, 180
Jorgensen's dilemma 71
judgement (*gnōmè*)
  as ingredient in ability 206, 208

Knowledge (*aisthēsis* or *epistēmē*)
  as ingredient in ability 206, 213–15
  *how* and *that* 200
  theoretical and practical 14

Latin 25
law, imperative theory of 18–20, 29
laws of nature 144–7
liar paradox, analogue of 151

Match, direction of 24, 29, 220
meaning, utterer's 219–20
method, scientific 21
methodology, philosophy as 21
modals 105–06, 113, 117
  epistemic and root 6
mood 46
  pragmatic 23, 97

Negation 60, 64–71, 164–5
non-abilities 204–05, 213

Orders 5

Passive constructions in imperatives
  49
performatives 22–3, 100
permissives 30–1, 68, 110, 125, 164,
  189
  ambiguity of discretion in 31, 69,
    228
  varieties (distinguished) 30–1
permissions, obstructed 168
permission-unobstructedness 168,
  194–6
persuasions 44
philosophic wisdom (*sophia*)
  as ingredient in ability 206, 207
philosophical statements as
    procedural rules 21
plans 18, 32, 39
pledges 33
plots 39
pointfulness 161
possibility
  active 149
  logical 141–2
  physical 144–8
  temporal 148
practical syllogism 168
practical wisdom (*phronesis*)
  and ability 205
predictions 104, 112
programs 32, 151, 214
promises 33–4
promptings 44
proposals 32
propositions, traditional 3
pseudo-quotation 63
pure science 14–16

Quandaries 167–99
quandary-freedom 168
  absolute 178
  legislative 178–9
  minimal 181

strategic 179–80
questions, imperative 78, 201
  as imperatives 27

Recipes 12–13, 39
requests 7–10, 51
research, paradox of applied 205
resolves 42
responsibility, joint and several 166
rights 190
Ross's paradox 77
rules 167
  procedural, philosophical
    statements as 21
  of skill 12, 15

Satisfaction
  extensional 153
  second-best 154, 165–6
  wholehearted 158–60
schemes 32
science, pure and applied 3, 14
seductions 44
sincerity-conditions 7–8
Spanish 50
strategies 155–7
  partial 157, 213–4
subject, understood 47
  indeterminate 53
suggestions 11, 25, 29, 51

Tags 48, 52, 106
tense, future 105
tenses of imperatives 25, 50, 80–82,
  116
threats 34

Understanding (*sunesis* or *eusunesia*)
  as ingredient of ability 206, 210
undertakings 33
  varieties (distinguished) 35, 45, 225
universals, separable (resemblance to
    conjunctions) 73

Verbal nouns 88, 108–10
verbs
  agentive and stative 54–8, 203

mental-act 33
mental-state 33
virtue (*aretē*)
　as ingredient of ability 206, 209
vocatives 51–3
　and subjects 52

votings 29
vows 33

Warnings 23
will, 36, 81, 210
wishes 24, 42